W9-AVC-910

Caravan to Oz

a family reinvents itself
off-off-Broadway

by

Ann Harris
Walter Michael Harris
Jayne Anne Harris-Kelley
Eloise Harris-Damone
Mary Lou Harris-Pietsch

1/26/18

Holly — Thanks for your support with our "Nothing Personal" chorus! It has a bright future ahead. Peace, love and HARMONY — Michael

Cover design by Mary Lou Harris-Pietsch
Edited by Walter Michael Harris and Mary Lou Harris-Pietsch
Interior design by Mary Lou Harris-Pietsch and Walter Michael Harris
Graphic production assistance by Jodi Steele
Text set in Calibri and Helvetica Neue

Our book was written and designed in Apple's Pages™ program
and prepared for publication using tools provided by CreateSpace™.
We thank the staff of CreateSpace™ for their help and support.

© Copyright 2014

by the co-authors:

Ann Harris
Walter Michael Harris
Jayne Anne Harris-Kelley
Eloise Harris-Damone
Mary Lou Harris-Pietsch

ISBN-13: 978-0615997520
ISBN-10: 061599752X

EL DORADO

B O O K S

USA

NEW YORK - SEATTLE

All rights reserved. No part of this publication may be reproduced or used in
any form or by any means – graphic, electronic, or mechanical, including
photocopying, recording, taping, or information storage and retrieval
systems – without written permission of the publisher.

caravantooz.com

*Dedicated to our fabulous
friends and family in the arts,
here and in paradise.*

Photo © Andrew Sherwood

There was no grand announcement. No one came home one day and said, 'Let's go have this amazing life.' No one came home and said, 'I'm gay' or 'I'm an artist.' Somehow this wonderful, intoxicating and yes, at times, nail-biting life just happened. We followed our hearts by saying, 'Let's put on a show!'... and somehow found the portal to the epicenter of other colorful abstract souls.

- Mary Lou

Table of Contents

The Harris Family

Father   George Edgerly Harris II, aka George, Sr.
Mother   Ann Marie Harris
First Child   George Edgerly Harris III, aka G3, Hibiscus, George, Jr.
Second Child   Walter Michael Harris
Third Child   Frederic Joseph Harris
Fourth Child   Jayne Anne Harris
Fifth Child   Eloise Alice Harris
Sixth Child   Mary Lucile Harris, aka Mary Lou

Caravan Voices
(guests in order of appearance)

Ellen Stewart
Tim Robbins
Susan Dale Rose
Robert Heide
Scott Morris
Robert Patrick
Crystal Field
Angel Jack Coe
Ritsaert ten Cate
Mike Figgis
John Bernhardt

Judson Poets Theater

Caffe Cino

Photo © James D. Gossage

I believe that we are one big world and that all of us are connected.
It's as if there were some kind of genetic residue in each of us that binds us all together. If we could find a way to communicate through the part of our common geneticism, so to speak, there'd be an almost umbilical understanding among people. To find a way to do that – to strike a chord inside you that makes you respond to me, is what should be happening … I love to see and be part of what comes out. Now that's what I like.

– ELLEN STEWART, Founder, La MaMa Experimental Theater Club

I don't know how it was that I wound up in a vortex of the culture that would later define us all.

I ran spotlight at the Theater for the New City in the early 1970's for a show called the Angels of Light. I was 13 years old and the reason I was there was that I had a crush on Eloise Harris, an angel in her own right, and sister of George Harris, Jr., who I knew as Hibiscus, the creative force of this troupe of freaks and weirdos that were making theatrical magic in

Tim Robbins

Greenwich Village with their combination of glitter and outrageous talent. It would be disingenuous to compare the Angels of Light to anything within our modern perceptions of entertainment because they created the mold.

They were doing things in the 1970's that had not been done before. No one had lived as large in the utter joy of free expression as the Angels. They brought it like rock stars. What they were bringing was a beautiful combination of 1930's Hollywood musical numbers, camp before there was a camp sensibility and a radical commitment to a new form of entertainment fueled by an extreme pride in an alternative sexuality. Add in a little LSD and a lot of glitter and imagine the minds being blown and expanded in the audiences that were lucky enough to see them live. And there I was, present behind my spotlight at 13 years old, witnessing this spectacle.

We all think of Greenwich Village, in retrospect, as a place where this would naturally happen, but those of us that lived there during this time know that it was more complicated than that. The Village, for all its progressive thought and free thinking inhabitants, was also surrounded by old world thinking, conservative strains that resisted the freaks and the weirdos, second and third generation Italian and Irish that saw the Angels and all these other hippies as a threat upon their catholic sensibilities and upon their own conceptions of sexuality. In other words, it wasn't a safe or easy thing to do, even in Greenwich Village, to dress in glitter drag and to own one's homosexuality. It was, in fact, a radical act, not for the faint of heart. This flaunt hadn't been done before in such a brash and prideful way. To produce this kind of theater one needed real men, the kind of men that had real balls, the kind of man that would walk up to a soldier and place a flower in the barrel of a loaded gun.

I remember being intimidated by Hibiscus and Jack and by the other members of this wild company. I was a jock at the time and the intimidation didn't come from a fear that they would hurt me. The intimidation came from a feeling that these were fiercely committed individuals that had determined their path, a path I did not understand at the time. They were on the road of freedom with full knowledge of the dangers that lay ahead. They owned every inch of who they were and were not waiting to be legitimized by me or society or law. They were singing out and singing loud and they were kicking ass theatrically. All those that followed in their wake owe a huge debt of gratitude to Hibiscus, the Angels of Light and the Harris family.

Anyone that has, in the last 40 years defied societal expectations, pushed the envelope of sexuality, or lived courageously in the freedom of their skin should say a prayer of thanks, light a candle and line their eyes with glitter for George, Jr. and the Harrises of Greenwich Village.

With much love,

Tim Robbins

The Little Prince at Theater for the New City, circa 1972. Tim is sixth from the right. Also in the lineup are the following Harrises: Ann, Eloise, Jayne Anne and Mary Lou.

In 1946 my father, George Edgerly Harris II, returned from soldiering at age 25. Young people at that time were anxious to put the world war behind them and get on with their lives. The country was blooming with post-war prosperity and intoxicated with the promise of The American Dream.

Within the year George had met Ann Marie McCanless and they were married in June of 1948 in Bronxville, New York, just '45 minutes from Broadway.' The newlyweds took an apartment there and, a year later, their first child, George Edgerly Harris III, was born. He was nicknamed 'G3.'

- Walter Michael

Chapter 1
The Burbs

The world will hail the golden girl of the age
The great sensation, fantastical rage
We're gonna show them all, just give us a stage
And we'll be the toast of the town!

"Toast of the Town" from *Sky High*
Music and lyrics by Ann Harris

Walter Michael:
The family quickly outgrew the tiny apartment. Mom and Dad bought a house on Cross Street, in Bronxville. My brother Frederic Joseph, sister Jayne Anne, and I were born there. Dad commuted to Manhattan to work for a fabric wholesaler in the fashion district, while Mom looked after the home, the kids, the Catholic Church and the Cub Scout meetings.

Mom's aunt, Ella Driscoll O'Connor, lived with us. She was a merry Irish soul and a powerful presence in our family life. We kids called her "Yaya," so Yaya she became to all. She baked fresh bread every week, played a mean barrelhouse piano and taught us Irish songs. We were entertained and inspired by the joy in her playing and singing. Yaya was Mom's closest connection to her Bronxville family and a wise elder in our growing tribe.

Dad had played drums since high school in a band with his cousin Berrie, so there was always a drum set in our house. Mom wrote songs, so there was always a piano. Our parents encouraged music, art, enterprise and creativity. They were always ready to help with our projects, at school or otherwise, championing a "do it yourself" sensibility that inspired self-reliance and risk-taking. Like Rumpelstiltskin we learned to weave straw into gold. We rarely had money but always had magic.

Mom admired the great American songwriters: Irving Berlin, George and Ira Gershwin, Jerome Kern, Dorothy Fields, Cole Porter and dozens of others who wrote for Fred Astaire, Judy Garland, Bing Crosby and many other swing era vocalists who set the world on fire with their style. She also loved Broadway writers including Rodgers and Hammerstein, Lerner and Loewe and Frank Loesser. As far back as we kids remember, powerful rhythmic music poured into the house from the radio, the record player, and from Yaya's piano. We improvised dances to the beat.

G3 and I had Miss Myers in first grade, the same teacher Mom had. We walked to a red brick school every day, past Mom's grandfather's house where she lived as a teenager. It seemed idyllic, well-rooted. Yet, trying to live all-American in the 1950s suburbs became a struggle because our family just didn't fit in.

By the time Jayne Anne was walking, we were feeling restless.

So there I was, a princess in the midst of an all-boy family. There was Boy Scouts, Little League, Kiwanis, the bridge club and everything that goes along with suburban living. (1957)

- Jayne Anne

Dad's musical heroes were big band leaders including Benny Goodman, Lionel Hampton, the Dorsey Brothers and the stellar instrumentalists Gene Krupa and Chick Webb. (1942)

- Walter Michael

George and I were best buddies in Bronxville. Although we had our own interests and hobbies, we collaborated on projects that were entrepreneurial. Before theater became the family's focus, we were neighborhood regulars, doing everyday stuff that brothers do.

- Walter Michael

Jayne Anne:
My brothers raced soapbox derby cars and dressed up for Halloween. I'm told that my father would really do it up for that holiday, answering the door as Dracula or Frankenstein. He was a master at makeup. But the trick or treaters would look at him and say, "Oh, hi Mister Harris." I'm sure it drove him nuts after spending all that time transforming.

Walter Michael:
Born 20 months apart, G3 and I were close enough in age to share playpens, toys, clothes, and activities. We attended the same school, were instructed by the same teachers and played with the same friends in Bronxville, a well-heeled suburb of New York City. We were raised on Dick and Jane, Howdy Doody, Captain Kangaroo, the Pledge of Allegiance and American public school curriculum. Mom read to us regularly from Rudyard Kipling and Winnie the Pooh. She sang us to sleep with wonderful songs she knew or made up.

In Bronxville George and I were Cub Scouts, co-conspirators and blood brothers. Even as a little kid he was a fountain of ideas and a risk-taker, and I his willing collaborator. He was a magnet for neighborhood kids who would come over to play. Fred and Jayne Anne were younger than our friends, but no one was excluded. He simply gave each kid something to do and off we went!

Susan Dale Rose (our cousin):
We came to visit you in Bronxville, my mother, brothers and I. Christopher was an infant, and we were escaping my dad, who was drinking very heavily by that time. You were still living a suburban lifestyle then, and yet the glitter was already there, floating around. When we got home, Mom permed my hair to give me curls, so I could have some of the wild beauty you all had. I hated it, but understood.

Ann:
In the summer of 1958 the family bundled into a wood-paneled Chrysler Suburban, left the Cub Scouts and bridge games behind and moved to Florida, where George, Sr., had served in the Army Air Force as a radio operator, training pilots how to make emergency landings. His soldier buddies kidded him – "A plane a day in Tampa Bay!"

George Harris, Sr. near Tampa Bay, 1943

Chapter 2
The Beach Calls

Oh, how I like striped bathing suits
They make me feel so fine
I wear them in the summer
When the sun begins to shine.

"Father's Song" from *The Sheep and the Cheapskate*
Music and lyrics by Ann Harris

Ann:
Landing in Clearwater Beach, an island community on the Gulf Coast, we checked the family into The Gulf Apartments and set up camp. It was magical. We could see the beautiful white sand beach and blue water, catch the Gulf breeze and hear the seagulls from our tiny kitchen table.

This sleepy Florida tourist community was used to annual hurricanes with devastating winds of up to 100 miles an hour. This was nothing compared to the arrival of the Harris family. We found a suitable house on the mainland, in a residential neighborhood called Harbor Oaks. Another daughter, Eloise Alice was born in Clearwater, and the boys started school. The family subsequently bought a house in a Clearwater suburb called Belleair.

Jayne Anne:
It was a white house with yellow shutters and a stream next door. The Sunbeam commercial bakery wasn't far from us and looked like a giant loaf of bread! At that time we were still attending church and always stopped at the A&W Root Beer place afterward. You could sit in your car and order food that they would bring on a tray and attach it to your window. I thought that was so exotic.

At church, where I made my first communion, the Sister told us during practice that it was time to confess our sins. I told her I didn't have any sins to which she replied, "Make one up." I liked getting all dressed up in my Sunday best dresses, hats and gloves to go to church. I didn't really pay attention in church or Sunday school. My brothers would always be fooling around in the pews.

Walter Michael:
The family soon discovered the Belleair house was built on top of a swamp. Dad remembered it as one of the lowest points economically for him, because the house was a bad deal to begin with, funds were low and work was scarce. The boy next door contracted scarlet fever. Aunt Ella died during this period. Of Belleair, G3 said, "my parents lost everything in the subdivisions that sank." What a celebration we had when Dad sold an insurance policy and received an advance from his boss. We all yelled and screamed and jumped for joy. With the advance money in hand, Dad took the family on a grocery-shopping spree and bought anything anyone wanted.

Settling in to Florida beach living, 1958-59

Belleair became a turning point for the family in several ways. We kids began staging holiday parades. On Memorial Day we marched to the cemetery and placed a wreath on the grave of an "unknown soldier" (any tombstone we could find engraved with the American flag). On the Fourth of July we staged a red, white and blue parade with G3, our intrepid Pied Piper, leading as the drum major. For our Thanksgiving parade we were Pilgrims and Indians. G3 rounded up every kid in the neighborhood to participate in these events, which took on the magnitude of a Macy's Thanksgiving Day extravaganza, complete with floats, marching band and young "Shriners" on bikes.

Ann:
The kids started a neighborhood newspaper, "The Belleair Blab". G3 was the editor, and Walter did illustrations. News and commentary was of local interest with a column called *The Clothesline.* It was in Belleair that G3 responded to a newspaper ad for the Clearwater Little Theater Junior Workshop, an event that marked the beginning of the family's love affair with theater.

Walter Michael:
The Francis Wilson Playhouse became theater boot camp for the family. Harvey Warren directed adult programs and John Mayo was the director of the Junior Workshop, an innovative children's theater program. His specialty was kids performing Shakespeare in full Elizabethan English with no modifications. G3 and I made our theatrical debut at ages eight and seven as witches in *Macbeth* – an early exercise in gender bending and a testament to Mayo's faith in young actors' ability to absorb and interpret sophisticated literature.

George, Sr.:
Mayo cast the kids in *Macbeth.* And he didn't dumb down the lines or anything for them. Except that it was cut a little to shorten the running time. The kids also made the costumes and the props and the sets and everything. So that was the experience.

The Elves and the Shoemaker was the next show I remember G3 being in. I remember how exciting it was to see him up there on that stage with a man who was absolutely brilliant as a director. John Mayo treated the kids as his equal – not exactly as adults, but there wasn't a "schoolish" atmosphere about the whole thing. He talked to them as young professionals.

Walter Michael:
The family became regulars at the Playhouse, which often featured children in its mainstage plays. Mom and Dad co-starred in *King Lear* while G3, Fred, Jayne Anne and I acted together in *Hop O' My Thumb and the Seven League Boots.* These shows gave us our first opportunities to explore our potential as theater artists. It was great. I played Hop, my first lead role. Fred and Jayne Anne were Munchkins. G3 and our friend Scotty Church played Twinklefoot and Lazyfoot, forest faeries who outwit the wily witch and save us all.

George, Sr.:
The whole thing was beautiful. The theater itself was an old community theater of the type that I love best. Wooden stages – old-fashioned theaters with that theatrical smell you don't get in modern chrome places. All the children were young.

John Mayo's philosophy was 'learn everything' about stagecraft: acting, improv, makeup, stage management, combat, set and lighting design, technical theater and even front-of-house.

Lucille 'Lutie' Mayo, John's mother, was our savior from the "sinking subdivisions" of Bellaire. She lived in an upper floor apartment of her beach house, which doubled as the costume shop for Playhouse productions.

'The Nuremburg Stove,' a play for children based on a German fable, is a good example of Clearwater Little Theater's penchant for pairing youth and adult actors. Here's Dad as King Ludvig of Bavaria, G3 as Gustl Strehla, an aspiring artist, and John Mayo as Karl, his father. Our brother Fred made his stage debut in this play at age six, ca. 1960.

Jayne Anne:
I was three years old when I did *Hop 'O' My Thumb,* my first show. All of my brothers were in it too. The two things I remember from that show are standing on a table top and pouring water over someone - and sitting at that same table eating chicken noodle soup out of a bowl. The soup was cold and I remember vividly thinking, "Why don't they warm it up?" We were always welcome to attend the theatre and watch our parents perform. My brother George always picked out my outfits and had me curtsy for Mrs. Warren, the owner's wife.

Walter Michael:
Warren and Mayo drafted Dad and Mom into their traveling repertory company. The company played local hotels, Kiwanis lodges and schools throughout Florida, performing Oscar Wilde, Shakespeare and Moliere. While on hiatus between shows our parents and their theater friends founded an improvisation troupe called The Mad Hatters. Hats pulled out of a barrel at random suggested characters. The Hatters would create an original comedy piece on the spot for a dollar a minute. The Mad Hatters became the darlings of Clearwater's secretary clubs, earning babysitting money for its company members. What started as a lark became an epiphany for the family – the possibility of supporting oneself with one's art.

George, Sr.:
We might as well get down to the nitty gritty - we had a big family and wages were low. I worked in sales for an office supply company and worked in these plays at night. We got acquainted with Lutie Mayo, John's mother. She offered her big house for rent, so we ran out and lived with Lutie on the beach. It was great!

Walter Michael:
When Lutie's tenants moved out she offered to rent her house to us and we accepted in a flash. There again we could hear the soothing sound of Gulf of Mexico waves lapping at the most beautiful white sand beach on the planet.

Outwardly gruff, Lutie was always nice to we kids, teaching us a million ways to play cards and giving us nickels to buy candy. She chain-smoked Lucky Strikes while playing an intense game of solitaire. It was her meditation. She was a tough survivor who had long ago dispensed with the meaningless social niceties that keep people from communicating honestly.

Lutie was a Grande Dame of the theater, at least in Clearwater. Her tiny attic apartment was a magical place, alive with glittering sequins and shimmering fabric. There you could see, in progress, a suit of armor, a page's tunic, Lady Macbeth's nightclothes or a beautiful princess' wedding gown. She was happy to show us her ways of making costumes that make fantasy look real under stage lights. Her fingers spun first-class costumes out of the commonest threads.

Lutie was acknowledged as the elder of our theater tribe, an important link in the chain of events that propelled the Harris family into the gypsy life of show people.

Ann and Mary Lou on Clearwater Beach, ca.1963

When Mom became pregnant while on tour playing Gonnerel in 'King Lear,' Lutie Mayo simply made her a beautiful maternity costume. We can therefore say with certainty that my sister Mary Lucile, born on my birthday during the run, and named after Lutie, was the youngest Harris child to take the stage.

- Walter Michael

Chapter 3
El Dorado Players

Mr. Stanislowski, you took me all apart
Won't you put me back together again?
When I first came out-ski I gave it all my heart
You said that I would graduate, but when?

What good am I to anyone in sections?
My indicating friends are making dough – so,

Mr. Stanislowski, won't you let me out-ski
I swear I'll recommend you when I go, oh
I swear I'll recommend you when I go.

"Mr. Stanislowski" from *There Is Method In Their Madness*
Music and lyrics by Ann Harris

Jayne Anne:
When I was five or six and we needed more space, we moved to Eldorado Avenue after my sister was born, Mary Lucile, who we called Mary Lou. The landlady, Mrs. Meminger, lived in the back portion and we lived in the front. We lived right across the street from Clearwater Beach.

Our days were spent in school, on the beach and rehearsing plays for our newly formed children's theatre group called The El Dorado Players. Many of the neighborhood kids were in it. We performed in the garage of the house, made our own lighting and put folding chairs in the driveway. We did original musicals and Broadway shows such as *Camelot*. Halloween was always a fun time. We would dress up and go into Carlouel, a gated community for the well to do. Chic Young, the creator of the comic strip Blondie, lived there. He gave out pennies and nickels – you could take two handfuls! His neighbor, Mr. Haig, had a lioness and let us pet her until she got too big. The Baumgardner family, who owned The Kapok Tree Inn, a fabulous upscale restaurant, lived in Carlouel as well. Their son, Billy Baumgardner, became G3's best friend and was in most of our shows. He and my brother Walter started The Cobra Club. Us little kids went to a meeting once in Billy's dark attic. There was candlelight, chants, rattles and all kinds of mysterious noises. G3 and Billy were done up in Cobra Club drag!

Eloise:
From early childhood I remember fragments. My tricycle with plastic ribbons on the handlebars. My brothers were consistently in and out of the frame. They were always bringing dead critters home to dissect. Nasty kids down the street blocked my way and tried to boss me around. As a kid in Florida I did not have much of an understanding of the world around me – so it goes like this: tricycle, a screen door, weird kids and tropical, hot days, going to the beach with Mary Lou, who was a baby in Mom's arms, and me walking next to her in diapers.

Theater
HERE!

Audience
HERE!

After a year with Lutie we found a larger house on Eldorado Avenue further up the beach. Like Lutie's house, it was within earshot of the surf. Its garage was just the right size for a neighborhood theater. We moved there in the summer of 1962 and started our own family theater in the garage.

- W.M.

Walter Michael:

George viewed the world through myth-colored glasses. Upon landing on Eldorado Avenue he mused we had arrived in the fabulous land of Inca gold, Spanish conquistadors and Voltaire's *Candide* – the Land of El Dorado. G3 read about the legend of a king who covered himself with gold dust before jumping into a lake as part of a ritual. The name "El Dorado" translates literally as "the golden one." He dubbed us all "The El Dorado Players."

Eloise:

The scripts, written by our mother, were dreamy, complete musicals that she wrote while in college and carefully preserved in her trunk. The audience was our neighbors who sat in the driveway and cheered.

Walter Michael:

Our first "trunk show" was *Bluebeard,* Mom's musical adaptation of the legend. Her sense of whimsy transformed the gory fable of the murderous ogre into an amusing, un-bloody children's story about a nasty nobleman who, upon tiring of his many wives, disposed of them by turning them into pieces of furniture. The furniture "wives" decorated the set and spoke and sang to the live actors.

Billy Baumgardner, having the right body type and attitude of pomposity, was the obvious choice to play Bluebeard. G3 chose the glamour part for himself, Bunko, a handsome leading man who defeats the ogre and gets the girl, thus establishing a casting pattern which would endure through decades of Harris family musicals. The girl next door, Tina Keig, was drafted to play Paula, a plucky bride who outwits Bluebeard by dyeing his beard pink. This breaks the magical spell, restores the "furniture wives" to life and ends Bunko's servitude, leaving him free to marry Paula. From this moment forward, there was nearly always a big wedding scene at the end of G3's shows.

Eloise:

Bluebeard was an instant success! No sooner had the curtain (garage door) gone down to thunderous applause than George was planning the next show and begging Mom for new material. Mom reached into her trunk and out came *The Sheep and the Cheapskate*, a generation gap musical set in the 1950's. Our *Bluebeard* cast was drafted into service with Billy starring as the fuddy-duddy father who insists on wearing his old-fashioned striped bathing suit on the beach. Tina played Jane, his modern-minded daughter, who also happened to be a knockout in a bikini (the latest Florida fashion rage). And whom did our director select for the plum role of Dick, the handsome lifeguard who wins the hand of beautiful Jane? George of course.

Walter Michael:

The El Dorado Players were off and running. Having successfully produced two original musicals we set out to cover Broadway. George noticed that liner notes on Broadway record albums contained a detailed synopsis of each show. This was all he needed for a working script. From the notes we improvised an adaptation of Lerner and Loewe's *Camelot*. Billy played King Arthur, Tina was Guinevere, and George took up Robert Goulet's part of Sir Lancelot. Fred, Jayne Anne and I assumed our usual supporting positions of knights, pages and kitchen wenches. Eloise made her stage debut as a palace page, and Mary Lou as a village babe-in-arms.

Stunt work fell to Fred and I. We transformed our bicycles into war horses, made armor out of cardboard and silver spray paint and made clever use of convincing fake blood. We staged such a realistic joust battle on Eldorado Avenue astride our "horses" that a doctor jumped up from the audience and rushed into the street believing we were hurt.

The Eldorado Players all-child cast presents its adaptation of Broadway's 'Camelot.' G3 and Jayne Anne are in the middle.

Beach News, a mimeographed community newsletter, gave us a favorable review, our first! Emboldened by the success of Mom's two original musicals, plus *Camelot,* and drawing on our Junior Workshop experience, we tackled Shakespeare (and Elizabeth Taylor) with an adaptation of *Antony and Cleopatra,* retitled *Cleopatra, Queen of the Nile.*

For the first time G3 assumed the role of playwright for our little group. Taking inspiration from a history lesson in school and from Elizabeth Taylor's hit movie, he created a visual script, a storyboard consisting of pictures, drawn by him and cut from magazines, and pasted into a notebook. This creative process would repeat again and again in his career. Each tableau formed the basis for a scene in the play. Tina was cast as the infamous Nile Queen, Billy B. as Julius Caesar, G3 as the treacherous Brutus (he was stretching as an actor), and I moved up from the chorus to play Caesar's personal physician. Our garden hose became the infamous asp whose bite sealed Cleopatra's doom.

What I remember best is the death scene, my first appearance in a principal speaking role. Prior to my entrance, the traitor Brutus had stabbed Caesar to death. Entering, I saw the audience and forgot my opening line.

Falling back on my character's professional composure I observed my beloved master laying there in a pool of blood, life ebbing away, the murder weapon protruding from his back. Improvising, I exclaimed, "My liege! What seems to be the problem?"

Chapter 4
Unsinkable

It's such a beautiful day
The seagulls are flying in the sky
It's such a beautiful day
And if you must know the reason why
The sun is shining on us
And no one's making a fuss
It's such a beautiful day
A beautiful, wonderful day!

"It's Such A Beautiful Day" from *The Sheep and the Cheapskate*
Music and lyrics by Ann Harris

Walter Michael:

Having mastered Shakespeare and Broadway, what was left to conquer but Hollywood? My brother George saw *The Unsinkable Molly Brown* on television's *Million Dollar Movie* and recognized a story of mythic proportion. For our next project he envisioned a film about the sinking of the Titanic. George recruited our neighbor, John Lowell, to shoot the film with his home movie camera. Another neighbor, Harry Strenglein, not only owned a boat, but also could hold his breath under water a long time. Because of this remarkable talent, Harry scored the longest scene in the film. As the captain of the Titanic he went down with his ship and was on screen floating face down in the icy Atlantic (the warm Gulf) for almost two minutes. Harry's boat appeared snaking its way through a grim field of drowned passengers and picking up survivors.

Once the script was written and the casting set, our garage theater was transformed into staterooms, boiler rooms, and the bridge. Our front hallway became the Grand Staircase. Dad created a realistic balsa wood scale model of the Titanic, complete with its famous four smokestacks and other historical details. Mom was cast as the "unsinkable" Molly Brown, G3 was the chief steward and Fred played the Titanic's frantic telegraph operator. Everyone on our street came on board as socialites, sailors and stokers. When George cast me as the iceberg, my range as an actor expanded exponentially.

Finally it was time to film the final climactic scene. I was positioned in a folding chair in the Gulf of Mexico, covered with a white sheet and slathered with paper maché for a jagged ice look. My special effects assignment was to create the illusion of Titanic's crash and slow descent into its watery grave. We were down to our last roll of film and waited for the fading daylight in order to simulate the night of terror. Dad carefully placed the "Titanic" in the water. The tide began to recede as if orchestrated. The model luxury liner slowly edged its way toward the killer iceberg. Fumbling around underwater I struggled to get hold of the model Titanic. On the second try my hand found its way to the ship and gradually pulled it under. "It's a wrap!" cried George as he ran home to work on the narration. Our cameraman rushed to get the final reel developed.

G3 was fascinated by the Titanic's opulence, the contrast between social classes, the epic scale of the disaster and the enduring appeal of its legend.

— *W.M.*

Mom explained that, after the Titanic went down, the world changed. The generation that had built the "unsinkable" ship was sure of itself, its wealth and its technology. Before the disaster society was split into distinct classes, as reflected in levels of the great ship. Afterwards, nothing was the same.

- W.M.

Walter Michael:

At last the great day came for the premiere screening of *The Unsinkable Titanic.* No expense was spared to make this the event of the century. The Clearwater press and neighborhood public turned out in force. As people arrived for the premiere, it seemed just like Hollywood. Harvey Warren, director of the Frances Wilson Playhouse, brought a full-size klieg light that lit up the night sky. He and his wife, Louise drove up in their Mercedes. We were thrilled.

The audience took their seats. The elaborate set made them aware that this would be more than a mere movie screening. Backstage, George, Mugsy and I heard the buzz of excitement and anticipation. We felt this could be the El Dorado Players' finest hour as a producing organization.

All three of us rose to the occasion, taking turns reading from G3's narration. From the launching of the grand ship, to the lavish upper-class parties, to the card games and simple pleasures of the second-class passengers and the work below deck – life aboard the Titanic came to life in the fullness of 8mm Kodacolor. Our premiere audience was swept up in the magic allure of the "unsinkable" floating palace. The optimism, technology and class struggles present at the dawn of the 20th Century were symbolized by the Titanic's maiden voyage. Our little movie captured them convincingly enough.

Particularly touching was a long, somber shot of the dead captain floating face down in the water. It went on so long the audience thought the actor must have drowned. They applauded the bravery of the stokers, cheered the pluck and courage of Molly Brown and held their breath as the Titanic shuddered and lurched toward certain doom. It was time for the grand climax, on the last reel, delivered too late to view or edit. We, the narrators, were seeing it now for the first time along with the audience

In a wide-angle shot, the balsa Titanic struck the iceberg again, began to sink from view and then suddenly bobbed back up to the surface like a jack-in-the-box. Clearly visible on the screen, a gigantic hand more than half the size of the Titanic itself, rose majestically out of the frozen North Sea, dwarfing the ship. Turning one way, then another, the hand wrapped itself around the Titanic like a Japanese B-movie giant octopus, and dragged the ship under.

We sat there speechless. The audience became restless. Mugsy looked over at me, as white as the iceberg. Fumbling with my champagne glass, I smiled weakly. Without missing a beat, George stood up and bravely delivered the concluding line of his narration as the president of the White Star Line: "What we have done here today can never be undone – but we shall try our best to undo it."

Here's how The Clearwater Sun of October 19, 1962 described the event:

'Unsinkable Titanic' Triumph
by Beverly Hutchins

George Harris Jr., 13 year-old producer of new plays, outdid himself in his debut as a film director Saturday night with the premiere showing of "The Unsinkable Titanic."

The movie began with panoramic shots of elaborate staterooms, the first class ballroom and elite passengers enjoying various activities unaware of the impending tragedy.

Included in the unfolding plot were the first signs of concern on the bridge, valiant efforts of the stokers in the boiler room endeavoring to remain at their duties, the perspiring wireless operator frantically jabbing the code key with pleas for help, and the sudden realization and ultimate panic of the passengers.

Most realistic and exciting were scenes in the lifeboats when passengers, foundering in the water were hauled aboard to safety. A gripping shot was that of the "dead" captain of the ship floating in the water. The final scene showed the watery grave of the Titanic.

Asked if he would like to continue his filmmaking hobby into adulthood, George said, "Yeah, but I'd rather do live dramas than make movies … It's a whole lot easier."

Chapter 5
Return to New York

Here's where you can sing your way to the top
Here's where you'll start dancing, you'll never stop
Don't tell your pop!

Say good-bye and hail a taxi please
I'll hob knob with great celebrities
I'll confess my new address is Broadway! Broadway!
Don't tell me, I gotta be on Broadway, New York!

"Broadway, New York" from *Razzamatazz* and *Sky High*
Music and lyrics by Ann Harris

Walter Michael:
Titanic's story was symbolic of an existential and financial crisis lurking just below the surface for our family. While Florida met our parents' expectations of a great place to raise kids, it failed miserably as a place to make a decent living. That ship was sinking fast. Prepare the lifeboats! A life-changing decision was taking shape.

Something was stirring around the edges of the family's creativity. The seed of an idea took root subconsciously and grew gradually, spilling out soon after *The Unsinkable Titanic* in the form of a family meeting. The idea was put forth and discussed: should we move to New York and try to make a living in theater? The response was unanimous: Why not?

With his family's blessing, Dad left for New York in January of 1962 to explore the possibility of making a living in the profession we had come to embrace. Soon we were getting letters from him written on the back of Caffe Cino menus, whose illustrations were so imaginatively drawn that we clipped ideas for our show programs.

George Sr:
I was hunting around for work in New York. It was pure luck that I ran into Ellen Stewart while looking for a place to live. She recommended me to her landlord and gave me my first directing job. Her theater, La MaMa Experimental Theater Club, was in the basement of 321 E. Ninth St., right next door to where the family was about to land. Thanks to Ellen I had a place to live, current New York credits and introductions to playwrights and producers.

Jayne Anne:
While we were living on Eldorado Avenue, my father went back up to New York to explore making a living in theater. After a while he came home to visit but was stopped by the Clearwater cops because he had let his hair grow long. Florida in the early 60's was no place for longhaired beatniks, artists and Greenwich Village types. Dad made it home but when we got up the next morning, his hair was short. He proposed that the time had come to

29

move back up north. We decided as a family to undertake this enormous task. Dad returned to New York first, followed by G3.

In August 1964, just weeks before my ninth birthday, G3 came back down to Florida and talked me into going back to NYC with him. He dressed me to the nines in a sailor dress, tweed coat, straw hat, patent leather "Mary Janes" (with a button), white gloves (you wear one and hold the other) and a straw purse. We traveled in the coach car and my mother packed us a whole bunch of food for the 24-hour trip. We ate it but George also took me to the dining car with its tablecloths, flowers and exotic train food! There we ran into a bunch of nuns who were riding in the sleeper cars. They took us under their wing and we spent the rest of the trip with the Sisters.

Dad met us at Penn Station. I had never seen anything so glorious. It's a real shame it was torn down years later. I was in total culture shock when I arrived in New York. Here I was, a beach kid used to bare feet, now living in a fifth floor, two room walk up with no bathtub! Dad had to build a shower out of a galvanized metal tub and a rubber hose. I went to school at Public School 122 which has since become Performance Space 122, a performance art venue. George took me on all my auditions and bought all of my clothes with the money he earned by doing television commercials. We would shop at Lanes (a budget store) and S. Klein's department store on Union Square. I had an art teacher, Jim Grasso, who lived in a little two-story building behind ours in the courtyard. Jim would make his own canvases, so big you could not get them out of the apartment!

He would throw all kinds of paint, paper, and food at them and create these strange works of art. He taught me the basics of drawing but would get mad at some of my drawings and tear them up on the spot. I think he might have been hitting the bottle or perhaps other substances. Needless to say, I didn't stick with him for long. The rest of the family came up from Florida right after Halloween.

Eloise:
We had just come from the tropical winds and gentle waves of the beach. Now, steam came out of the streets from the sewers and subways. The subway cars were fascinating when we first arrived. They had fans overhead and seat coverings that looked like linen. On the walls were bolts that jutted out slightly holding the steel panels together, all painted tan. I used to think I could predict when the door would open. I'd shut my eyes and say *Nowwww!* And they did.

The first apartment was dank and dark with freaky smelly hallways and daddy's incessant jerry-rigging of overcrowded plugs and showers made of hoses - proving what doesn't kill you will make you stronger. Always willing to explore her new world, my mother would make the best of almost all situations. Often our East Village neighborhood was scary, but Mom had a knack for magical thinking and humor, making it all right. Our parents were from the generation of "just make the best of it and keep going, don't stop. Here, have some Haagen Dazs!"

In 1963 George got a job with *The Dolphin Players*, an Equity company. He appeared in 'Treasure Island' at the Paper Mill Playhouse and in Westport. He started to get a lot of print work (modeling) and in1965 was cast in a Broadway show, 'The Porcelain Year,' with Barbara Bel Geddes and Martin Balsam.

- *Ann*

Dad, G3 and Jayne Anne were already in New York. Mom and the rest of we kids (ages three, five, eleven and thirteen) traveled from Florida by train and reached the Lower East Side on All Soul's Day, November 1, 1964. It had not yet snowed in the city but the festive air of Christmas had begun to work its magic on minds and hearts. Subway tokens were fifteen cents in those days. Pizza was a quarter a slice. For five cents you could ride the Staten Island Ferry or get fresh hot chocolate at the Horn & Hardart Automat in a real china cup. New York City was an urban Disneyland for us to explore and discover.

- Walter Michael

The Harris Family exploring New York City at Rockefeller Center in 1965. It was our first summer after arriving from Clearwater, Florida.

Left to right, front row: Eloise, a friend, Jayne Anne, Fred, Mary Lou, unknown elbow. Back row: Walter Michael, Ann, George III.

Jayne Anne:
The East Village was both a hotbed of artistic freedom and a very scary place. This was the beginning of my NYC-induced Post Traumatic Stress Disorder, which is with me to this day. Lots of people there had fallen on hard times – bums, drug addicts and runaways, along with the writers, actors and artists. Cultures were a mixed bag as well and we were all living in close quarters.

Mary Lou:
In the 1960s the East Village of New York City was bustling with all kinds of intense political and cultural movements that touched our every-day lives. The Vietnam War was raging leaving scarring images of bloody and terrified people in my mind. The Civil Rights Movement affected our schooling as violence and tension grew inside the local parks and schools. I remember the random racial riots that would emanate from Tompkins Square Park. Eloise and I would turn around and run home. In those days there were a multitude of reasons to run home and not return to school: gang violence, racial rioting, flashers, or hippie stoners with kaleidoscope eyes wanting to touch your hair (at 7:30 in the morning). Women's Liberation was creating a shift in gender identities, which would influence the life choices that my two sisters and I would eventually make.

Simultaneously, New York City was flourishing with young artists of all genres. The artistic revolution included painters, dancers, writers, choreographers, actors, lighting and sound designers, film directors… and all degrees in-between, and blended with each other. I don't think anyone can actually describe the amazing, talented and sometimes tragic artists that were filling the streets, cafes, loft spaces, clubs and theaters in the 1960's. These artists came from all over the world and from all walks of life. With all the turbulent and scary revolutions going on around our family… this was the escape, the beautiful Garden of Eden… a place to create your own world… essentially it was the ground floor of the utopian society that the Harris family was about to build for itself.

Eloise:
Ellen Stewart, who founded La MaMa, was eager to help Dad's family of theater gypsies come to New York. Ellen found a large affordable apartment and got the landlord to hold it for a couple of weeks. When the apartment fell through because we couldn't move quickly enough, Ellen found a smaller apartment on the same block, a teeny 5th floor walk-up studio at First Avenue and East 9th Street. It was cramped, leaky, creaky and stinky, but our next-door neighbor was an artist! Farewell to the gentle sound of beach waves, hello to police sirens, loud neighbors, garbage trucks, construction clatter and taxi drivers leaning on their horns. Winos slept in our hallway and a gang of glue sniffers held their weekly meeting there too. We were home!

Ann:
After two months in our one room on First Avenue our "super" who serviced a lot of buildings in the area told us about a three room, first floor around the corner at 319 East Ninth Street. We ran! La MaMa was in the basement right next door and we learned that Ellen was responsible for our good fortune by referring us. George, Sr. built sleeping lofts with ladders easily accommodated by 14-foot ceilings so – voila – nine rooms!

George Sr:
This apartment that we lived in was very strange. It was small, so I built little lofts, one for each kid. It was kind of like a houseboat.

Jayne Anne:
It was a nice three-room apartment on the first floor in the back of the building. The ceilings were high and the rooms were large. We roller-skated through doorways that connected the living room, hallway and bedroom. My parents built sleeping lofts attached to the ceilings so that we would each have our own space. Dad and Mom slept under us in the living room. We had a piano in the kitchen and built a Japanese Garden out back in the alleyway. Since we were all involved in theater, school and jobs, our house ran 24 hours a day, seven days a week.

Above: Mary Lou's 9th St. loft with Suki the cat. Below: Mary Lou crocheting at the foot of the ladder leading to her loft.

Mary Lou:
319 East Ninth Street was a small apartment, but a wonderland to a little kid. It seemed quite magical to have my own loft with a small crawl space to pass dolls and notes to my sister Eloise. My life and memories really began in that apartment in the East Village. My vivid recollections were, wanting to decorate our apartment and make clothes with the sewing machine that my mother had given to me. My mother would take me to Woolworths on Broadway practically every weekend. She would let me buy a new pattern, bolt of fabric and matching thread. We would always end our shopping spree with an ice cream soda at the counter. I don't know where she found the money or the time, but this was our special time together… just us!

Ann:
G3 and I uncovered the "brick" by pulling the plaster off the wall in the kitchen where our rented upright piano stood. There was a window with the fire escape in the back and we had a little garden that first year.

Photo © Andrew Sherwood

Gradually the shock of the big city began to wear off and we began to adjust. For the kids I found the little old fashioned playground outside of Judson Church in Washington Square Park. It's not there any more.

- Ann

Clockwise from top left: Ann, Jayne Anne, Mary Lou, Eloise, ca. 1965.

Ann:

In the front of the building on our floor lived a great guy – Charles Caron. He was an actor in the summer with the Kenley Players and a photographer all year round. He came to the door on our first day with the makings of cocktails and cokes and proclaimed he was the Welcome Wagon.

Charles Caron

He and his lover cooked great dinners and he played show tunes on his piano and we all stood around and sang just like they did at the club, Rose's Turn, over in the West Village. *No No Nanette* was revived on Broadway and Charles photographed Ruby Keeler. As I was the lookout on the steps outside, he introduced me to her. It seems she had lived in that neighborhood years ago. She had very nice beautiful eyes.

When we arrived in New York City, young George had a real acting job as the juvenile in the Dolphin Players. They played theaters such as The Paper Mill Playhouse, Bucks County, and Tappan Zee. George, Sr. had already scored his Equity card in *Wide Open Cage*, directed by Bob Dahdah.

George, Sr.:

Dahdah is the master of keeping a show running. *Wide Open Cage* ran six months during a newspaper strike. My contract for $75 a week was written on a brown paper bag. Doesn't sound like much now, but $75 went a long way in those days. Forty years later that bag turned up in an old file at Actors Equity. It was just enough to prove I'd earned my pension.

Ann:

We went up to Central Park and discovered a wonderland of green grass and trees complete with a little stream. It was almost like being in the country. We went up there lots of times and later, I found out it was The Brambles, a gay trysting place. But like everything else in New York there's room for all and I guess nobody minded us playing Deer and Hunter on their turf.

On the other side of the park near the *Alice in Wonderland* statue is the small boat lake where George, Sr. took us to sail his model boat. Near the exit on Fifty-Ninth Street was a huge rock to climb. Walter, Fred and G3 had a great time extracting mica from the rock and sliding down the side. Their corduroy pants became totally smooth in the back.

Photo © Andrew Sherwood

Left to right: Eloise, Jayne Anne and Mary Lou in the light well of our building at 319 East 9th Street.

Photos © Andrew Sherwood

Settling in to their new life in New York City, clockwise from top left: Walter Michael, George, Sr., Eloise, George III, Jayne Anne, Mary Lou.

Eloise:

As a child you are really not cognizant of your surroundings. It is more sensory, like the warm disgusting water that came out of the school fountain. Being tired and at times confused because you became used to doing what was in front of you, sometimes, I just wanted to sleep. Other times, I was full of energy and ready to meet the challenges of the day.

Once we mapped out the city we would venture up to Central Park to a place called The Brambles that had a little hiking trail and a stream that trickled like a brook - a beautiful setting. I played there with my sisters and brothers. Always Mom would weave mythical tales of the enchanted forest that it was.

Years later we learned about something Mom may have been aware of already. At night, The Brambles was a cruising place for the gay community. We would play there during the day and the nocturnal boys at night. During the day there was no sign of their romping encounters, a testimony to NYC in those days.

There was a whole event calendar for the gay boys - the bathhouses, the bookstores, the dance clubs, The Anvil (a bar), The Brambles and what they called "glory holes" (enjoy the visual). Many of these places faded to black later on when AIDS began to wreak havoc on the gay community.

Walter Michael:

319 East Ninth Street became our family's residence and home base for the rest of the decade. The East Village was a magnet for artists and theater people thanks to the low rents. Our new neighborhood was culturally and economically diverse. Working class Ukrainians lived side-by side with more recent arrivals from Cuba, Puerto Rico, China and elsewhere. Long ago, this stretch of the Lower East Side had been the heart of the Yiddish professional theater, with venues up and down Second Avenue. Now it was becoming a hub for artists, activists and iconoclasts.

Once we attended to the necessities of enrolling in school, furnishing the apartment and signing up for free government cheese, we were able to build on Dad's initial contacts and Bob Patrick's enthusiastic branding of us as "the Lunts of off-off-Broadway."

G3 and Jayne Anne had several months' head start. George had already landed a good role in *Treasure Island* at The Paper Mill Playhouse and found work as an underwear model, while Jayne Anne landed a co-starring role in a new musical at Judson Poets Theater, in a big church at the start of 5th Avenue, across from the Washington Square Park arch. After a few days of getting oriented to the incredible change of terrain, we set out next to visit the Caffe Cino, the birthplace of off-off-Broadway and source of Dad's interesting stationery.

Joe Cino, upper right,, nurtured writers, actors and artists at his Cornelia Street coffeehouse theater. Photos and Images courtesy Robert Patrick, Ken Burgess, Conrad Ward and James D. Gossage.

SING HO FOR THE SIXTIES!
A Historical Overview by Robert Heide

The ten-year period of the l960's, like the l920's, was a breakthrough decade when all hell broke loose in the sense of a sea-change in America. It was the time of the Vietnam War, of the assassination of John F. Kennedy, Robert Kennedy, Martin Luther King as well as the mysterious death of the legendary Marilyn Monroe. Valerie Solanis the notorious author of "S.C.U.M. - The Society for Cutting Up Men" shot Andy Warhol; but he survived. In Greenwich Village where I lived everything was breaking down and opening up at the same time in a new way. The old guard Bohemia which included Maxwell Bodenheim, Edna St. Vincent Millay, Dylan Thomas, John Reed, Marcel Duchamp and other early 20th century icons gave way to 'The Beat' movement which included Allen Ginsberg, Jack Kerouac, Ted Jones, Gregory Corso, Jack Michelline, Taylor Mead, and Diane Di Prima all of whom were reading their poetry in places like the Gaslight on MacDougal Street as early as l958 and throughout the l960s. The Village at the time reflected and paralleled the Left Bank in Paris where Existentialism was all the rage and Jean-Paul Sartre, Simone de Beauvoir, and Albert Camus represented a new intellectual elite. Village writers like myself and H. M. Koutoukas, wearing beatnik black sweaters and pants, sat in Cafés like the Rienzi, the Figaro, and the Feenjon reading Sartre's thick philosophical tome "Being and Nothingness" from cover to cover with serious intent. Martin Heidegger's Being and Time was also a must read in those smoke filled cafés on MacDougal Street where we drank endless cups of black coffee, espresso, and cappuccino. The "Love Generation" as it was called, was an enthusiastic and driven lot and the motto was "never trust anyone over thirty." The influence of the "Theater of the Absurd," a term coined by writer Martin Esslin, entered when the plays of Ionesco, Beckett, De Gelderode, and Genet were produced all over the Village. These new European absurdist writers influenced new American playwrights like Jack Richardson, Arthur Kopit, Jack Gelber, and Edward Albee, who were grouped together by the news media as 'four on a new wave.' Mostly one-act plays were the order of the day in off-Broadway theaters and they were also done in the many places that eventually became known as 'off-off-Broadway.'

In 1958, Joe Cino opened the Caffe Cino coffee shop on MacDougal Street, later moving it to 31 Cornelia Street where it was then tagged by the Village Voice as 'the off-off-Broadway Shrine.' Joe was the first to do original one-act plays in his small cafe where new American writers like myself, Sam Shepard, Robert Patrick, William Hoffman, David Starkweather, Doric Wilson, Lanford Wilson, H. M. Koutoukas, Tom Eyen, John Guare, Michael Smith, and others followed in the footsteps of the four-on-a-new-wave group. In particular these Cino writers were inspired by the early one-act works of Edward Albee like *The Zoo Story, The American Dream* and *The Death of Bessie Smith* all of which became big off-Broadway hits in the early l960's.

The pinnacle for me was the mid-point year of the decade l965 when my play *The Bed* opened at The Cino. It featured two dissolute young men who could not get out of bed and who seemed to be forever lost in time and space. Produced many times at the Cino and elsewhere in the City it was also filmed by Andy Warhol who was a regular at the Cino. When my play *Moon* opened at The Cino in February of 1967 it had been immediately preceded by *A Funny Walk Home* written and performed by the brilliant Jeff Weiss, a psychodrama starring Claris Nelson and George Harris III who as Hibiscus would later go on to produce The Cockettes and the glittering musical extravaganza "Angels of Light" in San Francisco and in New York to great acclaim. Georgie, as we called him, was a member of the first family of off-off-Broadway the Harris acting clan - led by mother Ann, father George Harris II, three sisters, Mary Lou, Eloise, Jayne Anne, and brothers Walter Michael and Fred. This extraordinary family celebrated life in the theater and the Greenwich Village Bohemia of the l960's to the fullest. Many refer to this as 'the last gasp' of creativity partly due to the fact that rents then were under $l00.

In the l960's everything was happening including the folk music of Eric Anderson, Peter, Paul, and Mary, Bob Dylan, Joan Baez, and Dave Von Ronk who were performing all over MacDougal Street. Village clubs like the Cafe Wha?, Cafe Bizarre and the Nite Owl featured early rock n' rollers like the Lovin' Spoonful, the Mamas and the Papas and the Blues Magoos. After Joe Cino opened his caffe along came Ellen Stewart who first opened the Cafe La Mama later called La MaMa ETC (Experimental Theater Club) originally at 321 East Ninth Street and later at 82 Second Avenue, 122 Second Avenue and finally at 74 East 4th Street where the plays of Paul Foster, Rochelle Owens, Megan Terry, Adrienne Kennedy and other new OOB writers found a home. Influential in this theater movement was Tom O'Horgan of *HAIR* fame who began his illustrious directorial career at La MaMa. Judith Malina and Julian Beck's Living Theater on 14th Street and 6th Avenue with plays like Jack Gelber's *The Connection* was among the most prominent of the new theater spaces. The Judson Poets Theater - where director Larry Kornfeld and composer Al Carmines prevailed - produced new work by Rosalyn *(Home Movies)* Drexler, Ron *(Gorilla Queen)* Tavel, and Maria Irene *(The Successful Life of 3)* Fornes. This was also the place where dance-theater flourished and Happenings happened as well as the 'Fluxus' movement, which included Yoko Ono and Dick Higgens who found a home base for their Dadaistic experimental theater work. An important group, Theater Genesis, was founded by Ralph Cook in l964 to develop and promote a new subjective realism enlisting writers like Murray Mednick, Tony Barsha, Sam Shepard, Leonard Melfi, Walter Hadler and Tom Sankey whose *The Golden Screw* became a commercial hit.

In the l970's and l980's rents in Greenwich Village and all over New York City jumped to a new high, severely limiting experimentation in the arts and today it is all about real estate. The creative Bohemia of the l960's now seems a long time ago akin to the days following the Civil War where the carpetbaggers moved in and all that was before was gone-with-the-wind. Yet the time of the sixties persists on so many levels that it is a decade that will never be forgotten and who knows? The real dawning of The Age of Aquarius may be just around the corner.

**Robert Heide, right, with John Gilman
at the Gershwin Hotel in New York City, 2013.**

Photo © Randolph Graf

Poster art by Ken Burgess and Robert Patrick. Photos © James D. Gossage and Conrad Ward.

CAFFE CINO
AND IT'S LEGACY

AN
AMERICAN
CULTURAL
LANDMARK

EXHIBITION
VINCENT ASTOR GALLERY
MARCH 6 — MAY 11, 1985

LIBRARY & MUSEUM
OF THE
PERFORMING ARTS

THE NEW YORK
PUBLIC LIBRARY
AT LINCOLN CENTER

DAMES AT SEA!
or "GOLDDIGGERS AFLOAT"

CINO · 31 CORNELIA St · CH3-9753

Chapter 6

La Papa, La MaMa, and the Church on Washington Square

I'm betting on you to take a chance on my fantasy
Let's close the door on ennui
Take your chances and dance with me
I'm betting on you to be ready and willing and fancy-free
A spin on the floor would be
The start of romance, you see

Let's deal the cards for a mad affair
Go on playing chamin-de-faire
It's better than solitaire!
Let's spin the wheel while the night is young
Whirl around 'till the bells have rung
Bong! Bong! Bong! Bong! Bong!

And when we are through who knows
What fate has in store for us?
It may be a bore for us
But wasn't it marvelous?
That we took a chance
And started to dance
And started to dance.

"I'm Betting On You" from *Sky High*
Music and lyrics by Ann Harris

THE CAFFE CINO

Walter Michael:
We walked across town on St. Mark's Place in brisk winter air that makes the stars shine clearly. Following Mom like so many ducklings we made our way past the Waverly Theater, taking a right onto Bleecker Street and a left onto Cornelia, through a gust of warmth and fresh-baked bread aroma emanating from the Zampieri Bakery and finally to a doorway that lit the street with a magical, friendly glow. It would have looked like any other storefront except for the colorful aura cast on the cold night air by the Christmas twinkle lights out front and the inviting vibe of the place itself.

Once inside, we were swept up in the enchanting atmosphere. The lilt of opera was playing on a vintage Victrola. Hundreds of gleaming, twinkling, fluttering items of theater ephemera stuck to the walls and hanging from the ceiling danced wildly with the breeze from the front door whenever someone came in. The Cino walls were a mini-symphony of sounds and visuals prior to show time. They all fell silent once the doors closed and the show began, out of reverence for the cherubic guy who presided over the goings-on.

Photo © Herve Gloaguen, Rapho, Realities

"It's Magic Time!"

Joe Cino at his espresso machine, circa 1967.

Joe Cino was the Caffe's proprietor and muse. He cheerfully dispensed hot and cold drinks, sandwiches, pastries, song and laughter from behind the espresso machine. Dad's autographed photo was pinned on the wall behind him. Joe noticed us immediately, called us "bambinos," and showed us to our seats.

That night we tasted our first cappuccino and discovered the power of glitter. We marveled at the efficiency of the effeminate waiters, swishing from table to table, totally stoned, with trays piled high. We gleefully ordered the tasty drinks and pastries we had seen beautifully illustrated on the backs of Dad's letters to us in Florida.

In Joe and his Caffe we recognized the magical through-line of our family journey. He stepped over to the record player and replaced Maria Callas with Kate Smith singing "God Bless America." He stood listening so solemnly that the house grew quiet and listened too, filled with a blend of patriotic pride and high camp. As the last strains of Kate's "... my home sweet home..." faded, Joe lit a handful of red, white and blue sparklers, swept his hand across a curtain of wind chimes and glass beads and proclaimed "It's Magic Time!"

Joe's three words articulated how we understood theater. Once a play begins, it has to be Magic Time or all your best efforts are in vain. For our family and for many others Joe Cino embodied the emotion, excitement and commitment required for artistic success. Like Ellen Stewart, Joe chose artists on instinct alone. We saw him as our high priest, celebrating his counterculture Mass from behind the counter, dispensing culture. He was a generous man who accepted us as family.

The play that night was Paul Foster's *Balls.* The set was a bare black stage with two ping pong balls suspended by invisible thread and illuminated by a white light, like two souls drifting in radiant darkness. They represented two people who had died and were buried and were talking about what was going on in the cemetery above them, like a bunch of school kids getting off a bus for a picnic, one of them peeing on the grave.

We weren't "in Kansas any more!" How completely we experienced the play, forgetting we were sitting at a table in a tiny hot room, elbow-to-elbow with other people. At the Cino you were swept off your feet into whatever flight of fancy the playwright conjured. You could count on being enchanted, absorbed, annoyed, tickled, provoked, amused, outraged, pacified, ambushed, aroused, nauseated and ultimately entertained by schemes, themes and dreams. There were no sacred cows. The only critic that mattered was the audience.

Having experienced the Caffe Cino, how could we go back to the Catholic Church?

Photo © Don Hogan Charles, New York Times

Ellen Stewart's theater was also a coffeehouse, a club, a laboratory and artistic home for new playwrights, tech designers and performers. It became our theater home upon arrival.   - W.M.

Ninth Street was my childhood home. We had a magical Japanese garden that my mother made in the courtyard there. She and G3 bricked the kitchen wall and made everything lovely. We lived in a funky area full of artists, junkies, Ukrainian kids and wild hippies.

- Eloise (right center in the military coat, late 1960's)

How it all began... I came to New York in 1950. Sundays, I'd get on the subway and go anywhere, exploring the city wherever I got off the train. One Sunday, I discovered Delancey Street and all those little shops with clothes and fabric. I wanted to be a dress designer and there was all this wonderful fabric! You could look at anything you liked. You could try things on. No one said anything to you. And this little man – my Papa Diamond – came out of this shop. He was wearing a little black cap on his head. He tried to sell me some fabric. I told him I had no money. He said, "Come inside, maybe you'll see something you like better." Finally, he understood I really hadn't a cent. Also, that I didn't have anybody, no family in New York. He adopted me on the spot. I became the artist daughter. My Papa Diamond told me that when he came to New York from Romania at age 11, he had a pushcart in the Delancey Street area. He said that I should have a pushcart, too. And if I pushed the pushcart for other people, it would take me where I wanted to go! Then I got very sick, I had many operations. I didn't know if I was going to live. I went to Morocco. My Papa Diamond came to me in a vision and told me to get my pushcart. So I left Morocco and returned to New York. I decided my pushcart would be a little theater where my brother, Fred Lights, and Paul Foster, could have their plays performed. That's exactly what I did. And that's why La MaMa is often referred to as a "pushcart." I believe young people must have a chance to start and learn, even if the work, the production, isn't remarkable. I feel strongly that someday we will have to do more than just say "hello" to other people. There has to be a visceral understanding among men – not just a greeting. So I try to use La MaMa as a pushcart to help push us in this direction.

– ELLEN STEWART

LA MAMA EXPERIMENTAL THEATER CLUB

Walter Michael:
Ellen started La MaMa so her brother and playwright friends could have a theater home and opportunities to experiment and collaborate, free from critical and commercial limitations. Ellen kept her uptown day job as a swimsuit designer, rented the basement of 321 East Ninth Street, and La MaMa Experimental Theater Club was born.

Ellen befriended Dad in 1962. In December that year he directed *The Collector,* an original play by Kate Hoffman, for Ellen's first

Ellen and Tom O'Horgan, ca. 1966. Photo © James D. Gossage

season in her new basement theater. It was Dad's first real theater opportunity in the city and the beginning of a beautiful personal, professional and family friendship with Ellen Stewart. Ellen Stewart not only found us a place to live, but gave us an open door to work in our chosen profession.

In his 1966 book *The New Bohemia,* John Gruen offers this profile of Ellen:

> The tinkling of a bell. A beautiful Negro woman steps in front of the audience: "Good evening, ladies and gentlemen," she says with a slight Creole accent, "and welcome to La MaMa, E.T.C., dedicated to the playwright and all aspects of the theater." The lights dim and the performance begins. Miss Stewart is La MaMa … for scores of actors, directors, designers, composers, technicians, and, of course, playwrights, all of whom look to her as the most sympathetic producer this side of heaven. Through her energy and dedication to the young and the untried, she has released the floodgates of creativity that might otherwise have remained untapped.

> Neither wealthy nor particularly schooled in the ways of professional theater, she simply felt a need to bring a new theater into being, a theater that is not based on commercial success or failure, a theater unafraid of expressing itself in any terms, a theater where the playwright learns as he does, where he can be involved in his work and world twenty-four hours a day if he so wishes.

> Miss Stewart is not a fanatic avant-gardist. She will put on a play of any style, if the seed of talent is there. Although that seed has often been infinitesimal, and a good number of the new works have been excruciatingly amateur, she has never stinted on her time, ingenuity, or enthusiasm, and she has given all of her productions the best presentation possible.

Being a Negro, and a woman, has complicated Miss Stewart's efforts to find permanent quarters for her venture. Time and time again she met with unsympathetic landlords and license commissioners, and she had to move a number of times before finding her present East Village quarters, which she has turned into one of the most engaging and atmospheric of café-theaters.

JUDSON POETS THEATER

Walter Michael:
Another off-off-Broadway venue that threw open its doors to us early on was Judson Poets Theater, located in Judson Memorial Church, bordering Washington Square Park. Led by co-

pastor Al Carmines, a brilliant composer and performer, Judson Poets Theater became known for its signature style of musical theater rooted in whimsy, social satire and art as spiritual expression.

Since the late 1940s Judson Church saw artists as a natural constituency in its Greenwich Village neighborhood. The congregation and its leaders encouraged artists to *be artists,* and supported them materially as well as spiritually.

Howard Moody, its visionary pastor, along with Al Carmines, took gutsy political stands on issues of the day,

L to R: Al Carmines - pastor, showman, composer, singer, actor and five-time Obie award winner. With Maria Irene Fornes, H.M. Koutoukas and Larry Kornfeld, planning the operetta 'Pomegranada.' Photo © James D. Gossage

and made Judson Church a sanctuary and venue for artists who resonated with its philosophy and style. The Harris family felt instantly at home there and became regulars in its productions. Judson was the first to give the reconstituted El Dorado Players a venue when we arrived from Florida. Ever since, the church figured prominently in our lives and careers. As winter 1964 turned to spring, our family began an amazing run of working nonstop as actors, musicians, directors, producers, writers and technicians, while balancing our developing careers with school, family life and making a living.

George, Sr.:
I'd take a nine-to-five job, but the job was always the lowest priority. So I'd leave in an instant for a paid show. It was always that thing of trying to make enough money to pay the rent and feed the family. My attitude, right or wrong, was that theater is a wonderful thing to be in. It's actually a privilege. And if somebody has the talent to be in it, there's no reason they can't pursue it and pick up their education as they go along. My attitude must have been OK, because everybody seems to have turned out all right.

GEORGE III (Age 19) EQUITY

WALTER (Age 17)
EQUITY-SAG-Local 802

FRED (Age 15)

JANE (Age 13)

ELOISE (Age 9) EQUITY

MARY LOU (Age 7)

Off-off-Broadway was a great place in which to grow up. We worked side by side with talented producers, playwrights, directors, actors, singers, dancers, lighting designers and more. As a child, I thought of them as my playmates. As a performer, I was treated as an equal. That also meant that the goods had to be delivered with no whining. We kids were expected to behave like grown actors. Schoolwork being done in between scenes, catnaps and meals on the fly were the norm.

- Jayne Anne

Chapter 7
The First Family of off-off-Broadway

Opening night is such a paradox
Where's my lipstick, where's my powder-box?
Hey, a guy from Twentieth Century Fox
Will be catching the show.

Zip my zipper, is my wig on straight?
Now's the time I start to percolate
Don't be shy, you really look just great
Celebrating to go!

Isn't it nifty, he's a bit shifty
I'll have diamonds and pearls
Takes me out dancing, dinner, romancing
I'm just one of his girls.

When he calls half-hour with a knocking at my door
And my knees are knocking like they've never knocked before

My whole future lies before me
Will the audience adore me?
When I hit the stage
Will I be the rage?
Will he call half hour evermore?

"Opening Night" from *Sky High*
Music and lyrics by Ann Harris

Walter Michael:
Our best Christmas present in December 1964 was Judson Poets Theater's musical adaptation of A.A. Milne's Winnie the Pooh stories, *Sing Ho! For A Bear.* With songs by Al Carmines and direction by the great Larry Kornfeld, the show was signature Judson magic. Co-starring with Carmines as Pooh was our sister, Jayne Anne, in the role of Christopher Robin. We hadn't seen her since she left Clearwater with G3. Now, barely two months later here she was, starring in a new original musical based on material we kids knew well because Mom read A.A. Milne's poetry and stories to us frequently. It was thrilling to see those stories and characters spring to life on stage, and especially to see Jayne Anne playing a lead role and a character we knew and loved.

Jayne Anne:
I played Christopher Robin in *Sing Ho for A Bear,* a musical based on A.A. Milne's *Winnie The Pooh* and *The House at Pooh Corner* at Judson Poets Theatre in 1964. It was a wonderful experience for me. I was the only kid in the cast and I was treated as an adult. Claris Nelson,

prominent actress and writer, once said that we Harris family kids were always the consummate professionals. I don't know how long we ran but it was an awesome show. We met family friend Andrew Sherwood who walked us home after rehearsal one night. He was the window designer for Orbach's and had these Puss and Boots leather thigh high boots. We would go up to his apartment on Third Avenue above 23rd Street and listen to classical music and drink tea. Bob Dahdah, took the show to a cloistered convent in Connecticut where former movie star Delores Hart was a nun and would later become Mother Superior. The nuns watched the show through a latticed wall. Afterwards, we met the nuns and they shook our hands and spoke to us through the latticed wall. We stayed at Bob's sister's house and also visited a farm where Bob entered a field with a bull in it. He came tearing out of there pretty quick with the bull chasing after him!

I did lots of other things at Judson as well. Happenings were a big thing back then and all or some of the Harrises had a part in many of them. You would be placed in groups with specific music and told to do certain steps or placed in the park at outdoor ones and given certain tasks. There was one at St. Clements Church where I was placed (looked naked but was not) in a tub full of lime green jello and surrounded by dead rabbits hanging as if in a butcher shop (probably a vegetarian statement!). People filed by me on their way into the theatre. I was probably eleven or twelve years old. At that same happening, my father played a down on his luck bum, lying on the steps. People had to step over him to get into the church.

Dad would later reprise that role at Lincoln Center as part of oboe soloist and family friend Bert Lucarelli's *Lemonade for an Angel* concert and "happening" in 1971. He prepared by wearing a suit that he'd laid around in for a week so it got all stained and wrinkled. He poured a bit of alcohol on himself and lay in front of the entrance. He got arrested but would not go out of character in front of the audience streaming in. Producer, director and composer John Herbert McDowell had to go to the station house and talk the cops out of the arrest!

Ann with classical oboist Bert Lucarelli

At that same show, we had to walk and balance on thin walls that separated sections of seats in the theatre. I had Alexander Bartenieff on my back in a back carrier. Alex is the son of George Bartenieff and Crystal Field, co-founders of Theatre for the New City. I was twelve or thirteen at the time and he was an infant. It was Alex's theatrical debut. The show ended with everyone who had been given a segment to perform on stage in the theater.

We balanced school, day jobs and theater. Any one or a combination of the eight of us would be doing shows at any given time. Home life was a revolving door. The older kids would take the younger kids to their auditions if Mom or Dad were not available. All of us attended Anthony Mannino Acting Studio for lessons across from the Flatiron Building on Fifth Avenue at 23rd Street. On Saturdays my mother, myself and my two sisters traveled to the Upper West Side for singing lessons with our coach Tom Rosinsky. He was a barrel-chested baritone opera singer with a gorgeous voice. He taught me so much about the art of singing. Afterward, we would go to Central Park to the playgrounds or to paddle around the lake in a rowboat. We would go to the carousel and ride seemingly endlessly on it. Other times we would go to the museums.

Walter Michael:
We also took singing lessons from Mom's new friend Andrew Sherwood, a piano teacher, vocal coach and superb photographer who provided us with high quality publicity photos. Armed with our new skills and photos we hit the audition trail, seeking any kind of work we could find to improve our skills and build our resumes, while keeping up with schoolwork, day jobs, laundry and navigating the new world of New York City. G3 liked to say "we pounded the pavement with our portfolios." Building on Jayne Anne's Judson success, George and Mom cooked up a revue called *Remember the Thirties,* and convinced Judson to give us a stage. Although only a modest success, it was the first New York appearance of the transplanted El Dorado Players.

Andrew Sherwood

Jayne Anne:
Ellen Stewart heard about it and immediately offered the El Dorado Players a home at Café La MaMa where we developed and performed children's theater. Ellen called it her "Young Playwright's Series" and of course called us her "baybeez." Wow!

Walter Michael:
George and Mom dusted off our two original musicals from Clearwater Beach. *Bluebeard* and *The Sheep and the Cheapskate* transferred easily from our garage theater in Florida to La MaMa's café stage in New York. Thanks to G3's enthusiasm, Mom's songwriting talent, and our "can do" attitude, the El Dorado Players soon created two more musicals: *MacBee,* our take on *Macbeth,* set in a modern advertising agency; and *There is Method in Their Madness,* based on our experiences in acting school. The latter was reviewed favorably in the Village Voice by Michael Smith, a leading theater critic and later a family friend.

Jayne Anne:
Our children's troupe did several shows at La MaMa. Ellen treated us as equals in the theatre world and taught us a lot about theatre. Everywhere we performed we were kids but treated as adults. When you needed a kid you could always call the Harris family. I performed in and saw many significant original plays at La MaMa.

Ann:
Walter learned to play the piano in one show! We got into La MaMa, had all this music with no accompaniment, so Walter taught himself the piano and played. He would go from the piano, run up onstage to act a part, and back to the piano. Later he was playing drums for Tom Eyen's musical *Miss Nefertiti Regrets* at La MaMa. When leading man Jackie Curtis walked out in a huff, Tom asked Walter to step in. He had the paradiddle *and* the part!

Walter Michael:
In *Nefertiti* I got to act and sing opposite the wonderful, talented Bette Midler. She had recently arrived from Hawaii, as we had from Florida, and this was her first New York show. Bette was 19 and I was 14. She played Queen Nefertiti and I played the archangel Tobias, sent by Ra, the sun god, to seduce the queen and cause her downfall. It was so much fun performing with this powerfully talented young woman who was (and is) warm, generous and joyful on stage and off. In our roles we sparred, flirted, delivered hilarious Tom Eyen one-liners to the audience and sang a lover's duet. Seeing through the ploy, Queen Nefertiti orders me put to death - at which point the blackout provided cover for me to return to the drums in time for the next song. It was a blast. Thank you, Jackie Curtis!

Not long after *Nefertiti* Bette told me she had landed a part in the smash hit Broadway musical *Fiddler on the Roof.* We all felt tremendous pride that one of our own had made it to Broadway. She started in the chorus and soon rose to the lead role of Tevye's eldest daughter Tzeitel, where she could really shine. I saw *Fiddler* several times to enjoy Bette's performances and celebrate her success.

Mary Lou:
To me, off-off-Broadway felt like playing dress-up ... EVERYDAY! Now, to a little kid, this was magnificent. To some of the other members of my family, I am sure it must have felt like a roller coaster ride of pressure, euphoria and feeling incredibly lucky to be "on the scene." We all became skilled at taking direction, remembering lines and choreography and working with a variety of personalities in a variety of artistic genres.

I remember being cast as baby Alice, supporting Joy Bang's grown-up Alice in Tom Eyen's *Alice Through The Glass Lightly* at The Electric Circus on St. Mark's Place. Bette Midler played The Red Queen. I remember feeling so important at the age of four with my yellow Alice dress, going to the theater every night, having photographs taken of me and feeling fabulous that such a big fuss was being made over the production.

George Sr:
Everybody always seemed to be doing something. Ann was doing something, each of the kids was doing *something*. Our lives were a whirling kaleidoscope.

Photos © James D. Gossage

Bette Midler and I had fun performing in Tom Eyen's 'Miss Nefertiti Regrets'. She played the fabulous, fearsome Queen of Egypt who sent "too many men" to their doom. I played Tobias, an angel sent by Ra, the sun god, to depose the Queen with love's temptation. But she turned the tables. - W.M.

Jayne Anne:
Caffe Cino was a magical place. The walls were covered with photographs of the people that performed there. There was a mysterious looking menu of food and drink and an unbelievable cast of characters at any given time. We kids were welcomed there as well and saw lots of groundbreaking theater. I did several plays there, one of them being *The Death of Tintagiles* by Maurice Maeterlinck. It was a play originally written for marionettes to perform. In the beginning, we rehearsed in the director's apartment and there was a scene where I was supposed to be locked up in a dungeon.

The director, believing in the "method way," put me in the bathroom and barricaded the door so I couldn't get out. She lived on 13th Street between First and Second Avenues in the East Village, quite a seedy block. Anyway, there was a junkie on the fire escape looking in the window as I was screaming to get out.

The director kept saying how well I was doing and how I sounded so fearful. I finally convinced her to let me out and never let her do that again! In that same play during a performance, the very "method" leading lady Suzanne is supposed to be pushing on that same door which is supposed to of course be very heavy. Well she was pushing on it with her pinky and playwright Harry Koutoukas started to giggle. Once he got started he couldn't stop. Finally, Suzanne picked up a sword and raised it up over her head exclaiming, "If you laugh one more time I am going to cut you." She repeated that several times and it just made Harry laugh so hard he was crying! Suzanne threw the sword down and stomped off the stage leaving me and Tanya Berezin out by the front door, unable to make our entrance. Since no one knew what she would do next, Charles Stanley, the lighting designer, walked calmly across the stage, took Tanya and me by the arm and calmly escorted us to the area where they made the cappuccinos so he could keep an eye on us!

Ann:
Much to the delight of the audience, the house lights came up, and we were back in a cafe again.

Walter Michael:
The sudden departure of the leading lady left the Cino temporarily without a show, so the united forces of off-off-Broadway rallied to fill in. OOB artists from every venue rallied with readings, monologues, and acrobatics, anything to give the Cino audience something special. The result was the infamous *Spring Gala*, a.k.a. *Spring Horror Show* a.k.a. *Palm Sunday Spectacular,* a.k.a. *More, More, I Want MORE!*

Dad, dressed as a priest, performed a hilarious Alan Bennett monologue from *Beyond The Fringe* called "A Piece of My Mind." G3 and I performed songs from The El Dorado Players latest musical at La MaMa, *There is Method In Their Madness.* Other performers included Robert Patrick, John Herbert McDowell, Michael Smith, Remy Charlip, Johnny Dodd, Jeannie Lanson, Al Carmines, Deborah Lee, Mary Boylan, Robert Dahdah, Lanford Wilson and H.M. Koutoukas. It was a fabulous affirmation of everyone's love for Joe Cino.

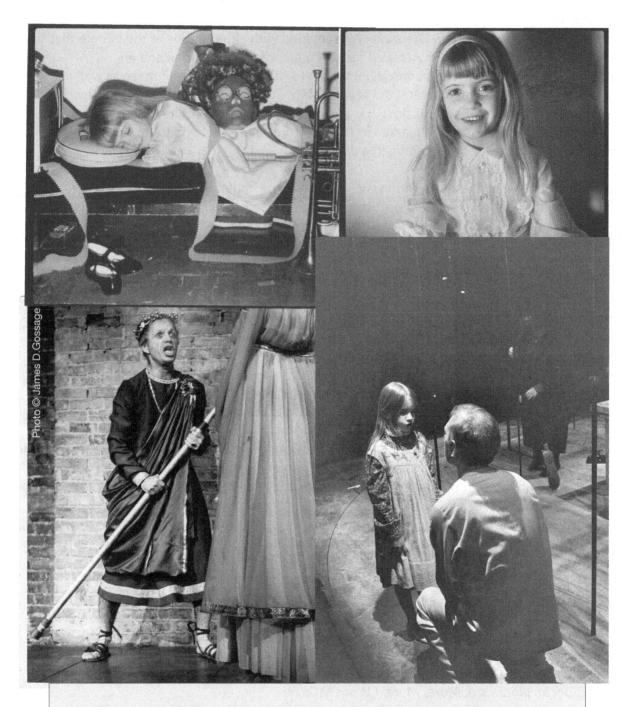

Photo © James D.Gossage

Clockwise from top left: Two images: Mary Lou as Young Alice (supporting Joy Bang's grown-up Alice) in Tom Eyen's 'Alice Through The Glass Lightly' at The Electric Circus on St. Mark's Place (1968); Eloise with John Heffernan in 'Invitation to a Beheading' at Joseph Papp's NY Shakespeare Festival's Anspacher Theater (1969); Dad in 'Myrtilus' with Kay Carney at La MaMa ETC (1967).

Ann:

One night at the Cino, Lanford Wilson stopped me and asked me if I would like to be in a full-length play he had written. Earlier, George, Sr. had acted in his one-act play, This Is The Rill Speaking, at the Cino. This new full-length play, *The Rimers of Eldritch,* was an extension of Rill. I'll never forget when we finished our first read through, the whole cast stood up and applauded Lanford. It was a gorgeous play and I was proud to be in it. We reprised it years later at a La MaMa celebration.

Jayne Anne:

At the Cino I also acted in Claris Nelson's *The Clown.* I played a prince (I was always called to play boys, foreshadowing of cross dressing to come!). That show was truly magical. It featured an all-star cast – myself, Lanford Wilson, Robert Patrick, David Starkweather, Soren Agenoux, Marshall W. Mason and others. Marshall was the director and Michael Warren Powell designed the costumes. I went for a fitting and came home with a lute in a case that I had to learn to play for a song or two. The lute played itself all night long and when we got it back over to the Cino a little mouse came running out!

Ann Harris (inset) in the premiere of Lanford Wilson's 'The Rimers of Eldritch' at La MaMa. (1966)

Photo © James D. Gossage

Walter Michael:

We had *momentum.* Our acceptance by the off-off-Broadway community inspired us to press ahead with our dream. As winter 1964 turned to spring 1965 the family individually and collectively answered opportunity with achievement. We had the great good fortune to work with producers and artists who reshaped our industry, transforming its entrenched ideas and institutions.

Ann:

Ellen Stewart was there for us from the start, and all the way through to her passing in January 2010. She was not only a sympathetic producer, but also a compassionate human being. Walter recalls that, during costuming for *Miss Nefertiti Regrets,* Ellen became aware of his extreme insecurity about showing his legs in tights due to a disfiguring bone condition. She brought a pair of hip-length leather boots to the theater for him to wear. The boots covered all, looked great and fit the character. Problem solved.

Walter Michael:

My family's extraordinary output during our first three years in New York propelled us into the heart of the city's creative community. We all worked continuously as actors off-off-Broadway, on television shows and TV commercials, including a Dove for Dishes spot in which Dad and I played a father and son trapeze team!

The El Dorado Players in 'There Is Method In Their Madness' at La MaMa, Young Playwrights Series, 1966

Photos © James D. Gossage

Photo © Andrew Sherwood

Photo © James D. Gossage

Left: Walter Michael at La MaMa's vintage grand piano.

Below: The El Dorado Players successfully transferred their debut musical from a Florida garage to a New York City coffeehouse theater with a new production of 'The Sheep and the Cheapskate' at La MaMa, Young Playwrights Series, 1966.

Photos © James D. Gossage

George, Sr. performs 'Take A Pew,' a monologue from 'Beyond The Fringe,' at the Cino Spring Horror Show, 1967

Walter Michael making his New York debut in Lanford WIlson's 'The Sandcastle,' 1965

Walter Michael:
We worked in summer stock, in movies, and on the radio. We performed in "happenings" and dance recitals. True to our Clearwater training we were often busy behind the scenes running tech, working front of house, doing publicity, sewing costumes, and serving as stagehands. We were often performing in one show and simultaneously rehearsing and/or writing the next. Plus squeezing in our school homework when we weren't needed on stage.

Susan Dale Rose:
In junior high I carried around a *Sixteen Magazine* article about George III. We were children of divorce living in a Russian Orthodox neighborhood; our living room was a studio and our house smelled like turpentine and we never had quite enough to eat. You all were the epitome of glamour and artistry. You lived in my mind as high wire artists, trapeze dancers, spangled and misted with the dust rising from the circus floor.

Photos © James D. Gossage

Clockwise from top left: Harry Koutoukas, Linda Eskenas, Robert Patrick and Walter Michael on the Caffe Cino stage; W.M. and Eloise in 'Method'; G3, Claudia Tedesco, W.M. and Elena Mattei at rehearsal.

Photos © James D. Gossage

Top: The El Dorado Players in rehearsal for 'There Is Method In Their Madness,' La MaMa, 1966. Fred is in profile, front left, and Mary Lou, age four, right. Right: Walter Michael with George Bartinieff in Paul Foster's 'The Madonna in the Orchard,' La MaMa, 1965

Eloise:
Mary Lou and I were sharing a role in a production of *The Little Match Girl* at Judson's Poets Theater. At the end of the show, the little girl (us) dies and goes to heaven, while carrying her doll. It was the saddest show that we had ever been part of and it affected us both profoundly. We would live this absolutely believable scenario on stage and then go to school during the day. It was difficult to separate these two worlds, and at the time, felt very surreal. The alternate reality would haunt us both in the middle of the day when we were trying to learn how to add and subtract. At the end of the run, the director gave us the doll as a gift. We named her "Yum-Yum" after a doll my mother had loved when she was little. She was soft and precious to us and we never questioned the idea of sharing her.

Jayne Anne:
I don't know how my parents hammered out a living with six of us, but we all had things like acting, singing and dance lessons. I even got to ride horses regularly out in Clove Lake Park on Staten Island as that was my passion. In between acting jobs, my mother worked as a temp at places such as S. Klein's (a department store) during the holidays where she was nearly crushed by ladies rushing the sale tables!

My father worked as a waiter in the cafeteria at the Metropolitan Museum of Art. When we went to the museum we would go there for lunch. We of course thought it was a four star restaurant with a huge fountain in the middle of it all. Dad also worked at the Sherry-Lehmann Liquor Store during the holidays, as many actors did, to cover Christmas presents. He didn't drink but sold a ton of wine by using his acting skills to describe the bouquet of the bottle in the customer's hand.

Walter Michael:
Dad leveraged his waiter job at The Met to try out exotic foreign accents on his customers. While they bore little resemblance to the actual languages, they did increase his tips. He tells a funny story about one holiday season at Sherry-Lehmann. Paul Newman came in shopping for a fine wine, so Dad outdid himself, laying his charm and B.S. on Paul, going on about the attributes of fine wine: strong oak, hints of cranberry, nice "legs" and so on. Early the following year Dad was working as an unbilled extra on the movie *Fort Apache, The Bronx*. In the scene, precinct captain Paul Newman is reviewing a line of uniformed cops, his steel-blue eyes narrowed in stern scrutiny. When he gets to Dad, Paul mutters under his breath, "hints of cranberry?" and flashes a subtle smirk to Dad, his fellow actor and would-be wine salesman. It was all Dad could do to not crack up with the cameras rolling.

Mary Lou:
My sister Eloise and I are very close in age (less than two years apart). Our young theater years in New York City seemed like an endless cycle of waking up at 7:00 a.m. for school, leaving for the theater at 5:00 p.m. for a variety of reasons (rehearsals, performances or those brutal cue-to-cue tech rehearsals) and finally returning back to our apartment on Ninth Street most often by 11:00 p.m. (sometimes after midnight). Eloise and I were SO tired and SO cranky. New York seemed to be geared towards artsy grown-ups and at the time it felt like the kids were used as the perfect ingredient of authenticity to any production.

Eloise and I saved our coins. Once, when we had enough money, we jumped on a Trailways bus bound for our summer home in Margaretville, New York. We really just wanted a break from the grind, but certainly weren't thinking about how out of her mind with worry our mother must have been. Running away served its purpose though. We got away from the theatrical rat race for a little while, but I know now how dangerous that action truly was for two little girls that were ten and twelve years of age, to be running around the mean streets of New York City in the early seventies.

Jayne Anne:
Going to public school in the '60's and '70's, one had to have a double personality. Theater training came in handy as one could instantly assume a "role" as needed. It is something I cultivated at an early age and still use to this day. I always feel as if I have my feet firmly planted in both bohemia and a typical existence. Bohemia usually wins out and I still feel out of place in many situations. In school and in day-to-day interactions in the East Village, much of my role-playing was safety related. If you were intimidated in any way, you became an easy target for the gangs, druggies and hooligans.

Our Ninth Street apartment had windows in every room and we lived on the ground floor by the basement that was always dark with the door ajar. Coming home from a date, a late night rehearsal, or a performance, you had to have your keys out and your wits about you. The front door lock was frequently broken. You had to run down the hall to the apartment door with your keys out praying that no one was standing in the basement stairwell. This

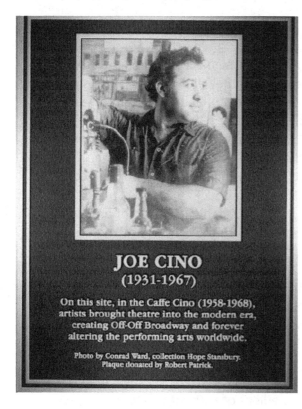

JOE CINO
(1931-1967)

On this site, in the Caffe Cino (1958-1968), artists brought theatre into the modern era, creating Off-Off Broadway and forever altering the performing arts worldwide.

Photo by Conrad Ward, collection Hope Stansbury.
Plaque donated by Robert Patrick.

went on for about thirteen years until I found an apartment on the Upper West Side.

Ann:
Without warning a knife literally struck at the heart of our community. Joe Cino stabbed himself on Friday, March 31, 1967, alone on the Cino stage. Apparently he was distraught over a lover's quarrel, but everyone knew how much stress was on his shoulders, trying to keep the doors open. Joe died the following Sunday, April 2.

Joe's death was a total shock to our extended theater family. I donated blood at St. Vincent's Hospital along with hundreds of others as Joe's life hung by a thread. A doctor there, amazed at the turnout, said, "I never in my life saw someone with so many friends."

Scott Morris, Filmmaker

I think of The Harris Family with great fondness as I remember Ninth Street, the piano in the kitchen, the loft-beds and musical instruments and Estes rockets in the living room, and the girls when they were, like, TWO, running around in their underwear. I heard a 45 of "Strawberry Fields" there for the first time (positively the strangest music I'd ever heard), and often stumbled upon your dad and his band playing honky-tonk on the street when I least expected it. We rode the subway to the High School of Music & Art while I tried not to burst out laughing when Walt had a conversation with his own reflection in the train window.

I visited The Electric Circus while it was under construction, and then Walt in his loft

Scott and Walter Michael in 1983

directly above the marquee at the Fillmore East (very surreal). That was when Walt said to me, "My Mom says you're a good influence on me..." I didn't say that I thought the Harrises were a good influence on me. I went to plays at La MaMa (the strangest theater I'd ever seen), and traveled in a mini-van to the house in Margaretville before there was any wallboard. I slept on the floor and was there when Fred crashed his Pacer. I visited some boyfriend who had a large, live wolf roaming around his apartment while I pretended I wasn't scared-shitless. Fred wrote and performed amazing music as a one-man orchestra for a whole bunch of my film projects.

I lost track of who got married, unmarried, and to whom (I think I've got it straight

now). I especially like the fact that Mary Lou married a video editor, but I don't take credit for it. Walt came back East to be my Best Man, and Nancy and I went West to visit Walter and Patty in Seattle. All of this was almost enough to make a middle class kid from Long Island EXPLODE.

But I didn't.

OFF-BROADWAY—George Harris and Selena Williams romp through a number in "Gorilla Queen," a new musical comedy opening tonight (Monday) at the Martinique Theater.

"'Gorilla Queen' is the avant-garde's 'Hellzapoppin' - outrageous nonsense that impresses you with its energy even when you are doubting its sanity." - The New York Times. "It is certainly going to leave those who are shockproof greatly shocked!" - New York Post

Chapter 8
Flowers, Guns and *Gorilla Queen*

(BRUTE disengages himself from the singing, exiting parade, and hops back up on the stage. He scampers over to the cuspidor and extracts the purple rose.)

BRUTE: Ladies and Gentlemen of every genus: Forget about dem durty minded fakes: Art ain't never 'bout life, but life is only about art. Dis rose? … oh, it ain't no symbol like ya mighta thought, an' dat's cause it ain't got nothin' to do with life either. Dis here rose is all about art. Here, take it --- (He throws the rose into the audience)

- Dad's closing lines from Ron Tavel's *Gorilla Queen*

Walter Michael:
By early 1967 our quiet working class neighborhood on East Ninth Street blossomed with the influx of actors, activists and artists of all kinds, attracted by the low rents. People watching from the front stoop became more and more interesting. Along with the neighborhood regulars and kids playing street stickball, on a given day you might see the poet Allen Ginsberg strolling crosstown, deep in conversation with his partner, Peter Orlovsky; the journalist-activist Ed Sanders, co-founder of The Fugs, a political rock group, en route to his Peace Eye Bookstore; and Ellen Stewart arriving with her artists to rehearse a new La MaMa show in its basement space next door.

It was a fantastic year for the family artistically. In February G3 appeared in Jeff Weiss' *A Funny Walk Home* at the Cino, after which he went straight into rehearsal for Ron Tavel's *Gorilla Queen* at Judson as a Glitz Ionas (ape). Dad was also cast as Brute, the lead ape, a principal role. Gorilla Queen became an overnight sensation and was transferred to off-Broadway, where it enjoyed commercial success and critical acclaim. Dad never forgot his admiration for Judson director Larry Kornfeld, who insisted that the producers take the whole cast for the commercial run – all or nothing. His courageous stance paid off, and gave the hard-working Judson cast a living wage paycheck for a change.

I was struggling to stay afloat in high school while appearing in a continuous string of shows. A standout gig for me that year was playing three roles in the pioneering science fiction radio drama, *The Star Pit,* by Samuel R. Delaney, on WBAI Radio. "Chip" Delaney was in his early twenties then, and his stellar career as a science fiction author was beginning to get traction. Delaney adapted his novella for the radio, and voiced the lead narrator role. This groundbreaking broadcast was repeated for about ten years in New York each Thanksgiving, becoming a holiday tradition.

Another highlight for me was collaborating with Robert Patrick on music for *Dynel,* his Christmas epic, at The Old Reliable Theater Tavern on East Fourth Street between Avenues C and D, and his follow-up, *Joyce Dynel,* an Easter spectacular at the same venue.

Photo © James D. Gossage

When Gorilla Queen moved uptown, Jayne Anne assumed George's role in Claris Nelson's 'The Clown' at the Cino in 1967. She delivered a beautiful, nuanced performance alongside a stellar off-off-Broadway cast. L to R: Jayne Anne Harris, David Starkweather, Soren Agenoux, Lanford Wilson and Arnold Horton. The director was Marshall W. Mason, who calls the Harris family "the Royal Family of off-off-Broadway." He muses," If either Neil Flanagan or one of the Harrises weren't in it, was it really a Cino production?"

Ink drawing, inscribed: *"George in a fur coat New York Dec '66"*
by **David Hockney *(inset)***

Nick Wilder had a beautiful gallery, and an apartment full of art and boys. A couple of them were actors and they would spend all day by the pool, in case their agent called for an audition. It was a time of hair issues. They had long hair, but most TV shows had short hair characters, so if they were offered a short hair audition they had to agonize over whether to have their hair cut. We all were refused entry to Disneyland because our hair was too long for their rules. One boy who arrived from New York was called George Harris III. He was seventeen.

- Mark Lancaster
(interviewed by Gary Comenas of warholstars.org)

**George Harris III and Mark Lancaster
in Beverly Hills, California, 1966**

(photo by David Hockney, with Mark's camera)

Walter Michael:

G3 was increasingly absent from the Ninth Street apartment, having flown the nest to explore the wider world, traveling and rooming with friends and lovers. In 1966 he met British artist David Hockney, who made an evocative drawing of George, capturing his look and attitude at the time as only Hockney can.

In December George acted in *The Peace Creeps* at New Dramatists, an anti-war play by John Wolfson, with James Earl Jones, Al Pacino and Paul Jabara, a former schoolmate of G3's whom I would later perform with in HAIR. This play raised my brother's awareness of the horrors of war and its danger to our nation, to the people of Vietnam and to young people our age who were at risk of being sent to fight, kill and die.

Signs of unrest around the war in Vietnam were becoming more visible in New York as demonstrations filled the streets and parks. One day a teenaged Polish boy in our building, a regular presence on our front stoop, disappeared. Not long after, we heard he had been drafted and then died in Vietnam. His mother was inconsolable. His death brought the war straight to our Ninth Street doorstep. My awareness of the war was soon expanded by a high school friend named Elliott Gertelman. He covered anti-war protests for our student newspaper and had his finger on the pulse of the protest movement. He encouraged me to get involved in demonstrations and agitate for peace.

The summer of 1967 kept me busy with back-to-back plays and efforts to start a rock band and make experimental movies with my best friend Scott Morris. It was the Summer of Love that produced the Beatles' *Sgt. Pepper's Lonely Hearts Club Band,* the Monterey Pop Festival, The Yippees and Abbie Hoffman, Timothy Leary and Krishna Consciousness. "All across the nation, such a strange vibration" sang Scott Mackenzie, inspiring young people to rise up against the war machine, agitate for peace, and "let their freak flags fly." Political activist Jerry Rubin, with poets Allen Ginsberg and Ed Sanders, led a loose coalition of community organizations called The National Mobilization Committee to End the War in Vietnam. They organized a March on Washington D.C., scheduled for October 21, with the intention of "levitating" the Pentagon. My school friend Elliot was going to Washington on a chartered bus and gave me a ticket to ride. George called from Washington the morning of October 20th, encouraging me to get on the bus and participate in the demonstration with him. At the last minute I elected to pass on the trip, a decision I would later regret.

The next day a group of demonstrators, including my brother, confronted fully armed National Guard soldiers deployed to guard the Pentagon and to keep the demonstrators under control. In that atmosphere of dangerous tension, my brother and his cohorts responded by gently placing flowers in the soldiers' gun barrels as a plea for peace. George proudly told Mom about his act of peaceful resistance and said, "I think photographers took our picture." He was right. The moment was captured by several photojournalists, including Bernie Boston, who was then working for *The Washington Evening Star.* Bernie's photo of George Harris III disarming guns with flowers became a runner-up for the Pulitzer Prize, and fixed the idea of "Flower Power" forever in the public imagination.

Boston's iconic image of George answering guns with flowers remains a metaphor for the message of the 1960s youth counterculture movement – that love can overcome political tyranny, unite the human family, break the war machine, and bring peace to the world.

David Montgomery, in *The Washington Post,* Sunday, March 18, 2007, wrote:

> The most enduring image from the last big march on the Pentagon, on October 21, 1967, survives in the collective memory as summing up an era. Carnations in gun barrels were the essence of Flower Power. "I knew I had a good picture," says photographer Bernie Boston, 73, who took the photo for the Washington Star. His editors, not imagining the significance, buried it deep inside the A section.

Boston told *Curio Magazine* interviewer Alice Ashe in 2005:

> "I saw the troops march down into the sea of people, and I was ready for it. One soldier lost his rifle. Another lost his helmet. The rest had their guns pointed out into the crowd, when all of a sudden a young hippie stepped out in front of the action with a bunch of flowers in his left hand. With his right hand he began placing the flowers into the barrels of the soldiers' guns. He came out of nowhere, and it took me years to find out who he was . . . his name was Harris."

Photo: Bernie Boston, © RIT Archive Collections, Rochester Institute of Technology

George Harris III places carnations in gun barrels during an antiwar demonstration at the Pentagon in 1967.

Robert Patrick

Playwright, novelist, Cino writer

Photo © Wren de Antonio

All I know about the Harris family is that when we needed a kid to act in our shows off-off-Broadway we called Ann Harris, a beautiful actress who appeared in such masterpieces as Lanford Wilson's *The Rimers of Eldritch* at La MaMa, and she sent over a pre-pubescent of the right size and gender. When she didn't have one of the right gender handy, they could double as the other, as Jayne Anne did when she played a young shepherd boy in Claris Nelson's *The Clown* at the Caffe Cino. I was astonished when I saw George and his siblings at La MaMa in a sharp, witty musical George wrote, and realized that they had independent existences of their own, quite apart from us egotistic playwrights' need of them to fulfill our fantasies.

I guess the standout Harris-kid moment for me was Walter's performance as Kenny, the youngest member of one of Lanford Wilson's sweetly dysfunctional families in a play called *The Sand Castle.* No one who saw it will ever forget him saying, "Hi. I'm Kenny. I get to open the play, and later on I get to close it." Walter donated his considerable musical gifts to composing and playing the songs for a show of mine that won a Best Play of 1969 award, due in no small part to his contribution.

I never knew if the Harrises considered themselves more actors or musicians. I visited the Harris home just once (I don't remember why) and I remember it as being dominated by Fred's huge set of drums. By the way, I may have been wrong, but I always got the impression that Fred was the one member of the family who did not -- shall we say -- have dual citizenship in both off-off-Broadway and some marvelous Disneyland of the mind.

Certainly George projected his inner Disneyland most conspicuously. As Hibiscus, he shattered everyone's ideas of theatre and gender, and as the maestro of the Angels of Light, he put on shimmering, breathtaking spectacles that can neither be accurately described nor satisfactorily revived. George was an aggressive, creative Alpha Male in a red sequined sheath with purple glitter in his beehive wig. It only hints at his poetic breadth of soul that he was also the blond-banged hero daring to step forth and insert the famous flower of peace into a National Guardsman's rifle.

I spent some time with the three girls in the late seventies. I wanted to adapt a popular novel about a theatrical family into a movie for them, and spent months trying to buy the rights to the book. No one seemed to know who owned the rights, and the project dissipated in a general atmosphere of regret and realism. But I have always kept a wonderful drawing of the girls on my wall in Los Angeles, hung over a mural from Crete of three priestesses.

I think the whole Harris family acquired from Ellen Stewart, Joe Cino, and George, an awareness that theatre is a sacred and important rite, worth working and sacrificing to make.

Robert Patrick on the
Caffe Cino stage, 1966

Photo © James D. Gossage

Robert Patrick is the author of the Broadway hit 'Kennedy's Children' and many other popular plays and novels. He is a tireless champion of the Caffe Cino and all that it represents. Mr. Patrick is universally acknowledged as a pioneer of gay and experimental theater.

Photo © Dagmar

Walter Michael relaxing backstage during 'HAIR' at the Biltmore Theater, early 1968. Inset: The iconic poster for 'HAIR' on Broadway, poster design by Ruspoli-Rodriguez, courtesy Michael Butler.

Chapter 9
HAIR and *The Great White Hope* on Broadway

What a piece of work is man
How noble in reason
How infinite in faculties!

"What A Piece of Work Is Man" from *HAIR*
adapted from Shakespeare's *Hamlet*
by Gerome Ragni, James Rado and Galt MacDermot

Walter Michael:
After *Gorilla Queen,* my brother George left home and moved in with his older lover. I lost track of him until he called from Washington D.C. I was aware that he traveled back and forth between New York and California, where he settled eventually on the Sutter Street Commune in San Francisco. G3 set out to follow his star, and I longed to follow my own. I admired his initiative and courage.

We had in common a restless desire for love and enlightenment. Also we both suffered from a hereditary bone disease called multiple cartilaginous exostoses. Mom called it "bone bumps" – a mutated gene that triggers cartilage tumors near joints, hampering mobility and causing pain. In G3's case the bone bumps were small and grew in not-so-obvious places. Mine were large and most visible on my legs, causing agonizing self-consciousness and insecurity. The condition followed me like a black cloud.

I felt like a freak of nature. My earliest memories are of doctors, hospitals, extreme social awkwardness and the sense that something was deeply wrong. My bumps were visible on the surface of my extremities, making it embarrassing to wear shorts, bathing suits, short-sleeved shirts and sandals without socks. There was nothing to do for it except wear loose clothing and hope not to be noticed – or worse, touched.

Mary Lou:
At the age of eleven, I was beginning to realize that I shared the same medical bone condition as my father and brothers. My knees were growing large, painful bone bumps. Soon the bone bumps were pressing on nerves and disrupting the mechanics of my walking, sleeping and daily functioning. The orthopedic pediatrician advised removing the bumps surgically. The doctor warned both me and my mother that the surgery would hinder my growth. Of course, not knowing what that meant, I had the surgery, which cured my walking problems and the pain, however I would spend a lifetime aching for those two-to-three extra inches of height that would never happen for me.

Walter Michael:
My interest in education was waning. Exhausted from so much after-school theater, I was caught between adolescence and adulthood and surrounded by a seismic cultural shift. The youth counterculture movement was forcing the country to reevaluate its values and priorities. My brother was out there doing something about it. What was I doing? Although busier than ever as a working actor and musician I was unsure of my place in the world. I was a disengaged 16-year-old high school student with no girlfriend and no sense of direction. A despairing sense of hopelessness threatened to engulf my teenage brain. I missed my older brother's intense self-confidence and leadership but knew instinctively it was time to figure things out on my own.

Ann:
In autumn 1967 Walter was sixteen and attending the High School of Music and Art. A friend of his asked him to play piano for his audition for *HAIR*. Walter said "yes" and when the audition ended, Tom O'Horgan asked him if he would like to audition too. So Walt did, and got the part. He had worked with Tom at La MaMa before. It was a happy day. Walter was the youngest member of the original Broadway cast. *HAIR* rehearsed at Ukrainian Hall one-half block from our Ninth Street apartment, and opened April 29 the following year.

Walter Michael:
Suddenly the dreaming and risk-taking driving our caravan's journey from Clearwater made sense. My year with *HAIR* (April 1968 – March 1969) yanked me out of my insecurity and self-doubt and thrust me into the vortex of the youth counterculture, political awareness and a cathartic theatrical experience that changed everything.

It was bigger than me. I wrapped up my projects, dropped out of school (with parental permission) and began rehearsals in January, 1968.

The company included the co-authors, Gerome Ragni and James Rado, in the lead roles of Berger and Claude. A handful of actors from the initial Public Theater production were held over. New faces included La MaMa players like Jon Kramer and myself; plus amateurs, pros and people off the street. The chemistry between the authors, the composer and band, the cast and designers, our courageous producer Michael Butler and La MaMa director Tom O'Horgan, produced a hit musical that connected with audiences and critics. Clive Barnes, writing for the New York Times, declared that *HAIR* was "the first Broadway musical in some time to have the authentic voice of today rather than the day before yesterday."

The night before we opened, four of us eluded the security guards and spent the night in the theater. Our goal was to hold a creative vigil to purify the space, in the Native American tradition. So many references in *HAIR* are drawn from that tradition. Steve Curry, Shelley Plimpton, Steve Gamet and myself stayed awake from dusk till dawn – chanting, lighting incense, smoking the peace pipe (wink) and putting on a light show in order to sanctify the Biltmore Theater for *HAIR's* Broadway debut. As the morning sun rose over West 47th Street, mission accomplished, we cried, hugged, and scrambled over the stage door gate, releasing ourselves to go home and rest up for the big event now just hours away.

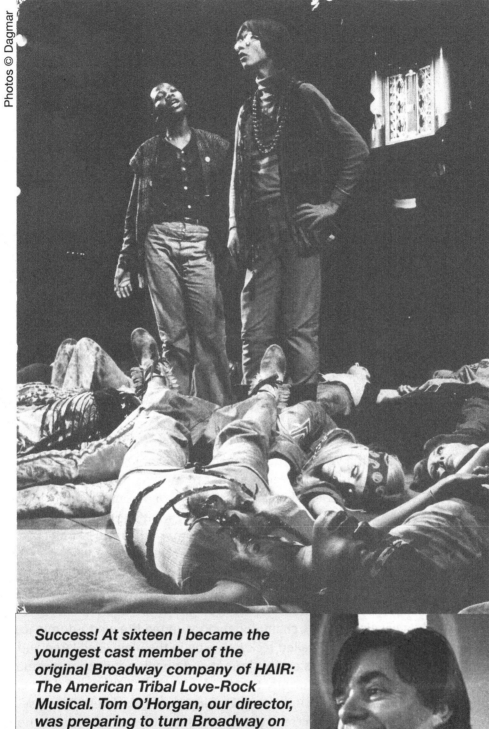

Photos © Dagmar

Success! At sixteen I became the youngest cast member of the original Broadway company of HAIR: The American Tribal Love-Rock Musical. Tom O'Horgan, our director, was preparing to turn Broadway on its head with a powerful anti-war message, La MaMa methods and a stockpile of rock songs that reflected my generation's aspirations and social concerns.

Walter Michael

Tom O'Horgan

Walter Michael:

After opening night our company knew that *HAIR* was more than mere entertainment. We believed it was an experience with the potential to end the Vietnam War, unite the planet and usher in the Age of Aquarius, as expressed lyrically by James Rado and Gerome Ragni:

> *Harmony and understanding*
> *Sympathy and trust abounding*
> *No more falsehoods or derisions*
> *Golden living dreams of visions*
> *Mystic crystal revelation*
> *And the mind's true liberation*
> *Aquarius ... Aquarius.*

HAIR was a smash hit. The cast enjoyed delivering and living *HAIR's* powerful message eight times a week, set to Galt MacDermot's pulsating score. Shows sold out months in advance. As a cast we experienced many highs and lows: from the euphoria of opening night to the assassinations of Martin Luther King and Bobby Kennedy, from a hit record album to an accidental death in our ranks. To add to the excitement, Dad was cast in *The Great White Hope* that fall, soon to be another runaway Broadway smash hit play.

As HAIR was a snapshot of America during the late 1960's Vietnam War years, Howard Sackler's *The Great White Hope* portrayed America fifty years earlier, in the decade leading up to World War I. Scott Joplin and Irving Berlin were ushering in the jazz age with ragtime rhythm. Henry Ford, Thomas Edison and the Wright brothers were transforming society with their technology. But workers labored twelve hours a day, seven days a week in dangerous working conditions for meager pay. Women were a decade away from winning the right to vote. Minorities were crowded into slums and ghettos, subject to discrimination on every level. The civil rights movement led by Dr. Martin Luther King, Jr. was forty years in the future.

The Great White Hope is based on the life and times of Jack Johnson, the first black heavyweight boxing champion, who stunned the white-dominated sports world by taking the title. Johnson (called Jack Jefferson in the play) lived large and free, thumbing his nose at the white sports establishment and openly conducting a romance with a white woman. His flagrant non-conformity triggered events that ultimately brought him down. Filmmaker Ken Burns, in his documentary, Unforgiveable Blackness: The Rise and Fall of Jack Johnson, said "for more than thirteen years, Jack Johnson was the most famous and the most notorious African-American on Earth."

The Great White Hope premiered at the Arena Theater in Washington D.C. in early 1968. It was so well received that it was brought to Broadway with its original cast mostly intact. A few lucky New York actors were added to the cast, including Dad, who played several roles. The Broadway company opened in October, 1968 and was a smash hit. The play went on to win theater's Triple Crown – the Pulitzer Prize, the New York Drama Critics Circle award and the Tony Award for Best Play. Its lead actors, the extraordinary James Earl Jones and Jane Alexander, became stars overnight.

On Broadway, in addition to his roles, Dad understudied the principal role of Goldie, Jack Jefferson's fight manager, played by Lou Gilbert. When Lou was out sick for two weeks, Dad got to play the part including intense scenes with Mr. Jones and Ms. Alexander, an experience he counts as a highlight of

Jane Alexander and James Earl Jones

his career. Later in the run, Dad signed on to a forty week national tour of *The Great White Hope* in which he could play a larger role with principal billing and better pay.

So Dad and I found ourselves in the happy situation of being fully employed as actors in smash Broadway hits. We sometimes took the subway to work together, amazed at our good fortune. These were no ordinary plays. Both *HAIR* and *The Great White Hope* confronted audiences with America's ongoing social struggles. Although our schedules were identical, eight performances a week, Dad and I managed to see each other's shows. We appreciated their importance in 1968, a year that shook the nation to its roots as people struggled for peace, civil rights and social change.

George, Sr. reads the news as Fred, a fight manager, in the national touring company of 'The Great White Hope.'

Jayne Anne:

Walt and Shelley Plimpton represented *HAIR* at the Obie Awards that year and my brother Fred and I got to go. Mom walked us over to The Village Gate and sat us at a table with fellow performers that we knew such as Jacque Lynn Colton and Sully Boyar. We got to see the The Mothers of Invention perform, led by Frank Zappa, with their lead singer, a woman called "Uncle Meat." Shelley sang her *HAIR* solo, "Frank Mills," with Walt at the piano. It was grand! There were crudités, desserts on the table and lemonade. However, Fred and I didn't know the lemonade was spiked. No one stopped us and we drank with gusto! Needless to say, it was a very long, peppy walk home. I saw *HAIR* quite a few times and it was such an experience. I even auditioned for Tom O'Horgan. He patiently sat through my renditions of "Frank Mills" at the open calls but I was only 13 or 14 at the time.

Walter Michael:

A few highlights: I understudied the role of Woof and played it several times. When our drummer, Idris Muhammad, was out sick I got to fill in for him for three performances. The band thought I did such a good job they asked me back to play *HAIR's* first anniversary concert in Central Park. We appeared on *The Ed Sullivan Show* and *The Tonight Show Starring Johnny Carson*. Our cast album on RCA Records won a Grammy and spent 13 weeks at Number One and 59 weeks in the Top 40 of *Billboard's* album chart. According to *Rolling Stone* magazine it was sixth in rock album sales for the entire 1960s, outselling *Meet The Beatles* and *Abbey Road* in the USA. Standing *HAIR* companies sprung up in Los Angeles, San Francisco, Seattle, Chicago, Toronto, Paris and

Michael Butler

London, a highly successful Michael Butler innovation unheard of while a Broadway show was still running. Tom O'Horgan was nominated for a Best Director Tony Award. Ellen Stewart regarded Tom O'Horgan's Broadway triumph with *HAIR* as La MaMa and off-off-Broadway and making their indelible mark on the mainstream.

For me it was a personal catharsis. I went in an actor and emerged a hippie.

My year with *HAIR* gave me renewed confidence and a sense of mission. Although I had to sit out for six weeks recovering from yet another bone tumor surgery, my soul-wrenching agony over my condition was held in abeyance by the runaway success of *HAIR*. Tom and my wonderful cast mates taught me that beauty is about who you are, not how you look – and love transcends appearances.

Rehearsing "Sodomy" with Steve Curry, Steve Gamet and Diane Keaton.

Photo © Dagmar

Photo © Kenn Duncan

'HAIR' cast members in New York's AFTER DARK magazine, December 1968. Clockwise from top: Paul Jabara (with baton); Walter Michael (with accordion); Kim Milford, Suzannah Norstrand, Linda Compton Dawson, Marjorie LiPari, and Bob Chapman (aka Chapman Roberts).

Dagmar Krajnc's awesome photography for HAIR on Broadway worked on every level and gave me one of the best images of my career - this portrait of Ronnie Dyson and I (above). We sang Shakespeare's duet "What A Piece of Work Is Man". Ronnie and I were seventeen in this photo, the youngest in our cast. Below right: Lynn Kellogg sings 'Easy To Be Hard.'

All photos this page © Dagmar

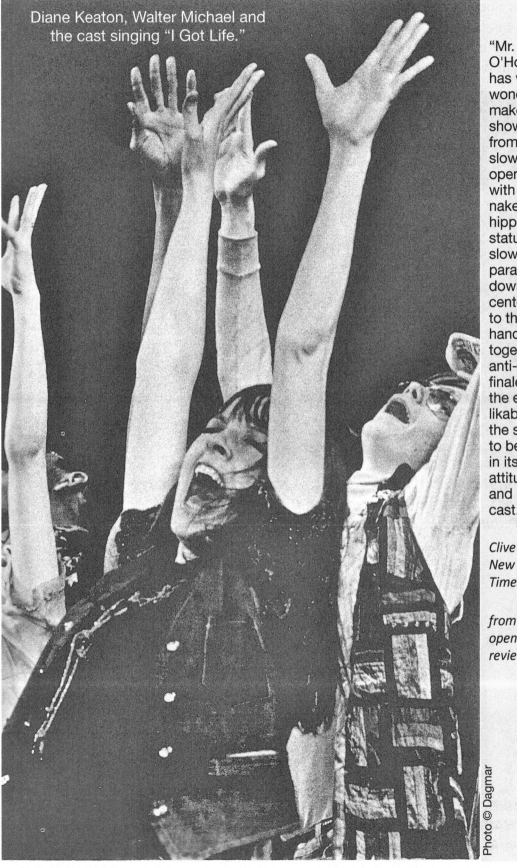

Diane Keaton, Walter Michael and the cast singing "I Got Life."

Photo © Dagmar

"Mr. O'Horgan has worked wonders. He makes the show vibrate from the first slow burn opening - with half naked hippies statuesquely slow-parading down the center isle - to the all-hands-together, anti-patriotic finale. But the essential likability of the show is to be found in its attitudes and in its cast."

Clive Barnes, New York Times

from his opening night review.

Now, 45 years since the Broadway opening, my character's name is still "Walter" and a new bit has been added to *HAIR.* During the war scene the lead character, Claude Bukowski, imagines that he is facing soldiers with their guns trained on him. He gently inserts flowers into their barrels, as my brother George did in 1967.

Photo © Michal Daniel

Above: Jonathan Groff (of 'Spring Awakening') as Claude, reenacting my brother's flower power moment in the New York Shakespeare Festival Public Theater's 2008 revival of 'HAIR.'

In April, 1969, I bid farewell to New York by playing drums with the show band for HAIR's first anniversary concert at the Wollman Skating Rink in Central Park. I departed for San Francisco shortly thereafter. - W.M.

Chapter 10
The Commune, The Cockettes and the New Age Monastery

Rainbow, all its colors make the earth glow
There's the green that makes the grass grow
The pink of the dawn
The yellow of morn
The blue of the ocean

Clouds white, turn to red with sunset's warm light
Change to purple of the deep night
The silvery stars
That shine from afar
All's right with the world -- it's ours!

"Rainbow" from *Enchanted Miracle*
Music and lyrics by Ann Harris

Ann:
It was a busy time. In 1969 Walter was in *HAIR,* George, Sr. was in Howard Sackler's hit Broadway play, *The Great White Hope*. Eloise, at age nine, was making her professional debut at the Public Theater.

Eloise:
In 1969 I joined the professional acting world at the New York Shakespeare Festival Public Theater in Nabokov's *Invitation To A Beheading.* It was directed by Gerald Freedman, produced by Joseph Papp and starred Charles Durning, Susan Tyrell, Robert Ronan, John Heffernan and, making her Equity debut, me! We rehearsed for eight weeks. During that time I learned how to play card games (Casino was my favorite) and how to make a solid gin and tonic for the adult actors. On opening night I received a huge bouquet of flowers from my parents and a small hothouse with mini cactuses. An additional bouquet was presented to me with a card from Joseph Papp. His note said, "You are lovely and loud." He was always screaming at me during rehearsal to speak up. One night during the show I completely and utterly forgot my lines. I had to roller skate across the stage, exit, and appear through another entrance and say my

Eloise with John Heffernan in 'Invitation to a Beheading'

line. As I made my entrance my mind went blank. Struggling for what seemed like an hour, my line popped out of my mouth – apparently on cue, because it was never mentioned in the notes we were given after each show. Funny the things you remember. The show was fun because I had the attention and respect of family, friends and other actors. At nine years old I got my Equity card and was part of the professional theater vortex that year. Dad got it acting in *Wide Open Cage* and Walter in *HAIR*. For the first time I became the center of attention for all my efforts. It felt great.

Ann:
Half of Eloise's salary was taken out each week to join the union and the other half was spent mostly in Azuma, a Japanese store on 8th Street. Baubles, bangles, beads and paper lanterns were the order of the day.

Eloise:
Speaking of beads and bangles – George hit San Francisco in the late 1960's. The war in Vietnam was raging. Thousands were dying, the civil rights and youth movements were transforming the nation, leaders like Martin Luther King, Jr. and Bobby Kennedy were soon to be gunned down, and new voices in theater, art and politics were shaking up society.

From Mark Thompson's profile of, and interview with, Hibiscus in his book, *Gay Spirit: Myth and Meaning:*

According to Allen Ginsberg, the precocious young actor had a circle of friends that included Irving Rosenthal, who had edited William Burrough's Naked Lunch at Grove Press, and filmmaker Jack Smith, whose *Flaming Creatures* remains a classic of independent cinema. Both men espoused controversial and visionary points of view through their work. "Jack Smith's film involved dressing people up in transsexual costumes with great adornment; veils and spangles and beautiful makeup. And Irving had the theory of having everything free," said Ginsberg. "So Hibiscus brought all that new culture west."

Hibiscus had an offer to drive west with Peter Orlovsky and another friend. [Hibiscus speaking]: "I was still very Brooks Brothers – you know, short hair and lots of madras shirts. I was lucky to catch the whole love-child bit just in time."

"We arrived in San Francisco, and one of my friends decided he was going to start a printing commune in Japantown. I started to grow my hair and became a vegetarian. I lived the life of an angel there. I was celibate and started to wear long hair and headdresses. I'd go down to Union Square and run around singing all my old Broadway show favorites: 'You Are Beautiful,' 'If I Loved You.'"

[Mark Thompson]: The headdresses kept getting bigger and bigger.

Photo © Robert Altman

The Haight-Asbury scene was drawing all kinds of flower-power people. George took on the name Hibiscus. He started slowly with a wreath of roses on his head, and it got bigger and bigger until it was headdresses, robes, and bare feet. He would collect flowers, go down to San Francisco's Union Square, and sing. (ca.1968-1969)

- Eloise

Photo © Ingeborg Gerdes

Hibiscus found his name in a Jean Cocteau novel. There is a line about a red hibiscus – a flower that blooms brightly but briefly and then is gone. We had several red hibiscus bushes in Florida.

- Ann

Still image © Gregory Pickup

Hibiscus de la Blossom

Being paid to play a hippie in 'HAIR' while my brother faced down loaded guns with peaceful flowers, made me feel hypocritical. In February 1969 I feigned illness, called in sick, hopped a plane to San Francisco and visited George/ Hibiscus. We spoke heart-to-heart and agreed that leaving 'HAIR' and New York might be the right move for my spiritual and personal well being. He offered me a place to land on his commune if I wished. I returned to 'HAIR' and contemplated my next move.

- Walter Michael

Walter Michael in 'HAIR'

Photo © Kenn Duncan

Walter Michael:
George sent me this letter:

Some other spring
Now I still cling
To faded blossoms

Thus sings Billie Holliday.

Hibiscus

Dear Walter,

A bizarre morning here in San Francisco. The wind howls as I howl. I remember last night running through China Town with flowers and glittering red Chinese banners flapping in the wind. Running from the horrors. I seek pure light, I seek the Kingdom of God. Life is so fleeting and I find myself leaving the path, then discover myself surrounded by darkness.

O to be crystalline - I have been living in a world of twilight... I lay on the scaffold like Christ on the cross. Sunshine, the stars, the moon, my view of Toledo, the glittering lights of Uranus and the hills of San Francisco. A mosque from my window.

So many new faces here at the commune. Rain pouring down at all the windows, I'm thinking of New York City. Wishing I could be there with you tonight. Sometimes when I wake up in the morning I think that you are still here on Sutter Street. So strange to be living up in the clouds.

I live with the angels of light. You have nothing to fear from the earthquake. And if death should come we shall all hold hands and descend into spirits. Come here and purify your soul. I hope for Fred to come here this summer, tell him a loft will be built in the sky.

Today is Tuesday. I find myself a kitchen slut crying at the fire by a burning rose. I collect orange peels and faded blossoms, O golden roses, a lost hand to make up for lost love. I have given up forks and chopsticks and eat with my fingers like some forest creature. Let all the animal in yourself flow, make no mistake. Look to the stars.

I shall fast and not break these vows of silence to find once more the grace of God and prayer. Feeling released from the shackles of Karma, waiting to hear love's magic music.

I speak to you through a veil of tears.
Love, Hibiscus

Walter Michael:
He closed with this postscript:

"The waitress held the rose and sniffed it ten times over, her life of longing had been fulfilled. I love to watch people on the streets to become them, to change their lives. All the children of Paradise."

My brother articulated what had been troubling me, even before *HAIR*. His words revealed my way forward. I wanted desperately to "hear love's magic music, let the animal in [myself] flow, and live with the angels of light."

I wasn't sure where that would lead, but knew I had to step out in faith to find out. I gave notice and left *HAIR,* and in July 1969 flew to San Francisco and joined my brother on the Sutter Street Commune.

Two brothers in San Francisco: Hibiscus (top), Walter (bottom): seeking to stay together.

Left: Walter Michael's self-portrait in a mirror on the top floor of the Sutter Street Commune, San Francisco, summer 1969. Right: Hibiscus dancing in the same room later that day.

Left: Hibiscus

Below: Divine with several Cockettes in a photo used to promote David Weissman and Bill Weber's acclaimed 2002 documentary, 'The Cockettes,' covering the group's trajectory from 1969 -1972.

Photo © Clay Geerdes

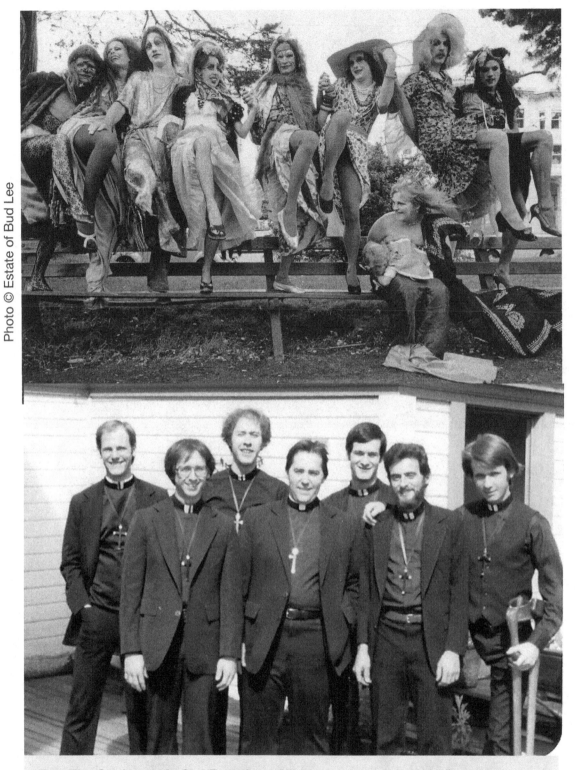

Photo © Estate of Bud Lee

Top: The Cockettes in San Francisco. Hibiscus is at the far left. Bottom: Brothers of the Holy Order of MANS in Seattle. Walter Michael is at the far right. Hibiscus and I were drawn to very different intentional communities, but shared the ideal of making a positive impact on the world. - W.M.

Continued, from Mark Thompson's book, *Gay Spirit: Myth and Meaning;* interview with and profile of Hibiscus:

[Mark Thompson]: The city was alive with counterculture entertainment. The Grateful Dead and Jefferson Airplane gave regular concerts in the parks, and groups like The Committee and the Floating Light Opera attracted large followings. A small movie theater in North Beach, The Palace, was also featuring Nocturnal Dream Shows at midnight. "I wanted to do a New Year's show," Hibiscus recalls, "and the Palace invited me to do it there. About eight of us – including Dusty Dawn, Scrumbly, Goldie Glitters and Kreemah Ritz – got up on stage in drag and danced to an old recording of 'Honky Tonk Woman.' The audience surged toward the stage, screaming. I was dumbfounded."

The 1970s had begun; The Cockettes were born. The Cockettes created a whole series of shows. The first few years were rough as the group got more and more popular and "everybody" became a friend of The Cockettes. Some of their "friends" included: Janis Joplin, the Grateful Dead, Jefferson Airplane and John Lennon. When it became too popular Hibiscus took a rest in the mountains. When he got back it was all different.

Somebody else organized it and in 1973 Errol Wetson produced The Cockettes in New York with a fraud masquerading in Hibiscus' clothes. "It was a bomb" exclaimed Silvia Miles. Hibiscus formed a new theater troupe in San Francisco called The Angels of Light. Hibiscus decided to return to New York and join his family and create original productions under this new name.

Walter Michael:
The Cockettes' success tempted some troupe members to break with Hibiscus and seek commercial success with the shows – a gambit which eventually bombed. Hibiscus, meanwhile, started a new group with a few faithful Cockettes and others. On New Year's Eve, 1969, the newly-christened Angels of Light rang in the new decade, the 1970's, with a concert at The Glines, a San Francisco cathedral sympathetic to the gay community. There a new direction for Hibiscus was born. Theater was nothing for George if not spiritual.

In 2002 David Weissman and Bill Weber created a feature length documentary, *The Cockettes.* Their web site for the film describes a brief history of the troupe:

"As the psychedelic San Francisco of the '60's began evolving into the gay San Francisco of the '70's, The Cockettes, a flamboyant ensemble of hippies (women, gay men, and babies) decked themselves out in gender-bending drag and tons of glitter for a series of legendary midnight musicals at the Palace Theater in North Beach. With titles like *Tinsel Tarts in a Hot Coma* and *Pearls over Shanghai,* these all singing, all dancing extravaganzas featured elaborate costumes, rebellious sexuality, and exuberant chaos.

The Cockettes were founded by Hibiscus, a member of a commune called Kaliflower that was dedicated to distributing free food and to creating free art and theater."

Walter Michael:

Our commune's weekly publication, The Kaliflower, carried news, essays, poetry, recipes and illustrations from some 300 communes in San Francisco. Hibiscus was a frequent contributor, especially with his florid illustrations. In keeping with "free" we bartered printing services for things our commune needed like food, clothing and auto repair.

Ann:

In the summer, George, Sr. was usually out of town in summer stock. His mother turned over the family house in Margaretville, New York to us. She moved to Lakeville, Connecticut, where she was the photographer for and wrote a column in the Lakeville Journal. George's maternal great grandfather had built the house. It was one of the oldest in town. As soon as school was out, George, Sr. rented a truck and dropped us off at the house. Then in the fall he came to pick us up.

We had some great times in the Catskills. We swam in the East Branch of the Delaware River where George, Sr. swam as a child. Our neighbor, Mary, had two kids and they swam with us in addition to the rest of the gang. Mary would sit on the Big Rock in a lawn chair and was the lifeguard. Come to find out years later, she couldn't swim. When she was a little kid her brother pushed her into the water and she almost drowned. She hasn't been in the water since. I love that story.

Walter Michael:

My three months with Hibiscus on the commune proved a mixed blessing. San Francisco and commune life were a refreshing change of scenery. On one hand I felt relief from my loneliness and from the grind of eight shows a week. On the other hand, the commune was free love, everyone slept with everyone, and lover's quarrels were a daily distraction. All that, plus being strictly vegetarian, was not my cup of tea. Yet I was grateful to my brother and his housemates for giving me a place to land and showing me how they were earnestly striving to live what we sang about in *HAIR*.

By September 1969 a bone bump on my right leg was beginning to grow again. I found an orthopedic surgeon who determined it needed to come out as a preventative measure. Once more I checked into the hospital and had a tumor removed from the same leg and location it was during my six-week absence from *HAIR*. After the operation a young X-ray technician named Jenny saw I was suffering and offered a visit by members of her community she identified as healers. I was skeptical but open to anything. Their visit instantly eliminated my pain, sped my recovery and sold me on their methods. When I left the hospital I instinctively accepted their invitation, choosing to join their San Francisco faith-based community called the Holy Order of MANS.

The order was founded by Rev. Earl Wilbur Blighton, a charismatic fellow in his late sixties who believed he was the reincarnation of St. Paul. His stated mission was to unite the world's religions. This meant bringing his followers through a series of spiritual exercises leading to various levels of enlightenment and connection to higher planes of being. Father Blighton's patent medicine blended eastern and western spiritual practice with Science of Mind concepts, Zen Buddhism, Rosicrucian philosophy, American can-do optimism and self-reliance (think Thoreau), poetry, psychology and a strong exhortation to serve one's fellow man. Blighton spoke like a Damon Runyon character, reflecting his coming of age during the Great Depression – when a job, a meal and a clean suit of clothes were hard to come by. He instructed his followers to be "*in* the world, but not *of* it."

Rev. E. W. Blighton

Grandfatherly in appearance, Blighton exuded charisma, charm, sincerity and inexhaustible energy. His background was murky and the source of his doctorate degree sketchy at best. Yet his "east-meets-west" blend of scripture, science, philosophy and spiritual practice attracted refugees from the counterculture who were seeking to effect meaningful personal and social change. He called himself a "cosmic roustabout" and ruled the roost with an iron hand, softened by his wife, the gentle and empathetic Mother Ruth Blighton.

Father Blighton had a working knowledge of the world's main religions and philosophies, old and new. His curriculum incorporated elements from all of them. He said that he received Holy Orders by direct revelation from "The Master" Jesus Christ - and further direction from "ascended masters" whose job it is to enlighten initiates here below. Validated revelations were posted on the hallway bulletin board at headquarters for all to see. We believed they were real.

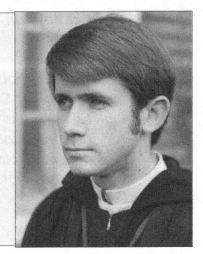

Like my Sutter Street Commune colleagues, the followers of Father Blighton yearned for a better world. What attracted me to his organization was the emphasis on service.
- W.M.

I was determined to start fresh. So I bid farewell to Hibiscus and his commune and vowed to save the world from itself, through the Holy Order of MANS.

Hibiscus, seated center, with The Cockettes in Steven Arnold's film, 'Luminous Procuress,' 1971

Photo © Ingeborg Gerdes

Detroit Abbey, 1974
Walter Michael on right

A spiritual yearning drew me to San Francisco as it had George. Thus, six months after leaving HAIR I began a thirteen-year journey with the Holy Order of MANS, starting with a three-month novitiate during which kitchen duty was de rigueur.

George and I were on parallel journeys. In San Francisco he scrubbed the commune's kitchen floor on Sutter Street while I scrubbed the Order's on Steiner Street. Both of us followed our hearts, hoping to find enlightenment and be proactive players in building a better world.

- W.M.

The Harrises and Me
by Crystal Field

Most of the Harris family has been a major part of Theater for the New City for many years. It really started with my relationship to George, the father, when I directed my first play at Judson Church. In the choir loft, George came to me and volunteered to play the lead and I welcomed the enthusiastic brilliance of him. He was plain. I was plain. But you know, the plainness – our plainness – allowed us a fantastically wild imaginational process. The honesty we both searched for and demanded of ourselves made us non-druggie madmen. We could hallucinate without help.

This quality he so richly exuded was soon found in his entire family. And I bonded very closely with his wife, Ann. She became, very soon, my confidante and leading actress, for shortly thereafter we founded Theater for the New City. We were soon thrown out of Westbeth, where we had started. Like gypsies, we traveled down West Street, piano and all, to our new digs at the Jane West Welfare Hotel on Jane Street that sat between the West Side Highway and "The Trucks" [a nocturnal trysting spot - ed. note] "Oh my God," I said to Ann, as we stood at the main entrance to the hotel (a set of stairs often covered in vomit and blood from its derelicts), "there's no one here!" "Hello out there!" I yelled to show her, and of course to repeat the name of one of America's famous plays. "Don't worry!" said Ann, turning to look at the empty warehouses that lined the street, "If you do good stuff, people will find you," and oh my God, was she right! We packed them in to our new theater home and one of the most packed in was the Angels of Light, a troupe that was led by one of Ann's and George's sons, George III and his lover Jack. The whole family was in the show, and I was as well. And oh yes, my mischievous son, Alex, and my ex-husband, George Bartenieff. We were quite a family. Actually, two families that came together to form a village. (Someone asked four year old Alex, "What's the name of your theater cult?" and Alex replied "Roadblock.")

The Harrises, especially Ann, and Weezy, Jayne Anne and Mary Lou, were in so many of our resident productions including Laurel Helsing's (my sister) adaptation of Saint-Exupéry *The Little Prince* – the musical which, by the way, opened the door to Tim Robbins, after his sisters Adele and Gaby had come to aid me as stage managers and good right hands. The wonderful production of *Morn to Midnight* by George Kaiser, the father of the avant-garde, featured Ann, Jayne Anne, Mary Lou and Weezy. So many more. But I remember Morn to Midnight most because we had all become rather attached to some of our neighbors who lived in rooms in the single room occupancy portion of our building. In *Morn to Midnight* Ann and I agreed to put some of them in the last scene in the play, which takes place in the Salvation Army Hall, in which the leading character is electrocuted at the Cross that stood at the front of the dias. During the play's run, one of these neighbors passed away. He simply didn't show up one night. They told us, he'd been taken to the hospital and then, later, he died.

So many near emergencies, near disasters, and actual disasters occurred, during these years. But our audiences never knew, because we'd clean up the mess – many times with the help of Ann, her sweet brood and Timmy, Adele and Gaby. The audience had their own entrance and never saw the men being carried out of the main hotel entrance – nor the remains of their insides, sprawled on the stairs or leading into the street.

And who buoyed us with her love and her talent? Ann Harris, who gave her family to art, as I gave mine. There's so much more to tell, about those years. I have only touched at the iceberg's tip at this writing. But here is a taste of a theater's early life. One day, I shall write it all up!

C F

Crystal Field is
co-founder and Artistic Director
of Theater for the New City, New York.

L to R: Crystal Field, George Bartinieff, George Harris, Sr.

Chapter 11
Theater for the New City, Summer Stock and *The Honeymoon Killers*

Mary Lou:
Theater for the New City (TNC) in New York was an essential ingredient towards our social education. The co-founders – George Bartenieff, Crystal Field, Theo Barnes and Lawrence Kornfeld – gave our family troupe, The Angels of Light, a theatrical home. The early years of our repertory work allowed us to portray and grapple with important human themes, such as the prophetic *Prosperall Rising,* a show about the aftermath of global warming, as well as supplementing our education with plays like T*he Little Prince*, by the poet and pioneering aviator Antoine de Saint-Exupéry.

At TNC we enjoyed working with the Robbins family. Adele Robbins was TNC's steadfast stage manager with boundless energy and problem-solving prowess. Her sister and brother (Gaby and Timmy), were good-looking, confident teenage actors – a friendship "score" for the younger Harris kids. It was rare to work with other children during the off-off-Broadway movement. Timmy played the title role in *The Little Prince.* My sister, Eloise played The Rose opposite Timmy in the production. A first-love romance bloomed between them behind the scenes as well as on the stage. I thank Crystal Field and George Bartenieff in particular for playing colorful hosts to SO many Harris family adventures and Harris children's firsts.

Eloise:
The best thing about being in a play is that not only do you meet great adults, but you meet other children as well. The Robbins kids were another family that were part of the theater experience and as it turns out, a wonderful life experience for me. Timmy Robbins took me on my first date and was my first boyfriend. He bought me a corsage and took me to see *No No Nanette*, a hit on Broadway, and later to a pub in the West Village for sodas. He was really fun to talk to and I was terribly nervous. It was my first time having so much attention from a boy. But the truth is, we were still just kids, making that the best of times.

I had only drag queens to advise me, so I thought on a date you were supposed to have a kiss no matter what. The date went great and I had my first kiss! We eventually turned our young relationship into a lifelong friendship. Timmy is theatrical kin and remains the dearest of friends who continues to weave in and out of the tapestry of my life.

Ann:
George, Sr. went out on tour and summer stock a lot. He did *The Great White Hope* national tour, *The Trial of A. Lincoln* with Henry Fonda and Billy D. Williams, *No Place to be Somebody* and many other bus and truck tours and lots of summer stock.

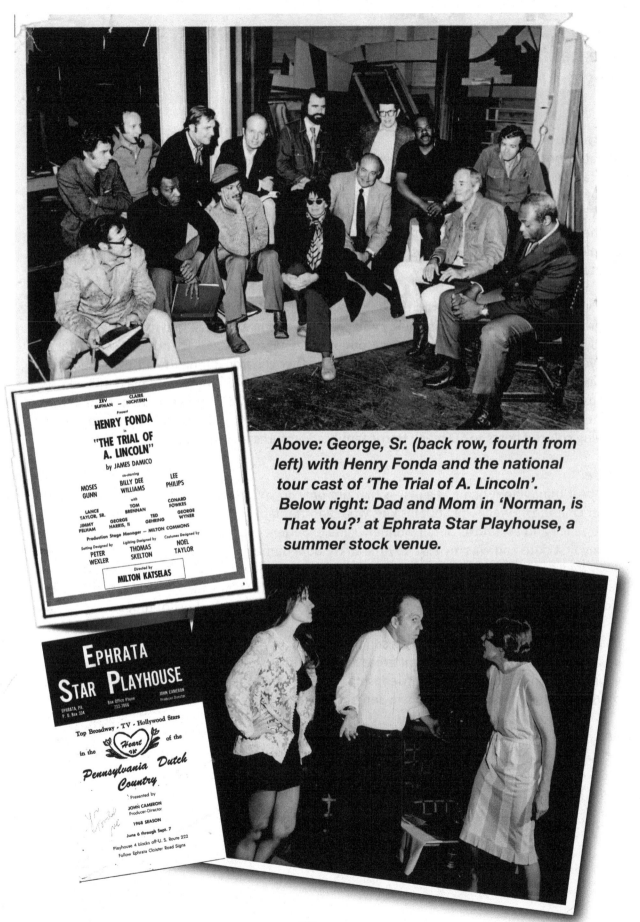

ZEV BUFMAN — CLAIRE NICHTERN
Present

HENRY FONDA
in
"THE TRIAL OF A. LINCOLN"
by JAMES DAMICO

co-starring

MOSES GUNN   BILLY DEE WILLIAMS   LEE PHILIPS

with

LANCE TAYLOR, SR.   TOM BRENNAN   CONARD FOWKES
JIMMY PELHAM   GEORGE HARRIS, II   TED GEHRING   GEORGE WYNER

Production Stage Manager — MILTON COMMONS

Setting Designed by   Lighting Designed by   Costumes Designed by
PETER WEXLER   THOMAS SKELTON   NOEL TAYLOR

Directed by
MILTON KATSELAS

Above: George, Sr. (back row, fourth from left) with Henry Fonda and the national tour cast of 'The Trial of A. Lincoln'.
Below right: Dad and Mom in 'Norman, is That You?' at Ephrata Star Playhouse, a summer stock venue.

EPHRATA STAR PLAYHOUSE

EPHRATA, PA.
P. O. Box 334

Box Office Phone
733-7966

JOHN CAMERON
Producer Director

Top Broadway · TV · Hollywood Stars
in the Heart of the

Pennsylvania Dutch Country

Presented by

JOHN CAMERON
Producer-Director

1968 SEASON

June 6 through Sept. 7

Playhouse 4 blocks off-U. S. Route 222
Follow Ephrata Cloister Road Signs

The many faces of George Harris, Sr., a versatile and engaging actor. With little formal training, Dad built a successful acting career and earned the respect of his peers. Here are just a few of the many characters he portrayed throughout the 1960's and 70's.

Susan Dale Rose:
When your dad toured with *The Great White Hope* we got to spend a little time with him. He was sweet and loving with us, though he and Mom were still at odds. Somehow when I was 13, we ended up at Aunt Dorothy's seaside house with G3. At that time we looked a great deal alike, he and I, and he announced that we were twins, telling everyone. Aunt Dorothy just looked at us and said, "Don't track sand upstairs." Uncle Dink in his study said nothing. So G3 and I went to the water and told the sea. My brothers were jealous, and suspicious of George after that, for trying to steal their sister.

Ann:
The kids and I discovered the Central Park rowboat lake complete with clubhouse at one end. Hot dogs and boating became our obsession. I remember, too, that Fred and I saw a tiny notice in the New York Times that a group of people from Venus (outer space) were going to land behind the Metropolitan Museum at 8 o'clock that night. So we went! Actually there was a small welcoming committee of people (about 20) but the Venusians never came. Another night Fred and I went to the park to witness a comet (shooting star display) hosted by the Hayden Planetarium. They showed up. It was a spectacular night.

Years later, when we were in Europe with the Angels of Light, on our days off Fred and I always looked to see if there was a zoo to visit. We found them in Amsterdam, Nancy, and the most spectacular zoo in Berlin. There, all the animals were in their natural habitats, so most of the time they were hiding.

One summer both George and I got parts at the Ephrata Star Playhouse in Pennsylvania. We took the girls along and they went swimming while we were rehearsing. We stayed in this old Revolutionary War era hotel in the park and the playhouse was next door. Our director was great and "old school." He remembered the time when actors stood on the corner, "Have trunk, will travel." The more costumes you had in your trunk, the better chance you had of getting the part. He was very strict – no pets and no cooking. We sneaked in a bowl of gold fish and hid a Sterno stove in the closet. One of the actors told me that the year before, a gay chorus boy put a ladder up to the window of his lover and our director came after him with a shot gun and made him come down.

Eloise:
During that summer in Ephrata Pennsylvania, Karen Carpenter's record "Close To You" was the big hit. It was a bountiful summer for us full of sweet grass, flower fragrances, Amish buggies and new surroundings to explore. Jayne, at thirteen, was becoming a budding teenager. Being four years younger (nine), the experience gap between myself and Jayne was wider at that time in our lives. Mary Lou was six years younger (seven).

There was a great public swimming pool down the street that Jayne took us to. Being the oldest she was in charge. We would don our towels and flip-flops and walk to the pool for summer fun. It had three diving boards – low, medium and a really high board that caught Jayne's eye as a summer challenge. Jayne was coming into her supermodel stage. She was and still is a beauty. But this summer she was Sports Illustrated!

Top: Theater for the New City's street theater summer company touring New York City's five boroughs. (1970's) (Top photo, back row, from the left: George Harris, Sr., George Bartenieff, a fellow actor, Tim Robbins. Front row: third from the left: Alexander Bartenieff)

Right: TNC's co-founders, Crystal Field and George Bartenieff profiled in 'Other Stages,' a short-lived but informative publication that focused on the off-off-Broadway scene. (1979)

OOB & Dance: Listings · Reviews · Features

OTHER STAGES

NEW YORK, NEW YORK   FEB. 22 - MAR. 7, 1979   VOL. 1 NO. 11

George and Crystal
Page 2

Caffe Cino, Part II - Page 8

Eloise:

Clad in a white bikini bathing suit, Jayne Anne was a vision of the quintessential blond surfer girl. That summer Jayne was a pure poolside goddess and had her first pure young flirtation and romance at the pool. She also taught Mary Lou and I how to dive which took long durations of coaxing from her. The pool was her stage that summer. She was the belle of the ball, mothering her two sisters and posing on her towel.

After several weeks of being coaxed to take the plunge, first me, then Mary Lou, we began our ascent into the bigger leagues learning to dive like the other kids. Jayne taught us to dive off the side of the pool. It took weeks of her saying, "come on, you can do it!" That summer she got us to conquer our fear. We learned to dive off the side of the pool. She also conquered her own fear, jumping off the high dive on our last day there.

Jayne was learning who she was that summer. She was struggling to become the matriarch of the Harris girls and wanted her rights as the oldest sister. She had her own room in the hotel that was connected to the room Mary Lou and I shared. Jayne insisted we not bother her, as she was "the oldest and needed space." We had to knock in order to enter her room and wait for her to perfect her beauty before leaving the room.

The hotel was old, creepy and creaky. It had been the same since the Civil War and according to legend was haunted. Jayne told us she saw a man standing in the hallway in a soldier's suit, so it was an exciting hotel. One night there was a big lightning storm. In the middle of the night a flying teenage body flew in between Mary Lou and me knocking us off the bed and onto the floor. We woke up to Jayne saying, "Did you see that streak lightning?" She said that she needed to sleep with us. Needless to say we teased her. "You need your own space, you can't stay in the little kids room, go back in your own room." However, we little kids wound up letting her stay, and like most days, after giving her a taste of her own medicine, we would relax and roll with laughter. In my life, I've had the most belly laughs with my sisters.

Ann:

I got my Equity card in summer stock and my SAG card with a film called *The Honeymoon Killers.* The audition was awesome. I walked in and they had me sit on the floor as if I was in the bathtub and sing "Glory Hallelujah." The part was Doris Acker, a gym teacher, and the only one who doesn't get killed.

I didn't hear from them for months and I didn't think I got it. Months later I got a telegram telling me to report to the film. They offered me a plane ride but at that time I didn't want to fly so they met me at the train station and drove me.

The film starred Tony Lo Bianco and Shirley Stoler. They were great to work with as was the director, Leonard Kastle, the producer Warren Steibel. and the cameraman, Oliver Wood. A lot of the scenes were shot as if you were hiding behind a chair witnessing the terror. The film was based on a true crime event that took place in New York.

Shirley Stoler, Tony LoBianco and Ann Harris in 'The Honeymoon Killers,' 1970. 'Our mother is a natural. She wins any part she auditions for and often is cast just by meeting the director.'

- Eloise

Still image © Warren Steibel/Roxanne Co.

Ann:
Back in New York City, the girls, George, Sr. and I acted at Theater for the New City in a lot of new plays, street theater and special occasions like Frederick Olmstead's (the founder of Central Park) anniversary. We rode around in horse carriages in costume and performed skits. We also performed in *The Expressway* for Joe Papp's Public Theater. The goal, I believe, was to save Broome Street from the planners who wanted to build an expressway over it. We would drive down in a van standing up in the back and set up when we got there.

Unfortunately, one day we inadvertently set up near a church where a wedding was exiting. I wonder what they served at the reception because we were pelted with hard-boiled eggs and Hostess Twinkies. Needless to say, we made a hasty exit.

Happenings were in vogue during that time. Tom O'Horgan, (director of *HAIR, Jesus Christ Superstar, Sgt. Pepper's Lonely Hearts Club Band*) staged a few of them at Judson and, of course, "rounded up the usual suspects." One of his happenings took place all over Washington Square Park. John Herbert McDowell, a fabulous composer, and James Waring, a dance master, staged happenings at Judson Church.

I remember, one night, John Herbert's mother came down from Scarsdale and John sat her next to me. The house lights dimmed and there were dreamy ballet dancers and a roaring chorus of voices when all of a sudden Eddie Barton, an amazing contortionist and dancer made his entrance upside down, walking on his hands, stark naked. John Herbert's mother looked at me and said, "To think, we used to go to church here!"

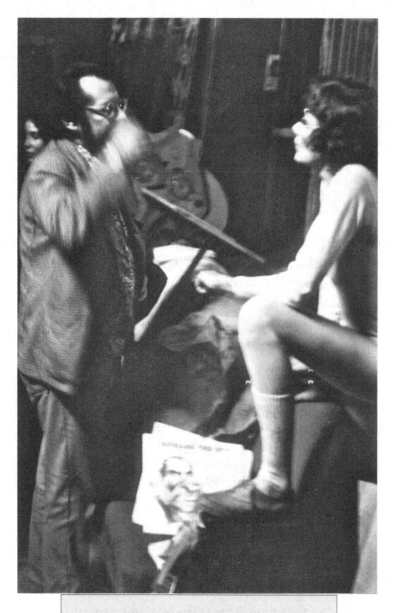

John Herbert McDowell, singing his latest musical creation to Ann Harris, backstage, ca. 1970

Chapter 12
Hibiscus and Angel Jack

Passions jaded, starlets faded
We'll be raided with the dawn
Trumpets moaning, lovers groaning
Wow that boy can blow that horn!

Room is reeling am I feeling
Higher than I felt before
I'm perplexed and oversexed
And really what I want is more and more

"Passions Faded" *from Gossamer Wings*
Music and lyrics by Ann Harris

Walter Michael:
Jack Coe first saw Hibiscus as George was re-enacting Jesus' crucifixion on a windy bluff overlooking the Pacific Ocean. As the magic of San Francisco seeped into Jack's sensibilities, a friend told him, "Hibiscus is being crucified by the bad Cockettes at Land's End. Wanna go?"

"Bad Cockettes" refers to members of the troupe that wanted to take the group commercial, the decision that led to Hibiscus' departure. "Good Cockettes" were members that stuck by Hibiscus' commitment to free theater and joined him in his new venture, the original San Francisco Angels of Light.

Intrigued, Jack made his way to the beach at Land's End, a bleak, windswept bluff at the edge of San Francisco, facing the ocean. Trees there are twisted and bent by the wind into grotesque formations, giving the place a fairytale quality, like something out of Tolkien. Country Joe and the Fish, a popular local rock band, provided the musical backdrop for "The Crucifixion."

It was Good Friday, 1971. On one edge of the bluff, the "good" Cockettes cried, pounded the earth and ripped their garments at the sight of Hibiscus, their "crucified" leader. On the opposite bluff stood the "bad" Cockettes in silent witness of his suffering.

Mary Lou:
The whole scene was captured in Gregory Pickup's documentary, *Pickup's Tricks.* It features Hibiscus and the Angels of Light, who blazed new trails as pioneers of San Francisco's underground queer theater in the early '70s. Hibiscus, Angel Jack, The Cockettes and the Angels of Light were glittering examples of the powerful and growing movement of the counterculture in America where freedom of expression thrived and gyrated wherever it (or they) happened to be.

Still images © Gregory Pickup

Images from Gregory Pickup's film 'Pickup's Tricks,' made during 1971-1973, featuring Hibiscus and the Angels of Light. Clockwise from top left: Hibiscus' "crucifixion", at Land's End, San Francisco; Hibiscus and his lover Angel Jack; Hibiscus dragging his cross to the beach; and the poet Allen Ginsberg, a momentary Angel of Light.

Allen (left) dated Hibiscus for a time, and complained that there was too much glitter in the bed.   W.M.

Walter Michael:

The crucifixion was staged for the film, but held extra significance for George because it symbolized his death as a Cockette. Legend says the "bad" Cockettes, led by the supposed usurper Sebastian, stood afar off on a cliff, watching the "good" Cockettes tenderly remove his body from the cross. Legend also has it that Hibiscus was seen adjusting his loincloth while ON the cross. Jack met George a few days later. Jack was on LSD when he beheld Hibiscus dancing in Golden Gate Park. "He looked as if he were on fire," Jack recalled. "I thought he was the Devil!" At the time George was appearing in an underground movie called *Elevator Girls In Bondage*. Although he was not the director, he invited Jack along as a player. "You want to be Carmen Miranda in a film?" asked George excitedly. "Who's HE?" asked the naive Jersey boy.

Mary Lou and Eloise:

Like Romeo and Juliet, Hibiscus and Jack fell in love and came to New York together to start an East Coast Angels of Light. That's when "Angel" became part of Jack's name. Angel Jack was from an upper middle class family who resided in Short Hills, New Jersey. He was the son of a wealthy bank president and a beautiful housewife who had been crowned Miss Long Branch in the early 1940's. Angel Jack had two brothers and a sister, Billy, Jimmy and Valerie Coe.

Hibiscus and Angel Jack were lovers, competitors, best friends and enemies all wrapped into one big glitter ball. Hibiscus was always free spirited and visionary. All he would have to do is envision some creative adventure and poof! Just like magic the universe and all of its foot soldiers on the ground would begin to spin and magically manifest Hibiscus' wishes to life.

Angel Jack, however, who had always been cast as the devil or more aggressive characters in the Angels of Light shows, would have to work extra hard (or throw a tantrum) to get any of his ideas or wishes to manifest.

Angel Jack:

The shows gave me something to *do*. George kept everything moving – a crazy-ass kaleidoscope of people and projects. He could draw things out of me, hidden talents. His genius was his way of bringing people together and his instinct for who was right for what task. George learned that nagging was the best way to motivate me. "I need 10 unicorns BY TONIGHT!!" I made everything to impress him. He knew I was the best, but wouldn't ever tell me.

Eloise:

Initially, Jack took non-singing roles in the shows because he could not carry a tune or dance, but quickly found his vocal footing after hearing Eartha Kitt and modeled his husky voice after hers. He was in fact a wonderful artist and produced sets and costumes that often were both magical and clunky. He was never afraid to try an idea. During our early years together he would do wonderful things like remember birthdays and make special costumes when he was feeling extra gushy.

Angel Jack:

There was the dichotomy. George could be extremely generous at times, an angel with a genuine kind nature. Other times he could be manipulative, like Diaghilev. When this side took over he was very megalomaniacal, self-centered, manipulative, and hurtful in order to gain. Somehow he could do a whole interview without even mentioning my name. He was extremely jealous. If someone else's sequined gown had more sequins, it drove him to do more work, more shows. I never knew if he could make it all work, but amazingly it did.

Walter Michael:

A sweet, shy guy offstage, Jack bounded onstage like a force of nature. His signature role was The Devil in *Sky High* – a swishing, swaggering, sequined spectacle. Decked out in a brilliant red body suit, Jack's Devil cut a commanding presence. Swinging a sequined trident, Jack gleefully intimidated everyone in his path. His Devil came on like a speed-driven dervish, sweeping his red rhinestone cape until it caught the footlights sending a shower of fireworks into the first row. He slunk towards Mother Nature and the Lost Little Girl, breathing heavily. "The time has come!" he hissed. "The world is succumbing to my power... and soon it will be mine. Nya ha *HA!*"

Never before was there a Devil like this, tall, menacing, masculine and wearing pumps! Jack's headdress had a horn span of about four feet, encrusted with red glitter. His pitchfork swung around and nearly clipped Mother Nature's bosom. Jack played the Devil with the physical skill of an athlete and a drag queen's aesthetic.

- W.M.

Angel Jack

Go to the Devil
you Devil Man.
You've been a Jonah
since the world began.
Go with your love
making voodoo,
You do not do what you
Used to do to me.

Go to the Devil
and dance in Hell.
You know the reason
and you know it well.
Down to the underground
then see what we
could be
If we were free to be we.

I'm on fire - with desire,
But I'll inquire
Where you're leadin' me to.
Boo-hoo!

Go to the Devil
I'm tellin' you
Down to the level where
the Hoodoos coo.
Go to the Devil you zero,
You go below,
You know I'll go
To the Devil with you!

"Devil Man"
from 'Sky High'
Music and lyrics
by Ann Harris

Top photo: Jayne Anne and Angel
Jack in rehearsal at the Angels' loft

George and I could sit for hours making sand castles out of dust. We shared a real innocence and childlike quality. He was incredibly superstitious. He would kiss each letter three times before mailing it. Walking past a tree, he would touch the tree, run back and kiss it, touch it again and then kiss his hand.

- Angel Jack

After the painful schism that broke up *The Cockettes*, George was ready for a new adventure. Jack came along at precisely the right time for their kindred spirits to ignite in a blazing collaboration that kept the potent magic of the hippie ideal alive well into the 1970's. Their love and friendship gave each of them the courage to take creative and personal risks.

-Walter Michael

Angel Jack and Hibiscus were like peas and carrots. They performed throughout Europe, in Provincetown, and endless shows in New York City. Between 1971 and 1979 they were interviewed in hundreds of newspapers and magazines including Andy Warhol's 'Interview

-Eloise

ANGEL JACK and HIBISCUS

They began as artist-hippies. Eventually Angel Jack morphed into a demanding diva, obsessed with the spotlight and convinced that no show could happen without him. What we can say is that Jack was an extremely talented set designer. His aggressive nature produced enough upheaval to fuel our Caravan to Oz through the worst of times and the best of times.

- Eloise

Bottom photo: Andrew Sherwood Top photo: David Loehr

Early Angels of Light shows were held on the full moon. Hibiscus called them 'The Full Moon Bash.' Throughout the middle 1970s, in New York and later across Europe, the Angels, led by Hibiscus and Angel Jack, left a trail of sequins, stellar reviews, and broken hearts.
- Walter Michael

Hibiscus

Angel Jack:
George was the darling of the underground set in San Francisco and could have almost anything (or anyone) he wanted. But he especially wanted what he couldn't have. I was one of the few people who stood up to him and spoke my mind, told him no, told him off. That made him want me more! George would "marry" people for a week, then dump them.

I didn't want to be part of that. We liked to eat at The Carrot Club, an organic restaurant. George loved three foods: carrot cake, carrot juice and Southern Comfort. George was drinking heavily. I wanted to leave San Francisco. The scene was too heavy for me. Too much drink and drugs.

Eloise:
Hibiscus and Angel Jack arrived from San Francisco in their long "Jesus robes" complete with a hole cut out where their backsides could be viewed, and matching glitter-beards. I had no idea of the profound relationship my whole family and I would have with Angel Jack. I would definitely call him my brother in-law and outlaw at the same time.

Walter Michael:
When Jack was younger he made award-winning Halloween costumes for his brothers and sisters. He never dreamed he could do it for the theater until Hibiscus learned of this particular talent and immediately drafted Jack as head costumer for the Angels of Light. Hibiscus liked to appoint newcomers to top-level positions. On little or no budget Jack conceived and crafted shimmering, larger-than-life sets and costumes that reflected his partner's visions. Together they conjured a powerful, magical stage experience, building on techniques that George/Hibiscus learned over time, from Clearwater through The Cockettes.

L to R: Angel Jack's mom, Bette, his brother Jimmy and his sister, Valerie., enjoying the moment. Photo: courtesy Valerie Coe.

Photo © Charles Caron

When Hibiscus and Angel Jack came home I remember answering the door at 319 East Ninth Street. We didn't know they were coming. I looked through the peephole in the door and saw George standing there. He yelled, "Honn – eey!" (his buzz word back then) and I opened the door. There was a bearded, longhaired George in a Spanish Wool cape with a fur piece around his head. Jack had on a rust colored Jester's top with bell sleeves. They were like whirlwinds. In the early 1970s they moved in and started immediately working on the East Coast as the Angels of Light Free Theatre troupe.

- Jayne Anne

Chapter 13
Angels of Light

Speak to me!
You're just the boldest sheik to me.
Ma never told me you'd shriek to me
Unending words of love.
I'm just a child to you,
Charming and undefiled to you.
Oh, but you drive me wild, you do!
Under the stars above.

In your eyes, dark as the black of
Midnight skies -- I see the edge of
Paradise, now coming into view.

Come on and carry me
Into your tent and marry me.
It's an event. Don't tarry, see,
There can be only you!

Fold your tent, go on to another
Fold your tent, go on to another

"Sheik Song" from *Sky High*
Music and lyrics by Ann Harris

Ann:
When G3, now Hibiscus, returned to New York in 1971, Crystal Field and George Bartinieff let him showcase his new troupe, the Angels of Light, at their Theater for the New City. Of course he rounded up his family and some friends he had worked with in San Francisco and we were off to the races. It caught on rather quickly.

George Sr:
Hibiscus had a wonderful attitude, I thought, toward the theater in that he could really put on a show. He would take people literally off the streets with no training whatsoever, call them Angels of Light, and build a show around them. I still can't get over the way he did that. Pure magic!

He had a theatrical mind that just shimmered and sparkled. This somehow sprinkled all over everybody who got involved with him. And the beautiful, incredible sets and costumes and everything else. He wrote the scripts as he went along. All he had was a frame! But he had a vision, and somehow he would just move straight towards that shining goal of his, whatever it was, and nothing could stop him. Our next-door neighbor, Charles Caron said, "I don't know what makes it work... but it *works.*"

Above: Two images from the original 'Sky High' at Theater for the New City, 1972 or '73. *A-Crystal Field. B-George Bartinieff. C-Ann Harris. D-George III. E-Mary Lou Harris. F-George III. G-Angel Jack Coe. H-Carolyn Graham. I-Rocky Roads. J-Eloise Harris. K-Chuck Dancer. L-Billy Rafford. M-Jayne Anne Harris.*

Hibiscus and the Angels of Light were beautiful and angelic.

Photo of Hibiscus' scrapbook © Richard Peterson

A page from Hibiscus' script for 'Gossamer Wings,' an Angels of Light show, hand-lettered by him and illustrated with wallpaper, glitter, markers, watercolors and ephemera. This large, jewel-encrusted book is also known as 'Hibiscus' Scrapbook.'

Jayne Anne:
Our first East Coast Angels of Light production was at a place called Studio M. It was a loft in the East Village where a man named Jack Tree was living. Costumes of course came from the thrift shop. We had no lighting then so my sister Mary Lou (10 or 11 at the time) simply asked the audience to close their eyes whenever there was a blackout. And they did!

Eloise:
During the day, my sisters and I were students, and at night thespians. There were two teachers that noticed the tired girls in their class, my fourth grade teacher Mr. Bregman and my fifth grade teacher, Mr. Ringel. They came to see my Public Theater performance and then subsequently the Angels of Light shows and said, "How can we compete with this?" So they made their demands more visual and less pedagogic. Now I realize what great teachers they truly were and how much of an impact they would have on my later life.

Jayne Anne:
Theater for the New City gave us a home, first in their space at Westbeth and later when they relocated to Jane Street. We did many productions there as The Angels of Light and continued to do TNC's productions as well. Each show had a rotating cast of characters from the downtown scene in New York as well as some of the people from the West Coast who had done Cockettes and Angels shows.

Eloise:
One Angels show that stands out in my memory is *Enchanted Miracle.* The set was a giant storybook. At each set change the page was turned.

The whole family was in it along with such off-off-Broadway notables as Crystal Field, George Bartenieff, John Herbert McDowell and Stonewall activist Marsha Johnson. One night Crystal had to send an actor outside dressed as a cop because there were so many people outside and they were tearing out the banister. Another time, during rehearsal, when Jayne Anne and I were sent to get food from the Opera Deli, John Lennon and Yoko Ono came out of their apartment, sprinkled glitter on us and ran down the street.

Jack was a talented artist with long curly black hair and brown eyes. A bit of a control freak, his costumes and sets became more and more grand as the shows progressed. He was doing everybody's make-up, including Hibiscus's. He would spit into the eyeliner and apply it with deep breathing patterns so the mixture of the cold spitted up eyeliner and his breath were the stuff theater kids would put up with and talk about fondly for years, "All for the show." They were a cohesive team, George in charge of the script, actors and scenery ideas and Jack making them come to life. Jack loved smoking marijuana. He called it "doobie." He would roll it up and "shotgun" it for the cast with big puffs of breath.

Mary Lou:
In the wings of theaters all over the world, I felt privileged to have a front row seat to the most amazing talents of the parade of boys in drag. Little did I know that these living figures before me were pioneers of gay free expression who were standing up for the rights of many artists to come (often in an intolerant and reprimanding city.)

Angel Jack and Hibiscus with their Angels of Light

They seemed like gods to us little kids.

- Mary Lou and Eloise

We lived our lives like a Hollywood musical. Top: Jayne Anne, Ann, Mary Lou and Eloise performing the military tap, choreographed by Ann. Bottom: A Busby Berkley-style underwater scene, ca. 1973.

Mary Lou:

In those wings I witnessed my brother Hibiscus, with glitter in his beard, wearing Kabuki Opera robes with a twelve-foot wingspan, singing excerpts from Puccini's *Madame Butterfly* – Holly Woodlawn, who is able to cry real tears on stage, just acting and singing her heart out in *Tinsel Town Tirade* – John Rothermel, delivering a heart-wrenching version of "When Your Lover has Gone" in a beaded cocktail dress complete with a feather collar and rhinestone pumps – Java Jet, who later became Bambi Lake, standing well over six-feet-tall in her stiletto heels, with her white goose marabou stole, singing Marilyn Monroe's hit, "Kiss Me" – Chuck Dancer, who would later re-name herself Sugar in *Romy Haag's Drag Burlesque,* dancing on toe shoes in Berlin, as the clown Pierrot, with all the technique and strength of a seasoned ballerina – and our great protector Marsha P. Johnson, a delicate Angel of Light on stage, but a force to be reckoned with when provoked or while looking after us theater kids off-stage.

Walter Michael:

Of the many talented performers who performed with the Angels of Light, none were more courageous or as comfortable in their skin as "Miss Marsha" P. Johnson. According to the web site for Hot Peaches, the New York City-based performance troupe with whom she also performed, "Audiences adored her. Critics also, to their great consternation. Her comedy – true, natural and startling – never missed. She embodied the early Gay movement proudly and very LOUDLY." Marsha was best known in New York City as a gay and transgender rights activist. She was a leader in the 1969 Stonewall Riots that united the LGBT communities to demand an end to police brutality. When asked what her middle initial "P" meant she replied, "Pay It No Mind" and this became her signature catchphrase. Following the 1992 Gay Pride celebration Miss Marsha was found murdered and her case was never solved.

"Miss Marsha" P. Johnson
June 27, 1944 – July 6, 1992
Artist - Activist - Angel of Light

Mary Lou:

On stage with the Angels of Light, Miss Marsha would be met with standing ovations upon her entrance without ever singing a note or dancing a step. She would inevitably break the fourth wall and start talking to the audience, which whipped them into a frenzied back-and-forth banter leading to another standing ovation. Hibiscus eventually stopped assigning songs and dances to Miss Marsha, because she rarely got to them. Just being Miss Marsha P. Johnson was enough magic to electrify the audience.

Clockwise from top, Jayne Anne making up backstage, Ann as a fabulous Angel of Light, and as a comet. (ca. 1973)

The 'Fourteen Angels' sequence from 'Enchanted Miracle' with music from the Engelbert Humperdinck opera. 'And the Angels carry the children to heaven...'

Mary Lou:
And who could forget Richard Goldberger, elegantly dancing his Martha Graham American Flag modern art piece in *Larry Ray's Trockadero de Monte Carlo* dance troupe? There were many, many more gorgeous boys who would show up at the theater looking quite normal (beautiful, but ordinary), then transform themselves into magical sparkling characters that would light up the stage and mesmerize the audience and me, the little girl standing in the wings.

Eloise:
The Studio M stage was a semi-circle with a light-up rainbow border and a mirror on the back wall making it look as if there were more people on the stage. Four people looked like eight. After Studio M, the Angels of Light gradually made their way through many interesting theaters including Theater for the New City and Theater for the Lost Continent, and performed many other new original shows. In New York, Hibiscus found the same popularity that had happened in the West. Famous people were beginning to be in the audience. The guest list included the Osmond Family who at the time had a variety show on television, The Rolling Stones, John and Yoko, David Bowie and documentary filmmaker, Shirley Clark.

Ann:
The shows always opened on a full moon. In one show Crystal made a spectacular Mother Nature and George Bartenieff was a fantastic devil. He wore his tail in front. I learned so much from watching them work. Hibiscus did the writing (and starring) in the Angels of Light shows, and Angel Jack made the costumes and sets and probably did the worrying.

Mary Lou:
One of my favorite memories of the Angels of Light shows was one winter's night when there was a full moon in New York City. Being only ten or eleven years old, every night at the theater seemed magical... but this was a particularly magical one. My family and much of the cast of the Angels of Light, were running down a West Village street hurrying to the theater, in full costume, for our midnight show called Enchanted Miracle. Our faces were fully made-up with crimson lips, flower shaped rhinestone eyes and glitter in the men's beards. As we ran down the street, car brakes were screeching, people were jumping out of the way, and some hippies joined the stampede and ran all the way to the theater with us.

Out of breath, we ran to the back entrance only to find the theater was already over-crowded with people chanting, "START THE SHOW, START THE SHOW!" The tension was building, when all of sudden, Hibiscus yelled, "PLACES EVERYONE!" The lights in the theater went black, the audience hushed. Suddenly, the fully glittered giant *Enchanted Miracle* set storybook opened to the first page. The audience calmed down once the show began, but it was so crowded that the audience spilled onto the stage, hung over the balcony and filled all the aisles and stairwells. They were mesmerized by the magic they were seeing. I remember the audience (young, old, men, women, gay, straight) being just as colorful and free spirited as the performers.

The show opened with a soothing Angels of Light sunrise song, with slow lyrical music and choreography, golden billowy costumes and body parts that magically transformed into sunbeams.

- Mary Lou

Eloise:

When we started the shows at Studio M we did a tremendous amount of work building sets, choreographing dances, making costumes and rehearsing songs with our colorful cast. Being around drag queens is like listening to cartoon creatures talking to you and giving you advice. Here was their best of all possible singing advice. On show nights, each person received their own tiny bottle of Southern Comfort for their costume trunk, to be used for medicinal purposes only (they believed it opened your throat). Although we were little girls, they considered it their responsibility to teach us their lore and show us the way.

My first sip was a fiery tonic that I sprayed in a hard stream of spit across the room. They laughed and commented proudly, "That always happens the first time." After that it was considered a show staple like wearing your tap shoes. Before each show the tradition carried on – we were never without these little bottles. The drag queens would come around and make sure that we had our supply as mother hens do with their young. "Honey, no one can resist a girl with crimson lipstick and Southern Comfort on their breath. You're going to be fabulous!" With all that attention from "beautiful boys" who look like Marilyn Monroe and Rita Hayworth, what more could a little girl ask from her fairy godmothers?

Eloise as Isadora Duncan in The Angels of Light's 'Gossamer Wings,' 1972

Photos © Andrew Sherwood

Photos © Andrew Sherwood, Sheyla Baykal

Top, The east coast Angels of Light family members: L-R Jayne Anne, Mary Lou, Eloise, Hibiscus, Ann and Fred. Bottom left, Jayne Anne and Mary Lou. Bottom right, Billy Rafford and Mary Lou.

I have often reflected on those days as an important and woefully unknown moment in time that I was fortunate enough to witness. The Angels of Light were way ahead of their time. These were liberated and free souls putting it out there for all to see, in a gloriously camp way before it was fashionable and, more importantly, before it was safe to do so. I remember their courage and their outrageous pride in who they were and how it contrasted with the rigid homophobic neighborhood swells in the Village at that time.

-Tim Robbins
actor and childhood friend

New York Angels of Light. Clockwise from top left, David Loehr, Chuck Dancer, Zomba and Brucie Flower (ca. 1973)

Jayne Anne:

Theater for the New City (TNC) was formed originally by George Bartenieff, Crystal Field, Theo Barnes and Larry Kornfeld. Larry had directed me years before in *Sing Ho! For a Bear* at Judson. TNC was first housed in the Westbeth complex on Bank Street and had two floors. The space upstairs was versatile and large. We acted in The Co-op by playwright Barbara Garson (*MacBird!*) as a reading and then a play. We performed in Arthur Sainer's *The Celebration: Jooz/Guns/Movies/The Abyss*, which was the history of the Jews since the caveman. The play was originally supposed to be six hours long and people were supposed to go to dinner at intermission. It ended up being three hours with two intermissions. It was an excellent show but never got off the ground. One night the audience consisted of Hibiscus, Angel Jack, and Arthur Sainer and his cousin. *The Little Prince* was also a lot of fun. I played the snake.

Walter Michael:

Meanwhile, three thousand miles west, my first year in the Holy Order of MANS in sunny California began with a trip to the country. Father Blighton believed I needed to decompress from being in New York for so long. The Order's farm in Sebastopol, Sonoma County, about an hour north of San Francisco, provided an idyllic setting in which to begin my new spiritual quest. I was assigned to cook for the brothers and sisters who lived and worked there, while also pursuing my Order studies.

It was the change of scene I needed. I rose before sunrise, milked goats and gathered eggs from the chickens, picked fresh produce from the garden and cooked three meals a day for twenty people. Evenings were devoted to Bible and philosophy classes, meditation and prayer. I had a dog and chewed straw.

Both Dad and Hibiscus visited during that year, 1969-70. Dad borrowed my clerical collar and performed Alan Bennett's "Take A Pew" monologue from *Beyond The Fringe* which had been such a hit at the Cino *Spring Horror Show*. Hibiscus visited following a weeklong LSD fueled vision-quest atop Mount Tamalpais, north of San Francisco. As the visit progressed he became very paranoid, believing that Father Paul could read his mind. That only prompted him to deliberately think nasty thoughts, which fed the paranoia. Although he was warmly received by my community, he departed after a day to return to San Francisco. Although our lifestyles had diverged dramatically, seeing him again lifted my spirits.

In the fall of 1970 I was sent on mission to Idaho Falls, Idaho, to clue in the Mormons on the illumination to come. Although mainstream Mormons were highly suspicious, I met a group of "jack-Mormons" (casual about sect rules) who met weekly to study flying saucers and other phenomena that could not be explained by science or scripture. I was invited to teach an Order-style philosophy class every other week, and felt right at home. These were friendly, family-centered people who opened their homes and hearts to us regardless of differences in our respective approaches to Christianity. We simply met to discuss life and enjoyed each other's company with no proselytization or pressure. It was good to be away from the big city and the Order's headquarters where daily life was proscribed. Turning twenty in Idaho Falls felt like a coming-of-age.

Toward the end of my mission year I began to have serious bone trouble again. This time I'd let it go far too long before asking to see a doctor. I was recalled to San Francisco, where Father Paul tried his best New Age healing methods to banish the tumor. In the end I was taken to San Francisco General Hospital where I was fortunate to come under the care of Dr. Kevin Harrington, then an early career internist, later a superstar orthopedic surgeon and educator. It was he who determined that my right leg had to be removed above the hip to save my life. I will always be grateful for the masterful job he did.

Now here is the strange thing. Losing my leg, traumatic as it seems, was actually a relief. At long last I was free of the recurring tumor that had tormented me since age four when I had my first surgery to remove it. I no longer cared how I looked, because now there was no way to hide. I became more comfortable in my skin and stopped worrying about being touched. Over the next couple of years I not only adjusted completely to being a one-leg man, I came to appreciate and even relish the new configuration. It gave me a way to demonstrate how unimportant the loss was compared to more important things like empathy, tolerance, and compassion.

My experiences during those years taught me that others did not see me as I had seen myself. Oddly, I felt whole for the first time, loved for who I was beyond the physical, psychologically free. Losing my troublesome leg was liberating, and remains so for me forty years on.

Eloise:
Hibiscus generated great interest in New York but still preferred not to go commercial. However, we were running out of glitter, and running on empty in NYC. Europe was the next most obvious step. Just in the nick of time, the Angels of Light caught the eye of Maurice Bejart, the French-born dancer, choreographer and Impresario of the Béjart Ballet Lausanne in Switzerland. Bejart financed the Angels of Light's first European tour and later requested that Hibiscus and Angel Jack join in his film project. On their first tour the Angels troupe traveled for a year and a half and then returned to prepare a second European tour, produced through the Mickery Theater in Amsterdam.

Jayne Anne:
Our show, *Sky High,* was picked up by Ritsaert ten Cate of the Mickery Theatre to tour Europe. We did the show at TNC and then that summer, George and Jack rented a house in Tannersville, New York, in which to build sets and rehearse. As often happens, the show was retooled and renamed *Enchanted Miracle.*

Ann:
The summer of '74 Hibiscus and Angel Jack rented a former inn in Tannersville, New York for rehearsal of *Enchanted Miracle.* We were booked to play Provincetown in August and slated to perform at the Mickery Theater in Holland, then France and Germany the next January. The building had eighteen bedrooms and a red telephone booth on the first floor. The girls and I drove over from Margaretville, NY, for rehearsal and the rest of the cast stayed in Tannersville for the duration.

Jayne Anne:
Our backers sent us to the Provincetown Playhouse to mount the show. We were put up in a nice hotel and fed breakfast every day at a local eatery. The first day we were allowed to order whatever we wanted. Miss Marsha proceeded to order everything on the menu, then announced that she always left something on her plate for the poor (she left most of her food!). After that we were only allowed to order pancakes which is what most of us ordered that first day. Upon our return to Tannersville we found that Rumi Missabu, an original Cockette, had re-rented the rented house we were living in to a woman who offered us tea and a place to stay for the night!

Ann:
Provincetown was great fun. We stayed at The Owl's Nest and staged a street parade up the main drag to the show every night. It was some kind of end of the summer celebration that went on for over a week. We were treated to disco at the A House Nightclub and a fabulous beach. The sand dunes were enormous.

Hibiscus and Jack were fighting over one of the cast members who was supposedly a former European prince. He was married and expecting a child but apparently that didn't matter. Always the intrigue! I think George won because Jack drove us back in a huff to Tannersville in my car, leaving George behind in Provincetown.

Walter Michael:
By 1973 I was in Wichita, Kansas, tutoring Spanish-speaking stockyard workers in English as part of my monastery service. I got a frantic call from Hibiscus at the airport in New York City. "Walt – we're leaving for Holland and I need another musician. We have an open plane ticket and it's yours if you want it." Although the prospect was tempting, I elected to remain loyal to my assignment and stay at my post. Part of me still regrets saying no to his invitation. Dad and I were the only family members not active in the Angels.

Mary Lou and Eloise:
Departing for a European tour on our first airplane ride was a glittery fairytale come to life!

Jayne Anne:
Europe was a whirlwind tour of Holland, England, Greece, Germany and France.

Ann:
The Angels of Light toured under the auspices of the Mickery Theater in Amsterdam. We left New York on Pakistani Airlines. This was my very first airplane ride. I had been avoiding it for years. The whole way over I sat in the middle of the plane, mentally willing it to stay steady. Our group landed in Paris and took a train to Amsterdam. European trains are a treat. I felt as if I was traveling on the Orient Express.

After a successful run of the Angels show at the Mickery, we were asked by Ritsaert ten Cate, the head of the Mickery Theater in Amsterdam, to stay on and take part in a show that he was directing called *The Boston Concept.*

Photo © Andrew Sherwood

**They were doing things in the 1970's that had not been done before.
No one had lived as large in the utter joy of free expression as the Angels.
They brought it like rock stars.**

- *Tim Robbins*

from an interview with

Ritsaert ten Cate

National Artist of Holland,
Founder and Creative Director of
The Mickery Theatre and DasArts

In the mid seventies the
Angels of Light were
operational in New York and
in San Francisco. If flower
power ever had an image this
was the one. Glitter galore
basing itself on a very thin but
utterly endearing story line.
The New York Angels lived
near La MaMa at East 4th St
and there were six of them,
two boys, three girls, and their
mother. An abundance of
costumes were made by the
mother and the girls, the boys
took care of set pieces
decorated in glitter and all
colors of the rainbow.

They came for the first time to
Mickery in 1973 with
Enchanted Miracle. A second
visit in 1975 gave us
Razzmatazz after which the
Angels left to be presented at
the Nancy World Festival.
When they were there, Jack
Lang, the Nancy Festival
creator and later Minister of
Culture of France, organized
a photo opportunity on the
steps of Nancy's Grand Hotel
for Mitterand to 'glitter' with
them as he visited the
Festival on his election tour.

Photo © Reyn van Koolwijk, The Guardian

François Mitterrand chez les anges de lumière

M. François Mitterrand a fait hier une « visite d'amitié » de trois heures du Festival mondial du théâtre de Nancy. Au Grand Théâtre de la ville, où était organisée la réception officielle des troupes, le leader du parti socialiste s'est mêlé aux acteurs et actrices venus d'Europe et des autres continents. La personne qui l'intrigue si fort (ici longs cheveux ondulés, maquillage appuyé, décolleté velu, est un travesti des « Angels of Light » (Anges de lumière) de San Francisco. Il s'agit d'une troupe à part dans ce festival, invitée hors programme, pour l'animation. Elle donne un spectacle de music-hall d'un très haut niveau quant au métier et aux costumes. Un spectacle à part au milieu du « théâtre de laboratoire » auquel se livrent traditionnellement et par hypothèse les participants à part entière du Festival.

(Lire en - Région -) (Photo Michel Bekhira).

Interview © Leiden University; Colleen Scott, Editor

◆ **RITSAERT TEN CATE** ◆

142

Ann:
The People's Theatre from London and one other group were also asked to participate. Three small stages were positioned around the space and the audience was moved around in giant boxes with bleachers for seats, floating on compressed air with technicians moving them around. The audience had to come back on three consecutive nights to see the entire show and we had to be in different parts of the room for different scenes.

Jayne Anne:
The grand finale of the People's Theater show was Mom, Eloise, Mary Lou and myself doing the military tap to "You're a Grand Old Flag" accompanied by a military band. Behind us slides were projected of President Nixon throughout the years and into his downfall.

Ann:
With Nixon looking more menacing as they went along.

Jayne Anne:
The rest of the company was onstage for the end as well after the tap. Mom taught us all kinds of tap routines she had learned as a child. She practically taught the entire West Village in NYC how to tap! We used them in every show.

Eloise:
We had many wild adventures starting with Amsterdam. If you were big enough to reach the bar you could drink beer in Holland. One night we were at the corner bar down the street from the theater, with a bunch of cast members and some very attractive Dutch boys. There was a fight outside the bar, which had nothing to do with us... we didn't even hear the commotion. Suddenly the police busted in and put everyone in the paddy wagon, including me, age fifteen, and my little sister, age thirteen. The police soon realized they had under-aged Americans in their midst and they had to have their parents pick them up. They did not yell at us or give anyone a hard time. They made us very comfortable and before long, we were all singing and laughing while sitting on top of the sergeant's desk. It was like something out of *Gentlemen Prefer Blondes.*

Ann:
At the end of *The Boston Concept* run we had a hiatus and everyone scattered. George, Angel Jack, Eloise and Mary Lou went to Mykonos in Greece. Jayne Anne returned to New York. Fred and I were invited to stay in Mike Figgis' studio at the Abbey Arts Center in New Barnett just outside of London. Mike is a writer, composer, photographer and director.

Besides Mike, Derrick and Laura of People's Theatre had studios at the Center. Derrick was an artist and we sat for two of his paintings. Laura had a TV so we watched a Fred Astaire and Ginger Rogers festival for several afternoons. Laura had a rabbit, Mr. Nose, that she kept indoors and believe it or not he watched with us.

Dear Harris Clan,

How nice to hear from you all. I've thought about you all from time to time. So great to read that you are all still involved in the Arts. We had such a great time in Amsterdam. Just the other day I was thinking about those tap lessons. I saw Ritsaert a couple of weeks. He's been unwell but is now fully recovered. I may be making a film in NY soon (as well as L.A) and will get in touch.

My love to you all.

Mike

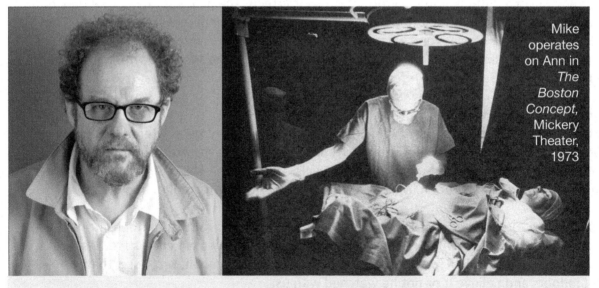

Mike operates on Ann in *The Boston Concept*, Mickery Theater, 1973

'I have such a clear memory of tap dancing lessons with your mother, the tune was 'Tea for Two' and the venue was probably upstairs at the Mickery. The Harris family was such a delight to be with.'

- Mike Figgis

Ann:

We were treated to an English pub experience and made a trip in to London several times. We visited the Tate Gallery, the Science Museum and watched the guard outside of Buckingham Palace. We also had time to write a couple of songs. One day we walked into town and bought some fish and instead of a bag, they wrapped it in newspaper, a great idea. We cooked on a coal stove, which also was our heat. If you wanted a bath, you had to go up to the main house and put a coin in the slot for a tub full of hot water, another great idea.

Walking around the neighborhood, everyone had a beautiful garden, even the smallest house. It was the beginning of spring and the apple and cherry trees were blooming. We got a call from the Mickery and left for Amsterdam. I will always be grateful to Mike Figgis for letting us stay there. In 1995, his film *Leaving Las Vegas* won Figgis an Independent Spirit Award for Best Director and Academy Award nominations for Best Director and Best Screenplay.

Mary Lou:

Eloise and I boarded The Magic Bus, a low-cost, psychedelic hippie bus, going from Amsterdam in Holland, to Athens, Greece. We were going to spend our six-week layover with Hibiscus and Angel Jack on the Island of Mykonos. The Magic Bus ride was long but adventurous. All the passengers on the bus were searched for drugs in Switzerland including me at age thirteen and my fifteen-year-old sister. I had my first taste of Greek coffee in Yugoslavia and needless to say I talked for the following sixteen hours to Greece. Once we arrived, Athens was amazing, we saw the Acropolis and quickly learned a few words of Greek to maneuver the fast paced city.

We only stayed for two days in Athens, but being short on money meant we had to stay at a pretty shady hotel. Angel Jack was always protective of us little girls, so while he and George went out to get food Jack instructed us to hide. Nothing happened while we were alone, but at some point during the night, a man had come into our room and was leering over Eloise's bed, when all of a sudden Jack popped up and punched him in the face and threw him out of the room. Thank God we were leaving for Mykonos the following morning. It's always refreshing to leave the scene of the crime.

Eloise:

We were relieved to leave Athens and board a giant ferry that made stops at several Greek Islands. The sights of each stop were a treat to the eyes. On board we learned Greek dances and began our relationship with Retsina wine, stuffed grape leaves and other Greek delights. Mykonos was beautiful, but we had no money left. Our first official act of the day was to get jobs. Mary Lou and I were immediately hired as 60's style go-go dancers, a la Nancy Sinatra, at an island hot spot. As young teen dancers we were able to attract tourists into the club, so we were a hit. We made enough money for a room with a sink, which is a luxury on the island, and two meals a day. Hibiscus and Angel Jack did not get any sort of job, but seemed to be able to take care of themselves for the six weeks. They proceeded to do what they always do... attract attention! Before long they were posing in full drag with

Mr. Greece 1976. Of course, they invited Mr. Greece to return to Amsterdam with us and continue the tour, which he did.

One day on Mykonos, Mary Lou and I met a kind man and his wife who invited us onto their yacht. They told us they had so much extra Greek money that they would not be able to convert it before leaving for home, so could we please take it off their hands? It took us a few years to realize that they knew we were teenagers, dancing in a nightclub, with little money and not a lot of supervision. Mary Lou and I truly believed that we were doing them a favor and accepted what turned out to be around five hundred American dollars. For the rest of the trip we ate like kings and queens and vacationed on Mykonos in style.

Thank you, Christopher and your lovely wife, wherever you are!

Left: Mary Lou and Eloise contemplate moons and stars in 'Enchanted Miracle' at the Mickery Theater. (1975)

Right: Hibiscus and Angel Jack as siren-mermen on the shores of Mykonos, and taking in the sights incognito with Mr. Greece. (1975)

Eloise:

As you can see, Mary Lou and I had an eventful stay in Greece. While getting ready to leave I fell climbing on the beautiful Mediterranean rocks and got a massive cut on my leg. The doctors gave me some cream to apply to my wound. Mary Lou and I only had one pair of pants each for the return trip back to Holland. My pants were filled inside with dried blood and icky medication – and I was suffering from the pain and cuts from my fall. The bumpy ride on the Magic Bus was about 72 hours, and my dirty pants were pulling on my wounds. Mary Lou turned to me and said, "change pants with me." I said, "No, we can't do that," and then she said, "I can take it… you can't." So we changed. She gave me her clean pants and wore my dirty ones all the way back to Holland. It was a kindness I will never forget. I felt we were two girls against the world. My sister kept those horrible pants on for two days and never complained once. I knew at that point that she really loved me. Even at our young ages Mary Lou, Jayne Anne and I would always come through for each other. We have the usual sisterly arguments, but when it gets serious they are always there for me.

Mary Lou:

In our tribe, traditional female role models were hard to come by. Mom and Jayne Anne were immersed in theater and nowhere to be found because of their commitments. The outlandish, almost narcissistic women of the off-off-Broadway movement presented a beautiful but toxic brew for Eloise and I, two budding teenage girls hoping for some female advice, guidance, or just a few tips on what to expect from our changing bodies. We were ushered into womanhood through a potpourri of revolutions like women's liberation, abortion rights and The Pill, and – let's face it – by a band of drag queens that hated and envied our emerging femininity. I remember menstruating in France in 1975. Oh my goodness, what an imposition to everybody. Angel Jack, always the problem-solver, rinsed out a makeup sponge, gave it to me and said, "Plug it up, girl! Rinse it out and use it again, honey." Voila, problem-solved. Well, it may have shut me up for a while, but that sponge made my vulnerable area quite sick. What could have been a quick and inexpensive jaunt to the drug store for some tampons turned out to be an emergency room visit, and of course the doctors thought the sponge was my brilliant idea. I was purple with embarrassment.

Eloise:

At the beginning of the Amsterdam tour, I had fallen with a mad crush on director Mike Figgis, not only because he was handsome but because he was a truly nice guy. He was very understanding. When the tour ended he said a special goodbye as I cried when we left Holland. He gave me a great pep talk about how wonderful life would be and how I would someday meet someone my own age. Although it must have felt awkward, Mike handled it beautifully like the gentleman he is. With a heavy heart, I moved on to the Nancy Festival.

Ann:

From Amsterdam we took several trains to Nancy, France for our next booking at the 1975 *Festival Mondial du Theatre.* Running up and down stairs to connecting trains was no easy task with our luggage. We simply had brought too much. We lightened our load in various trash cans and by the time we got to Nancy, we had gotten rid of nonessential clothes and it was much easier.

We arrived to find that the farmhouse we were supposed to stay in was bulldozed the night before. Another unexpected angel came to our rescue. An architect in town put us up in his loft apartment. We slept on the floor of this huge room. I felt right at home because I discovered a record album of *HAIR* with Walter singing, "What a Piece of Work is Man."

Eloise:

When we arrived in Nancy we had a modern white flat, someone's apartment where we were staying. He had all these great records, including Barbara Streisand, The Supremes, Judy Garland and Al Jolson singing Swanee. George loved to dance around and descend down the stairs lip-syncing, and rolling on the floor to Barbra Streisand's hit, "Stoney End." That was our entertainment, our TV. We girls and all the drag queens came down the stairs one after the other imitating all the moves. It made us all belly laugh so hard. The constant parade of lip-syncing idols that graced that apartment helped me to quell my big Mike Figgis crush and brought me back to the fun of the day. These parades helped me through many a broken heart.

Ann:

The Nancy festival was very political. One day we were lunching at a huge outdoor restaurant and suddenly a bunch of guys way down at the other end started pulling off tablecloths and menacing the diners. We ran before they could get to us. We took top honors at the festival and then began another no-income hiatus between bookings. This time the proprietor of the Café Duval, a posh restaurant in town, came to our rescue. We did a mini show there at night and he fed us all day. The food was out of this world. On the last night our host toasted us with unbelievable French wine and we all threw our glasses against the wall, as was apparently the custom.

Back to Amsterdam and off to Berlin. We took a bus with our theater manager. There were a lot of stops along the way. Soldiers with guns asked to see our passports. Each time they let us through. We looked pretty bizarre – something for everyone. I think they thought that by the time we reached Berlin we were headed for the insane asylum. We were put up at a lovely place. Our landlady was great and on Sunday invited the whole cast for dinner with her family. A great time was had by all.

Eloise:

George and Jack loved to gross out us girls. I'll spare you the details, but we'd be screaming so much that my mother would say, "What's going on in there?" George would say "the girls are bothering me Mom," and she would say "Girls, stop bothering George!" Even when we told her what was going on she would scream owwohh!! and "G.D.!" (Mom's shorthand for

On their third European tour the Angels of Light were encouraged to explore the furthest frontiers of their creativity and freedom. Ritsaert ten Cate, their patron and creative director of Amsterdam's Mickery Theater, recognized the importance of their artistry as a panacea for the social and political malaise of the mid-1970s.

"God damn!"). Then he would laugh so hard because we were all in trouble and he knew he started it. He was a prankster like that.

George loved a surprise attack. Sometimes you got caught in the blades of his fan and it was never very much fun. However, when you were feeling really bad he would do something nice, like take you out for ice cream or make you feel special. So it was a real toss-up what to do about him. But we were a family and took the bad with the good.

Mary Lou:
Although we were completely unaware of this dynamic at the time, Angel Jack was beginning to show signs of aggression and resentment toward the family. He was constantly teasing all the women of the cast, including me, my mother and my sisters. Any time a female came out of a bathroom, Jack would say that they smelled. "Whew... honey, change that rag!" He viciously accused my mother of being "old," often right before her cue to go

on stage. She was only forty-nine and could tap dance circles around any member of the cast. Ironically, Angel Jack died at age forty-nine.

Ann:
West Berlin was quite built up since World War II. There were a lot of new buildings, but you could see where the shells had hit on most of the older buildings. There was one church that was totally bombed out that the locals christened "the sore tooth." The Berlin Wall was still up in 1975 and we looked over to East Berlin and saw total devastation. Our theater manager pointed to a place in the rubble where he grew up. Our show was at the Academy de Kunst, a place very much like Lincoln Center in New York. We played to standing room audiences, and on the first night, who came down the aisle to greet us – ELLEN STEWART!

Six months of touring Europe went fast for us and it was time to go back to New York. The plane was overbooked and we almost didn't get on. The next plane was in four days and our lighting guy's mother was to meet us at the airport. A lot of the cast was staying on to do a show in Paris so there were just five of us: Fred, our lighting director, Rick, who by this time was wringing his hands big time, two teenage Harris girls and me. I begged the pilot and he bumped some of the airline employees off and put us on.

Mary Lou:
I must have been around fifteen years old and attending school in upstate New York, as public school in New York City was becoming dangerous and intolerable. My mother received a letter from Hibiscus, requesting that I come to Paris and be cast in *Les Angels of Light* at Le Campaign Premiere Theatre. God bless my mother, never one to question whether school or real life experiences were best... she made immediate arrangements for me to travel to Paris. From JFK airport to Charles de Gaulle, it didn't take long for me to transform from an American teen to a sophisticated Parisian. I had been lucky that my fifth-grade teacher, Mr. Ringel, gave me the choice of learning to speak French or participating in gym and of course I chose French. Now I had a chance to use it. Once I arrived in Paris, I rarely used my English, but vowed to struggle with the French I knew.

We settled into an apartment in Montparnasse: Hibiscus, Angel Jack, an English girl named Chandra, John Rothermel and several French boy dancers. We performed a traditional eight shows a week at night to very colorful audiences, while living a free and elegant lifestyle by day – shopping on the Champs-Elysees and sitting in French cafes for hours soaking in our new glamorous world.

My style became Marlene Dietrich (in *The Blue Angel)* and my favorite music to listen to was Edith Piaf. I shaved my eyebrows and wore French velvet dresses and delicate Little-Louie heeled shoes. During the run of the show an eccentric executive from the Mazda Light Company hired us to perform specialized concerts for corporate shows. The money we made from these shows turbo-charged our lifestyles. We were given a larger apartment in Paris, squired around town in private cars, and invited to chic events.

The Angels of light à Paris

● « The Angels of Light » avec leurs têtes peintes, leurs imaginations débridées, leurs paysages échevelés, entreprennent chaque soir au théâtre Campagne-Première (1), le même voyage à travers l'univers pailleté et fardé [...] Razzmatazz » est en effet le récit de pérégrinations [...] imaginaire, quand le show-business [...] splendeurs. Nostalgie...

SPECTACLE

HIBISCUS ET LES ANGELS OF LIGHT

au Théâtre Campagne Première

Je les ai vus la première fois tout au bout de James Street, dans le fond délabré de Greenwich Village, à New York. Elles étaient quarante. Elles balançaient une débauche de strass au bout d'un vieux hangar, gratuitement, à minuit, et pour deux mille personnes. On les appelait les « Angels of Light ».

Hibiscus trônait au centre, lançait ses arpèges, couronné d'orchidées, la barbe poudrée d'or, rapide dans ses voiles. Le bel Hibiscus inventait la Paillette augurait la décadence et révait du passé en se moquant d'Hollywood. Vous vous rappelez, il y a deux ou trois ans, David Bowie, Lou Reed, Le « glitter » ? C'était d'abord Hibiscus.

Autour de lui, Marlène s'avance d'un pas chaloupé, les petites roulent du muscle et du sabre, Judy Garland passe en moquelard, Fred Astaire joue des claquettes. En culotte de Tarzan un culturiste gonfle ses biceps en regarde avec l'œil ligne d'un discobole. C'est Monsieur Grèce 1975. Il n'a pas l'air d'un mou mais à même faire des mines. À sa droite, Roberta Black, éphèbe noir aussi comme un Nubien chante des mantras.

« Je ne veux pas mettre le monde à feu et à sang, je veux seulement allumer une petite flamme dans votre cœur ». (Photo de « The Organ »).

Roberta Black: Noire bien le colombeux, il explique tout. Roberta Black pour Roberta Black, chanteuse noire bien connue. Les « Angels of Light » font dans la dérision. Ils sont mordés les premiers au front et ce travestissaient sans être des travelos. Ils chantent la mélodie des années quarante. Ils se vautrent et si gaussant, ils regrettent. Ils rejettent, ils se moquent de la nouvelle religion, celle des vedettes du show business, celle des nostalgies de Judy Garland, dont ils expriment tout le sirop. Et, pour finir, ils se moquent d'eux-mêmes, et cette cinquième nous émeut. Angel Jack chante mal, très mal, faux, extrêmement faux, et l'horreur devient telle comme le cri d'un vieux toutou...

À l'intérieur du spectacle.

cevant l'onde. Hibiscus est un être touché par un doigt de fée. Avec lui l'artisan des cinquante costumes. Gas-spics papiers d'un rouge criard et d'un jaune citron...

quant, chapeau en forme de bâton de rouge à lèvres, ailes de papillon, grandes robes de gaze et de tulle, drapés en tissus bordés, bercardés d'argent et de perles. Hibiscus l'a rêvé.

FARDÉ COMME UNE COURONNE MORTUAIRE

Ils chantent des textes succulents, idiots, vides, en plats des années cinquante. « Où est mon poudrier ? », le chœur : « Où est mon poudrier ? ».

— « Où est mon rouge à lèvres ? », le chœur : « Où est mon rouge à lèvres? ».

— « Où sont mes bas ? », le chœur : « Où sont nos bas ? ».

— « Vite, vite, vite, on est la soir de la première », le chœur : « Où est mon poudrier? »

Hibiscus a traversé toute la belle époque de San Francisco. Il est arrivé en 67, complètement gaumé, flottant entre un verre de vin, un joint, un scotch, un fix et un mandrax. Il a titubé joyeusement sur High Street quand tituber c'était une fête. Fardé comme une couronne mortuaire, il offre pendant des mois des fleurs voilées dans les cimetières aux... jusaka » qui le trouvaient. Chaque jour, dans la rue, il comédiotte. Le voilà entouré de joyeux hommes fleurs enveloppés d'oripeaux empruntés dans les coulisses d'Opéra. Ils vivent en marge dans un joyeux délire, les hommes et les femmes et les enfants mélangés hors de tout contrôle. On connaît leur maison, le « Grateful dead » vient travailler, suivi de quelques zombis, des militants venus tripper un samedi soir, avec les hippies des poètes qui s'écrivent depuis qu'ils vivent, c'était High Street en 1960 et en 1970 les cocker-ces émergent, les voilà sur scène, deux ans à San Francisco, une orge de brexxuaté rinisse San Francisco devient la ville des Cockettes. Ils échouent à New York où l'on préfère les travestis des docks, dans le West End, à moitié en robe, à moitié en cuir noir, où chaque des mécaniques...

et chante plutôt dans les basses. C'est en 1973. Ils se dispersaient et les « Angels of Light » autour d'Hibiscus préparent la tradition à ric.

Le spectacle est enfin à Paris, quelques années après leur apogée de signification, on retrouve les cockettes et Hibiscus avec plaisir. À leur manière ils nous renforcent dans nos certitudes. Ils sont tendres souvenirs, en leurs enlacements fortent les modes et chatouillent notre désir. On les sent gaîs. Monsieur Grèce est content, et ça s'en foutent de la salle étroite. Je les avais vus à quarante devant deux mille personnes. Je les retrouve dix devant quarante personnes ! Des spectateurs de cabaret pour. Et quelle personnes ? Des types qui ont du mal à rire. Et aucun lecteur de *Libération*. Évidemment « Campagne Première » est administré par Jean Bouquin, qui n'a pas toujours été une merveille, mais les « Angels of Light » méritent votre joie. Ils nous ramènent au naturel de la caresse, ils fondent les questions des sexes dans leurs ambiguïtés, ils sont subversifs, encore aujourd'hui.

Et après le spectacle, Hibiscus reste là, en robe au milieu des confettis à ranger ses ailes de papillon avec la douceur qu'elles méritent dans des grandes malles quelques à vif avec ses cinq homos, une dame et sa sœur Lu Lu Bel, charmante et svelte. Hibiscus sourit, Roberta Black vous lance une œillade de braise. Ils veulent connaître des Français.

Monsieur Grèce arrive dans sa peau de Léopard, il enlève Hibiscus dans ses bras très qui se déplient sans fleurs, comme des grues. Hibiscus se blottit dans cette belle face. Ils partent vers leurs appartements comme de jeunes mariés et nous font un clin d'œil complice.

J.F. BIZOT

Théâtre Campagne Première, rue Campagne Première

THÉÂTRE

Angels of the light
de l'autre côté de la nuit

● Des matrones aux seins glorieux, aux visages peints de blanc vif et de rouge sombre, masques et grimasses féliniens, ombrés un instant par d'interminables faux cils, couronnés d'une tiare multicolore scintillante de mille éclats de pacotille, d'où sortent des voix d'hommes : ce sont les Angels of the Light, ces travestis dont certains sont des filles, découverts au Festival de Nancy en mai dernier, et qui passent enfin à Paris sur la minuscule scène du théâtre Campagne-Première de Jean Bouquin qui a le mérite d'avoir cru en eux.

La scène est trop petite, le travail se fait sans filet, les talons aiguille buttent parfois contre une marche, la coulisse est transparente : mais finalement, le spectacle passe, d'une façon plus émouvante encore, aidé par le recul volontairement maladroit que cette troupe américaine introduit dans sa rétrospective du music-hall des années 30.

Du rétro, encore ? Pas un instant : les costumes flamboyants des Angels of the Light, renouvelés à chaque scène dans un prodige d'inventions délirantes, n'ont rien à avoir avec une copie snobissement décadente du passé. C'est au contraire l'invention qui prime. On voyage, en fait : en compagnie d'une petite fille aux seins nus et à la peau de lait, dans un royaume qu'on trouve derrière les pages arc-en-ciel d'une bande dessinée qui chante. Surgis d'un rêve de Little Nemo, des êtres emplumés, drapés de lumière, viennent raconter aux hommes quotidiens un monde qui flotte tout près de nous, de l'autre côté de la nuit : le monde des anges, auxquels aucun concile ni aucun enfant n'est jamais parvenu à donner un sexe ou des papiers d'identité.

Quant à savoir si ce sont des anges de l'Enfer ou du Paradis, c'est une question à laquelle vous répondrez mieux que saint Pierre en allant les voir.

Bernard CHAPUIS

19, rue Campagne-Première, 23 heures.

The press fueled The Angels of Light popularity in Paris. Enthusiastic reviews with striking photos attracted an eclectic audience to Le Campaign Premiere Theatre.

The Angels of Light on tour in Europe, 1975. Top and inset: The Mickery Theater in Amsterdam. Bottom: at Festival Mondial 1975 in Nancy, France.

Mary Lou:

After four months, things got weird. The Mazda Light Company abruptly stopped showering us with cars, gifts and performance opportunities and we were told to vacate the apartment in two weeks. One by one, the cast members left the apartment to go back to their homes. Hibiscus and Angel Jack, never ones to panic, booked a show somewhere on the Ivory Coast of Africa. They had one last engagement to fulfill in Paris, and wanted me to fly ahead and meet them there, but I was too uncomfortable going to Africa by myself. So on New Year's Eve morning I secretly packed. Once again I thank my mother for the advice of always keeping enough money for a taxi to the airport and to hide my return trip airline ticket.

As I was sneaking out of the apartment in the early morning hours, Angel Jack jumped in front of me with an angry and demonic look on his face. He said, "Where are you going?" I said, "I want to go home!"

Jack became very agitated and started grabbing my suitcase. George jumped in, grabbed Jack's arm and said, "Let her go, Jackie!" Jack started punching George while screaming, "She has to go to Africa, you idiot." I was really scared. When they started to physically fight with each other, my brother jumped on him and screamed at me... *"RUN!"*

I was shaking uncontrollably, but that's what I did... I ran, jumped in a cab and sped off to Charles De Gaulle airport, sobbing the whole way. I knew that my poor brother probably took a bad beating. Angel Jack was furious that his bait for Africa had gone home. But secretly I knew George was relieved that he had saved his little sister from something really bad.

Mary Lou in Paris, age 15, in the production 'Les Angels of Light.' (1976)

DEAR DAD, MOM, JANE,
FRED, WEEZY, Lou Lou Belle,
Kitty Kat, LAKIE,
How ARE YOU?
FOR NOW WE ARE living
on a house boat in
AMSTERDAM on a beautiful
canal. WE ARE Waiting
FOR THE CHECK TO COME
SO WE Can RETURN
to NEW YORK. Autumn
is gorgeous HERE, all
THE leaves aRE
changing color. Its
starting to TURN VERY
cold HERE. I got a
dutch army coat to
KEEP WARM IN. Its been Raining quite often.
WE aRE anxious to RETURN to NEW YORK
To begin work on THE show
GREECE WAS WONDERFUL, THE MOST
beautiful place I have EVER been before
WHite Sandy beaches, crystal clear blue
ocean, hot sun and delicous food. All THE
PEOPLE in GREECE aRE allways dancing and
aRE all VERY friendly. The islands aRE THE
best. So far WE have been to two islands,
CRETE and Myconos. On CRETE WE lived in a
cave and on Myconos a stone house on THE
beach with a bamboo Roof. IN ATHENS WE
went up to the Parthenon and looked at all of

Ann wrote the beautiful lyric below, 'Soon As My Check Comes In,' inspired by letters from Hibiscus including the one at left.

I'm writing you from Holland
And I'm glad that I've been
To so many spots in Europe
And the beauty all around me
Dazzles me and frazzles me
And somehow soaks in

And I'll let the dazzle flow
And I'll put it in a show
And the show will be colossal
And I'm coming home to write it
Soon as my check comes in.

154

Chapter 14
Exile on Ninth Street

Walter Michael:
The Seventies were powerful and painful years for our family. In addition to the Angels of Light's triumphant tours across Europe, family members moved in new directions, sometimes in groups, sometimes individually. My brother Fred studied music in New York with master composer John Herbert McDowell. After that he moved upstate to Margaretville where he co-founded the rock band Jasper. The band earned a loyal local following and afforded Fred the opportunity to apply all he had learned, to grow as a musician and arranger, and to find his voice independent of the family "amoeba."

By 1974 I was living and working in the Order's abbey in Detroit, far away from the Caravan, missing the family and struggling with doubts about the path I had chosen. That spring Father Blighton died unexpectedly and his Order began to drift. A cabal of his protégés saw their opportunity, seized power and began to manipulate the organization in a completely different direction. Their self interest proved Blighton's often cited dictum: "Absolute power corrupts absolutely." If it wasn't for my family staying in touch via letters and postcards, the monastic life would have been truly unbearable.

In the midst of all the excitement around the Angels shows, the Harris family remained challenged to get the young ones through school, make a living and continue as working artists. We shared Dad's philosophy about education, that you can learn more by doing than you can in the classroom, especially in show business. Just as I left high school for *HAIR* my sisters and Mom ran with the opportunity to put the Angels shows ahead of school and "normal" family life, led by our whirling dervish brother Hibiscus. But fissures began to undermine the family's foundation. The ever-present scarcity of funds was a constant limiter of basic necessities. Dad was either too preoccupied or two stubborn to recognize that the tiny apartment at 319 East Ninth Street was no longer an adequate living space for my sisters as they advanced from elementary to junior high school.

Mary Lou:
Although the hippie movement changed the way we kids were experiencing the world, idealistic young people still met with resistance from yester-year people. One morning on my way to elementary school, walking down Ninth Street toward First Avenue, I remember a hippie running down the street, chased by a gang of 1950's type men with short greased-down hair, button-down shirts and black slacks. They carried pipes and tire-irons. When they caught the hippie... I am not sure, but they may have killed him. It was the bloodiest violence and most sickening image I have witnessed in my life and I was only eight or nine years old. Of course, frozen on the street and knowing I was halfway between the school and home, I just stood there hoping they wouldn't come for me. That one event altered my nervous system and activated my great fear of New York City into my teens and for many years to come. I had been raised in the tolerant artistic world and had no understanding of the intolerant outside world.

Dad's path through all of this was different. As much as he loved theater and off-off-Broadway in particular, he was determined to make a living with acting and music. He began to accept only paid work, and to turn down showcases. He made exceptions for the family shows when possible, and performed in Angels of Light shows at Theater for the New City. (1970's)

- Walter Michael

Top: Dad and Mom backstage at TNC. Bottom: Dad as God in 'Sky High,' Theater for the New City, 1970's.

Mary Lou:

Thoroughly distracted by being well-behaved students by day and being part of the thriving artistic downtown scene at night, in reality, we three Harris girls grew deathly terrified of our apartment at 319 East Ninth Street. The line-up of bums laying in front of our apartment door, the peeping toms looking through our small shower window (a window that was positioned so high off the ground that the peepers must have climbed seven or eight feet to get a good gander) and the basement door that was directly outside of our apartment shook us to our core. The basement door lock was continually broken and the door was cracked open just enough to see that it was pitch black in the stairwell down to the cellar. The vibe felt like a child-snatching torture movie.

As a little kid, our Ninth Street family apartment was a wonderland. But over the years wonderment gave way to reality. I became claustrophobic in my sleeping loft. Teenage moodiness filled the air and my sisters and I wanted girl stuff. We would spend hours in front of the tiny mirror, styling our Farrah Fawcett hair and dressing in sexy outfits, just to go to the grocery store. Little did we know that we were growing into women and restless to... dare I say it... leave the nest.

Eloise:

Dad had solved the problem of six children in a one-bedroom unit by building "lofts" for each of us to sleep in. However, they created other problems. Dad didn't want anybody, including repairmen, in the apartment for fear of the landlord discovering the lofts. If anything broke, Dad usually fixed it, unless he could not fix it himself. If appliances were in disrepair a hand written "out of order" sign was hung on them. Patches of cardboard theater sets repaired the ceiling. In my final weeks of living there he would leave the lights on 24 hours because there was a cockroach problem and they would hide from the light. At the end you needed a manual to carry around with you in order to understand Dad's series of notes just to flush a toilet.

Early on, I remember my dad lecturing my mom about ironing shirts and starching them just right. Everything was very 1950's (Norman Rockwell, move over!). But by the end of the 60's and into the 70's the apartment became worse as Daddy's expectations and avant-garde way of living conflicted with what Mom or anyone could tolerate. Daddy was paranoid about many things: the landlord, doing his tax return or someone coming in and seeing the lofts. It was a constant effort to keep people from coming into that apartment. The place went to seed as windows were papered over, cat food dishes were left unwashed on the floor and armies of cockroaches swarmed to feast on them after dark and lay their eggs.

By the time mom left even Mother Teresa would've cut a hole in the screen and run screaming. Unfortunately Daddy never understood why. He could not see the apartment crumbling around him. He only saw art and what that meant to him, a valiant idea. However, the day-to-day living was difficult. Everyone left at some point due to aging out, freaking out or simply shutting the door and walking into the unknown as my mother did.

Walter Michael:

Other dynamics were making married life increasingly untenable for both my parents. Dad's inability to see how his lifestyle choices impacted Mom and the girls led to unbearable tension and emotional distance.

The girls took matters into their own hands and found a small apartment on West 71st Street near Columbus Avenue, around the corner from the Dakota (of John and Yoko fame), a short walk to Central Park, and much closer to the theaters, agents and ad agencies. Soon Mom moved in too. Informally, perhaps, but decisively, Mom and Dad had separated.

Except for short visits I was far away from the family during most of the 1970s. Mom was focused on raising the girls and getting them through school, and acting when she could. Fred was forging his own independent path musically and the girls were struggling to find themselves personally and artistically. All this in the midst of a terribly challenging industry, a social scene driven by glamour, drugs and money, and with Hibiscus zooming in with energy and intoxicating ideas.

Dad remained at Ninth Street with his drums, cats and cockroaches for company. In a stream of letters to me from 1975 through 1980 he shared his daily activities and interests, occasionally pouring out his pain and frustration over the widening distance between himself, Mom and the family. Pain, because he truly loved the family and life together, and frustration because he was unable to admit that his stubbornness had forced his wife and daughters to seek higher ground in their own space.

At first Dad's letters rambled on about his favorite topics: restoring drums, playing music, and the never ending struggle to make a living.

July 6, 1978

"Dear Walter,

Happy 4th of July. Still doing the same things, a little film work, etc. Got the hardware back on the Gretsch snare drum. It's the most beautiful drum I have ever owned. I have one drum student, a very talented girl taking lessons once a week (am looking for more students). She also rents a set of drums from me at $15 a month. Sorry to bore you with drums. Also have friends, go to shows, movies, etc. and am enjoying myself. Am on my way to doing something in a Richard Donner film [*Superman* with Christopher Reeve].

Love, Dad"

By 1979 he began to express his feelings on the separation and his desire to reconcile with the family:

March 18, 1979

"Dear Walt,

How are you? I hear there is an article about cast members of HAIR in New York Magazine. Do you know what issue? Have been unable to find that Superman mag you told me about with my picture in it. I don't know why I'm telling you this except that I think you should know. My relationship with the family is strained to say the least. It's not unfriendly or hostile but they act as if I had bubonic plague or leprosy. I'm on friendly terms, but about the same kind of friendship you might have with an affable corner grocer (not very deep – it could be but I'm not spending any more time hoping or making overtures). I went through three years of depression and gloom. Even then I had plenty of happiness – I always seem to be able to find pleasure in small things – a dog, a cat, a walk, music (that's not small) etc. I'm not interested in living in squalor. I do want a different place to live and work in, plus a few niceties. But I never had any desire to be a millionaire or be famous etc. My desire, in addition to a decent living, is to be the finest actor and musician I can be. Enough said. After *Sky High* closes I'm going to ask them all to get together and kick it around to see if I can find out what the problem is. I still don't see why we can't have a close family relationship involving Ann and myself even if we are separated, and where we can work together. We should work together if possible."

Love, Dad"

Photo © Andrew Sherwood

Ann and George

Still images © Warner Brothers Pictures and courtesy Jim Bowers/CapedWonder.com

George, Sr. as Officer Mooney in 'Superman,' starring Christopher Reeve and Marlon Brando (1978)

Walter Michael:

The New York street musician movement was just getting started during these years. Dad experimented with various street band configurations in hopes of cashing in. At first he tried theatrical elements, forming a trio with Dad dressed as Dracula and the other two musicians as Lucy and The Wolf Man. I sat in on guitar as the pirate Long John Silver.

The act was a bomb. But, tinkering with the formula, he found the winning combination. He gathered eighteen first rate musicians, established a weekly practice, and began playing Big Band and Dixieland standards in choice locations like Battery Park, in front of the Plaza Hotel and on Wall Street during lunch hour. Whereas the Dracula-Lucy-Wolfman band had earned less than five dollars for an hour of street playing, Dad's new ensemble, The Ninth Street Stompers, could pull in eight hundred dollars in just one hour playing on New York City's streets. His double-share as bandleader was more than he could make at his day job. Soon the band was so popular that he split it into three bands that could play parties, weddings and bar mitzvahs in the evenings and on the street during the days. The Stompers were pioneers in Manhattan's burgeoning street music scene, and for over a decade were among its most popular practitioners.

However, Dad's delight at finally parlaying his passion for music into his livelihood was overshadowed by the widening gulf between him and the family. Although overtures aimed at reconciliation were made by all parties, there seemed to be no solution in sight.

Walt and Dad on a break with the 9th Street Stompers, mid-town Manhattan, late 1970's

Photo @ Michael Ian

George Harris

Photo @ James D. Gossage

George Harris Headlining

George Harris of Margaretville will be playing the role of "The Trainman" in "Prairie du Chien," a one-act play by David Mamet.

Presented by the Catskill Mountain Theatre as its premiere production. The play is being produced and directed by Rebecca Grow. Four other roles will be played by actors from the Actors Institute of New York City. Performance time is 7 p.m. on Saturday, July 19 at the D&URR station in Arkville.

George is a veteran character actor who got his start in school plays in Margaretville and doing a minstrel show in the Galli-Curci Theatre. He has worked on Broadway, off Broadway, musical comedy, off off Broadway, tours, summer stock, dinner theatre, children's theatre, etc. He has also worked in films, television and commercials.

George appeared in plays at the Cafe Cino, Cafe La Mamma, Judson Poets' Theatre for the New City and others. "Superman," "The Great White Hope," "Trial Of A Lincoln," "King Lear." etc. George has played opposite Henry Fonda, Billy Dee Williams, Christopher Reeves, Jane Alexander, Frank Sinatra, James Earl Jones, George Segal, Brock Peters, Cliff Gorman and others.

He was also a dance band drummer and blues singer and for many years, prior to returning to live last year in Margaretville, had his own band in New York City playing Dixie Land jazz and big band swing tunes. George has worked as an acting and drum teacher.

Storytelling, Music Mix

YVONNE'S

914 688-7340   Rt. 28 North
Phoenicia, NY 12464

CRISP DUCK OUR SPECIALTY
Roasted Plain or w/Fruit Sauces,

Photo @ James D. Gossage

Dad worked tirelessly as an actor. His willingness to try anything developed a versatility that made him easy to cast. Between acting and music he managed to make a living doing what he loved.

- Walter Michael

Chapter 15
We're All Gonna Blow *Sky High!*

Who cares if love will vanish tomorrow?
Let's dance and sing and play the night away! (cha cha cha)
Gringo, you follow me in a conga line
Shake your anatomy and we'll do just fine!
Pulsate to your heart's content
Till your mind is bent, it don't pay the rent
But you will be sent
Into paradise right away.

"South American Way" from *Sky High*
Music and lyrics by Ann Harris

Walter Michael:
After the last European tour, the Angels were tired. Hibiscus and Jack in particular felt the need to stay put. It was back to home base in New York.

Ann:
I wrote the music and lyrics for a show called *Speak Easy* about gangsters during prohibition. It opened at a theater on Thirteenth Street. The girls were in it. Hibiscus came to see it and made off with four or five of the songs for his new show, *Sky High*. I must say that his idea for scenes using the songs were much more fascinating.

Walter Michael:
Yearning for creative independence, George was beginning to move away from Angel Jack. George took up with a CEO of a successful New York corporation who knew George only as "Brian Wolfe," one of his many noms de plume. This new boyfriend cast himself in the role of protector and patron, and tried to school Hibiscus in the benefits of financial stability. It was heavy lifting to say the least. Like trying to interest Peter Pan in Wall Street arbitrage. George played along and gave everyone jobs.

The CEO boyfriend set up George in legitimate businesses including an antique store and a flower shop. Each venture was short-lived because George never let commerce get in the way of his art. Finally George convinced his boyfriend to bankroll an off-Broadway production of *Sky High*, a streamlined distillation of several Angels shows. All members of the family were in this show with the exception of Dad, although he hovered close by.

Angel Jack:
George could've got me to do anything. Across a crowded room, with a glance, we could have an entire conversation. We were friends, lovers and collaborators forever it seemed. But after he met the rich guy and decided he wanted to be a Jewish American Princess, George turned into a monster. The guy didn't know George as Hibiscus, only as 'Brian Wolfe', a svelte Madison Avenue model. I had to show the guy the Angels scrapbooks. George was no businessman. This rich guy gave George the means to manipulate people

using money, rather than with his sparkle, his twinkle, his charm. Because of this heavy business influence the new off-Broadway *Sky High* might have been done without me. I cried at the backer's audition, because I had to read for my Devil role!

The sugar daddy-produced version of *Sky High* was a "best of" compilation album of recycled Angels of Light material. I got 7% for my contribution and George got everything else while fucking his rich patron. The whole thing was bringing me down. George was beginning to pit me against his family.

Jayne Anne:
Upon our return from Europe, George re-opened *Sky High* at the Entermedia Theatre on Second Avenue at 12th Street. It was one of the old Yiddish theaters (now a movie multiplex) and gorgeous inside. We all joined AGVA (American Guild of Variety Artists) and ran there for twelve weeks.

Mary Lou:
Building *Sky High* for the Entermedia Theater in 1979 wasn't easy. Each family member had to learn much more script dialogue, songs and choreography than we were used to. But, each one of us also had extra duties as well. George was voraciously writing the script, and mom wrote songs day and night. Eloise was in charge of choreography, while Jayne Anne taught the cast how to tap dance and Angel Jack designed the sets and costumes. Of course, someone had to make the hundreds of various costumes, sets and headdresses needed.

Me, armed with my gift for sewing, the sewing machine that my mother gave me, and my big mouth, I volunteered to move into Hibiscus' loft on Twenty-Ninth Street, just off of 5th Avenue, and started making the costumes. Little did I know that I would be working 'round the clock (literally) for a month. I slept and sewed in cycles, two hours of sleep, ten hours of sewing and repeat, repeat, repeat.

Angel Jack and I made all the mathematical calculations of twelve-to-fifteen major scenes that included ten to twelve performers (that's 180 costumes so far), plus primary character costumes like Jour, Nuit, Devil, Mother Nature, Little Girl, Mrs. Gottrocks, Slit Dagger and others. This easily added up to over 200 garments. We set out to make the chorus pieces first, so that the settings on the sewing machine could stay the same for elongated periods of time. We made many trips to M&J Trimming on 6th Avenue and 37th Street for rhinestones, trim and brocade. After the first week we were exhausted! We were living on coffee, cigarettes, hamburgers and Donna Summer!

Idiotically, a cast member thought he would help us speed up the creative process and spiked our water pitchers with "black beauty" amphetamine. I drank quite a bit of water that particular night and before long I was vomiting into the only sink in the loft. I vomited on-and-off for the next two days. The drug sent me spinning. After all, I had not eaten much and was already sleep deprived. It put me out of the costume making game for a week. Angel Jack was furious. He had lost his BEST worker (me… always everyone's little helper).

Soon the entire loft was set up with various headdress building stations, hand and machine sewing stations and anyone who was foolish enough to walk in... was immediately put to work. And voila! Four weeks later, Busby Berkeley and Georges Melies would have been proud. The sets and costumes were more beautiful than we had originally thought they would be. I looked exhausted and confused, but damn it, those costumes were gorgeous.

Jayne Anne:
Sky High at the Entermedia was a great experience. The theater was huge and the stage was enormous. Timbo, our stage manager, built us a staircase in the center of the stage. We came down it for quite a few numbers just like *The Ziegfeld Follies.*

"SKY HIGH"

'Sky High' was Hibiscus' answer to Broadway variety revues like Ziegfeld Follies and Leonard Sillman's 'New Faces' series. It was a flexible framework he could decorate with any song or scenario. The off-Broadway editions of 'Sky High' in 1978-79 had songs and characters from almost every past Harris family show.

"SKY HIGH"

"SKY HIGH"

Beginning at the Entermedia Theater on Second Avenue, NYC, 'Sky High' continued at The Players Theater on Minetta Lane. Walter Michael signed on as drummer, playing alongside Fred at the piano. Except for Dad, the whole family was on board. (1978-1979)

Jayne Anne:
The problem was that Timbo had built the staircase to fit his tall frame and his large shoe size. We had to leap down like gazelles on a cliff! Our shoes were opened toed silver four-inch heels purchased at Paradise Bootery where all the "working girls" bought their shoes!

Eloise:
Angel Jack insisted on shipping the headdresses and costumes we left with Mickery Theater in Amsterdam back to New York. It was a crazy endeavor because it was more expensive to mail them than remake them. But Jack was determined. I think he was a little paranoid that someone else was using them.

We drove to some freight location at JFK airport and got all the way through the gate to the place where the boxes were delivered. We picked up two boxes and opened them to find only one scene's worth of crumbling broken headdresses and two or three costumes. I don't know what Jack was expecting. He put his head in his hands and began to cry.

We had to re-build the headdresses for *Sky High,* using strips of burlap dipped in acetone and placed around a bathing cap on somebody's head. I became the test subject for this headdress technique. I had to sit next to an open window with a cloth over my face with him dipping the acetone (which is like nail polish remover) and wrapping it around my head with a bathing cap covering my long hair. As always, Jackie would breathe heavily as he was applying the toxic strips to my head. ("Hold still, hold STILL!) He would always drink a large cup of Nescafé iced coffee. With his husky, breathy voice, growling as he stirred the coffee "umm umm umm!" We would begin our daily regimen of sewing crinoline costumes and endless headdress building sessions, fueled by Nescafé and Jack's usual raw energy.

Susan Dale Rose:
After I got back from Africa I settled in New Mexico, and a business trip took me to NYC. I was the only woman in a group of PR professionals and feeling the oddness until the Harris sisters turned up in the lobby of my hotel. The girls wore short shorts and tank tops and very high heels, and each was balancing a towering ice cream cone. It was a spectacle, and the men regarded me differently after that.

Before going home to New Mexico I partied with George and a lot of his friends at his loft. After days of being the lone female in the PR group, suddenly I was the least feminine being in the room. It was memorable.

Walter Michael:
I took a sabbatical and came to New York to play in the orchestra. Fred conducted from the piano, I played drums and everyone received a weekly paycheck. *Sky High* included nearly every song Mom had written and new songs as well. It was my return to the family shows after a ten-year absence and the beginning of the end of my career as a monk.

Ann:
Our shows at the Entermedia Theater were performed at midnight in Angels tradition. We had good reactions from the audience and the owners of the theater had big plans for us.

Our new producer had other plans however and moved the show to the Players Theater in the West Village to do a union run. We had to appoint an Equity Union deputy. Taking her responsibilities seriously she began threatening to complain to the union about no showers in the dressing rooms, etc. We asked her if she really wanted to do the show or have it closed, and she quieted down. The Players Theater was much smaller than the Entermedia and we had to scale down a bit and also tone down a lot.

It was like fireflies captured in a jar. Still giving off light but when free, not knowing where or when the light turns on, gives it a magic experience.

Eloise:
Little did I know when I started performing in *Sky High* that it would be a big lesson in learning how to be a choreographer. Not only did I help choreograph a lot of that show, but on top of it, I had fifteen costume changes and several dances to do myself, a lot of them tap dances. The Entermedia had a huge stage and the sets and costumes reflected the enormity of the theater. As you look at the pictures in this book you will see dancing horses, dancing poodles, people in huge feathered headdresses and a huge stairway with steps that you could almost commit suicide on in high heels or slippery tap shoes. I don't remember the making of the show very well because it was hours and hours of sleepless nights in order to get the show ready. Additionally, George and Jack were beginning to split apart, and so it was a very turbulent time for everyone.

Adding to the chaos was *Sky High* having to move from the Entermedia, a theater large enough to land a plane in, to the Players Theater with a stage the size of a handkerchief. Having to fit our large costumes and sets into that smaller house was unbelievable. That being said, we had gone off-Broadway, were under a union contract and it was a wonderful time for everybody. We received a great paycheck, got reviewed in the New York Times, and had fun. I really got my choreography legs on that show, a gift that keeps giving today.

Jayne Anne:
Our move to The Players Theater scaled us down a bit. We ran there most of the summer of 1979 and brought along our loving "cult" audience. We did eight shows a week, the union standard, including two matinees. For dinner on those days we would run to Emilio's a high-end pizza place, in full drag.

Ann:
There was one reviewer of *Sky High* who said the worst things. Hibiscus and Jack wrote on the wall of the men's room, "For a good time call," and her telephone number. Hibiscus was devastated. Our producer, however, kept the show running for several months and our faithful following came and loved it. We had loosened up considerably. Andy Warhol and his entourage (including a British royal son) came night after night to the theater.

"SKY HIGH"

Top: George Jr. (Hibiscus) as Jour, God of the Sun with his chariot and dancing horses. Bottom Left: George, Mary Lou, Jayne Anne, Angel Jack, Janet Planet, Tommy Mathews sing 'Auf Wiedersehen.'

''SKY HIGH''

Promo shot for 'Sky High' at The Entermedia Theater with Hibiscus flanked by Tommy Mathews and Jayne Anne as rainbows.

Mary Lou:

I had just turned eighteen. My character in *Sky High* was Nuit, Goddess of the Night, co-starring directly with my brother George's Jour, God of the Sun character. Many months into the run, we began to see Andy Warhol with his entourage showing up night after night to watch the show for about two weeks. One night after the show Andy made a request that his guest be able to come backstage to meet Nuit, my character. The guest turned out to be Charles James Spencer-Churchill, aka Jamie Blandford, eldest son of the Duke of Marlborough and heir to the Blenheim Palace estate in Oxfordshire, England. He was a handsome but notorious playboy who came to the theater each night until I said yes, I would go out to dinner with him.

Photo © Allan Warren

Our whirlwind year of dating, included late night dinners at Mr. Chows and Brasserie, weekend trips to his family's estate in South Hampton, VIP clubbing at Studio 54 and Xenon, as well as private invitations to parties around town. I felt like a true jetsetter, except when Jamie would force me to wear his sister's, (Henrietta Spencer-Churchill's) clothing in order to make me presentable to royal society. I wasn't sure whether to be insulted or exhilarated (who cares, the Champagne was fabulous and I felt like I had met everyone in the royal, celebrity and high society circles). The pinnacle of my schmoozing was when Olivier Chandon, a race-car driver and heir to Moet Champagne, passed me a pick-up note along with his telephone number, with Christie Brinkley, his supermodel girlfriend sitting right next to him.

Jamie Blandford

James and I broke things off for good during his visit to my home in upstate New York, due to his bratty demeanor and me meeting a man who I would later marry (and divorce) at a party that both James and I attended. We both behaved badly that weekend. I finally realized how hard it had been all along... I couldn't keep up with the partying, the schmoozing, the people, the fabulousness or having to wear his sister's clothing.

Walter Michael:

Sky High afforded me a much-needed sabbatical from the Order. It gave me distance from the disturbing paradigm shift there. When our show closed after two months we scattered temporarily to the four winds. I went upstate to the family's summer house to deal with the aftermath of bad winter tenants. They partied hard at our house, built cooking fires in the living room and basically trashed the place. Fixing the house was a daunting project, beginning with jacking it up and repairing the foundation. I hired some help and by mid-August the job was done. In my spare time I traveled to nearby Woodstock to research and perform Catskill Mountain music for *The Story of Woodstock,* written and directed by my friend, the poet Magie Dominic. It was a historical play presented by children at the local library. Fred came up from the city to set up and run the lighting. The rest of the family came up to see the play and to help clean and paint the Margaretville house before winter set in. It was great to do something non show-bizzy with the family after *Sky High*.

Reconnecting with the family planted the seed that eventually led to my exit from the Order. Even before Father Blighton died in 1974, I had begun to doubt my future with his New Age religion. I had come to view my grandfatherly guru as an inspired, but deeply flawed, flim-flam man who meant well but whose lapses in character and attempts to cover them up ultimately compromised his life's work. Predictably, individuals in his appointed leadership circle jockeyed for position, grabbed the reins and hijacked the Order and its resources. I grew weary of their machinations and of having my concerns dismissed. The prospect of resuming a self-directed life became more plausible as the Order unraveled.

My summer with *Sky High* and the family caravan cleared my head. At summer's end I returned to the Order and transferred to Seattle to try working for one of the few leaders I still trusted. He jumped the fence and left the Order within a month of my arrival. Slowly but surely I came to the realization that the time had come, no turning back. I left the Order permanently in 1984. Many of my colleagues there – good, sincere and well-intentioned people – also left, and most carry on doing good works all around the world.

Together again! Walter Michael, in tuxedo and striped shirt, re-joined his family on its latest creative adventure, the retooled off-Broadway 'Sky High.' (1979)

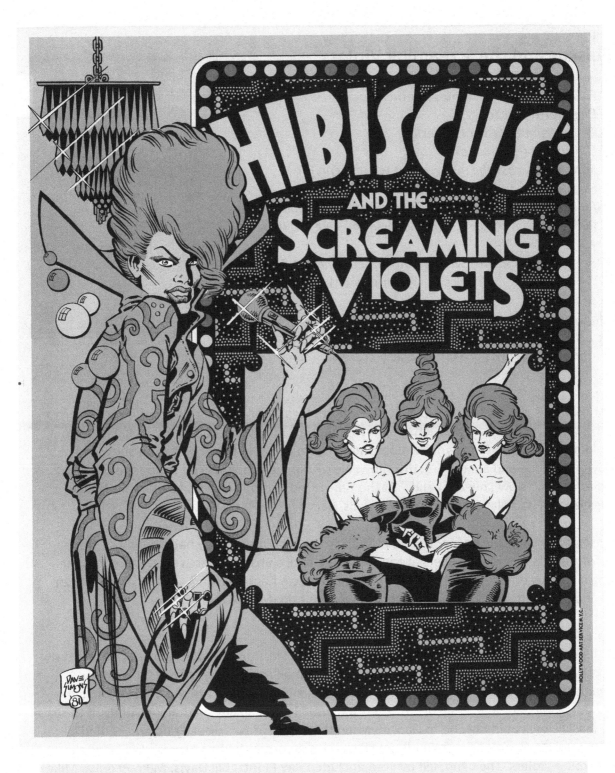

Hard to keep Hibiscus down. He was already envisioning a rock show.

- Ann

Chapter 16
Hibiscus and the Screaming Violets

Fill my arms with heather, Heathcliff.
Disregard their taunts
Thundering together Heathcliffe
Lightning strikes but once!
Sprawled across the moor, What we're living for
Fill my arms and all my charms with heather
Pull down the curtains, Mrs. Haversham, love is all!
Pull down the curtains, Mrs. Haversham, love is all!

'Heathcliffe,' written for *Hibiscus and the Screaming Violets*
Lyrics by Ann Harris, music by Fred Harris

Mary Lou:
Our brother George was eager to morph from his own Angels of Light theater style... to the theater of New York's growing music culture.

Ann:
First, Hibiscus put a billboard up over the Schulte Cigar Store in Sheridan Square to advertise his new act. His billboard was lettered with hundreds of sequins stitched in place by a group of elderly women in Brooklyn. He always gave them credit at the end of each show. It showed his face and announced the show. Next step, he brought Fred to see the billboard and told him, "Now I need a band." At the time, Fred was busy leading a marvelous band of musicians he had played with in the Catskills, backing The Harris Sisters.

Hibiscus was counting on his sisters for The Screaming Violets. They had already started performing as The Harris Sisters at top New York rock clubs and were reluctant to join the gang. Hibiscus told them that he was planning to use a Caucasian girl, an African American girl and an Asian girl for the Violets if they wouldn't do it. They folded.

Jayne Anne:
At the time, we were doing our own act, *The Harris Sisters and Trouble,* sort of punk, sort of rock. We played at CBGB, SNAFU and most of the small rock venues of the time. At the same time, I worked in the coatroom at Studio 54 and eventually ran the concession. I was also doing legit commercial work in television and film. Balancing all that was difficult to say the least! How could I say no to George when the billboard was already up and he had purchased the band's shoes? Our band, "Trouble," became the band for Hibiscus and the Screaming Violets. The band, led by Fred, included Ray Ploutz, Bill Davis, Mike Pedulla, Mike Kimmel and Josh Callow. It was quite the adventure. We played The Ice Palace on Fire Island and at the end of the gig, jumped into the pool in our purple sequined gowns and our marabou jackets. Studio 54 had us sing there a few times. The room had a bridge that we stood on way above the crowd. The bridge moved above the dance floor as we sang. There was no fence in front of us. In our stiletto heels it was frightening!

Eloise:

It was 1981 – the height of the disco era. Donna Summer was topping the pop charts. The Punk scene had just begun. The Screaming Violets embarked on a tour of New York City disco clubs such as Studio 54, Xenon, The Ice Palace, Danceteria, The Peppermint Lounge, Bonds, SNAFU, and The Red Parrot. We performed on the same circuit with Madonna, Lime, The Weather Girls and other up-and-comers. Additionally our group performed at underground punk clubs such as The Mudd Club and The Underground, alongside Nona Hendryx, China Davis, Blondie and The Ramones. To quote John Waters, "We were insane, but not permanently."

Mary Lou:

We were on the live performance circuit with Grace Jones, Michael Musto and The Must, Bobby Reed, Adam Ant, Holly Woodlawn, and Cyndi Lauper. We were scheduled to fulfill our weekly performances at SNAFU, make a video for the new MTV channel and to begin recording an album for a tour in Japan. By this point we were terribly jaded and bratty. We were interviewed by Robin Leach of *Lifestyles of the Rich and Famous* and had press junkets on Fire Island. We were poised and ready for the big time!

Ann:

In his "spare time," Hibiscus had a show running at Theater for the New City, which had moved over to Second Avenue to the Gate Theatre. The show was *Tinsel Town Tirade* co-starring Hibiscus and Holly Woodlawn. Opening night sported Kleig lights and a wet cement square for Holly to imprint her hand for posterity, just like Grauman's Chinese Theater.

Eloise:

We were on our way to George's house to pick up some equipment for a gig we had at the Mudd Club. It was Mom, Mary Lou, Jayne Anne and me crammed into a taxi. Jayne Anne was applying lipstick, Lou and Mom were gabbing and I was thinking about how long it had been since I had been down to see George's apartment. He had moved from West 76th Street, a beautiful garden rental on a lovely tree-lined street, to a large loft in Greenwich Village, a little deserted, but by the water and much larger.

Jayne Anne signaled to the building, we paid the cab and went upstairs. George and our dresser Albert were gathering mikes, stands and tapes for the show. George, who had been complaining of tiredness, had also been coughing for about a month. He was running to get everything together so we could get there on time. We did the show, brought everything home and went home ourselves. I thought nothing of it.

Center triad: Bobby Reed, Michael Musto and Mary Lou, at Studio 54 (1980's)

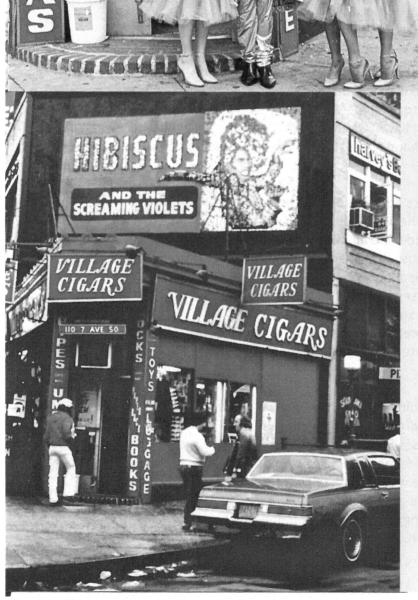

For sheer visibility in Greenwich Village, the Schulte Cigar Store on 7th Avenue and Christopher Street was the best location for the giant billboard.

Hibiscus recruited help from residents of a Brooklyn senior center in gluing thousands of sequins to his dazzling billboard. The sign rapidly became the talk of the town. (1981)

'Hibiscus and The Screaming Violets' were born. In the blink of an eye we were in the exciting downtown New York music scene, with a powerhouse rock-and-roll act. Fred, Jayne Anne, Eloise and I launched into tearing our t-shirts and jeans and booking ourselves into New York's funky music clubs. (1981)

- Mary Lou

Hibiscus and the Screaming Violets had a permanent performance home at Lewis Friedman's club, SNAFU, in the Chelsea neighborhood of Manhattan. (1981-82)

That year MTV launched its first broadcast. The first song that aired was The Buggles' 'Video Killed the Radio Star.' A whole new world was opening up for Hibiscus and The Screaming Violets.

- Mary Lou

An expert multi-tasker, Hibiscus managed to write and produce a full-length musical at TNC, 'Tinsel Town Tirade,' even while building his rock act and maintaining a grueling performance schedule. (1982)

**The press loved Hibiscus and his intoxicating energy.
"Get the queens talking!" was his P.R. mantra.**

Ready to make their video and tour Japan, Hibiscus and the Screaming Violets were rising stars.

Chapter 17
The Loudest Thud

Ann:
It started with a whimper – a small report in the newspapers about a strange new illness among a small number of gay men, they called it Gay Related Immune Deficiency (GRID). It was associated with a high level of stigma and discrimination, because it was linked to the gay population. The government did not respond to the crisis, but in New York City, The Gay Men's Health Crisis came to the rescue of victims of the emerging epidemic.

Hibiscus wasn't feeling well. He had a rash. They sent him home from the hospital with antibiotics but it only got worse. He was booked into a show at Magique and staggered in late because he didn't want Fred to have to explain his absence. He didn't want to let him and the girls down. It was a great show, among his best.

Jayne Anne:
Hibiscus was late and came in feverish and sick. On stage, I stood behind him and held up his purple sequined pants, which had once been form fitting.

Eloise:
My mother called me that night to tell me that the cough had gotten worse, but that George was in good spirits and would make the show tomorrow night and said I could go visit him if I had the time. I rushed to the gig, walked into the back door where the band usually loads in. I didn't see anyone but I overheard some voices that sounded familiar. I walked over to a table hidden by a wall, facing the stage, and found Jayne Anne, Mary Lou, Fred and the band in a state of confusion. "George is late and we can't get a hold of him. In desperation we are trying to think of who has the right range to sing in George's key just in case he doesn't make it." The family knew he had been ill. My mother had been helping him do things because he would go through spells of feeling well and then feeling terrible. Ten minutes before we had to go on, George came spinning through the door in costume, my mother holding him up. He was extremely skinny and looking frail. Without hesitation he pushed himself onto the stage and gave the best performance of his life. With the crowd still screaming he walked proudly off the stage and collapsed in an agonized state.

Ann:
Right after that he landed in the hospital on machines. He had pneumocystis pneumonia. It was the beginning of the AIDS epidemic.

Jayne Anne:
When I went to the hospital to see Hibiscus a doctor pulled me aside and asked, "Did you know your brother was gay?" Not knowing how seriously ill he was I quipped, "Is it fatal?"

Ann:
I remember going to the airport to pick up medicine sent by the Centers for Disease Control in Atlanta. George couldn't talk on his hospital ventilator, so he wrote us notes. He was

negotiating a tour of Japan at the time and recovering from a lost romance. He and Jack had broken up months before and this was a new boyfriend. He wrote, "Call him, make it sound worse than it is!" As if it could be any worse.

Eloise:
We took turns staying at George's place and going to the hospital a few blocks away. I spent a lot of time in his apartment. Painful as it was, staying there was a source of relief. I would sit in his closet among his shoes or under his clothes to feel close to him, and to cry.

The last day came. For some reason we were all there – which had never happened before as we visited in shifts. It was kind of like he summoned us there. We were called into the room. The machines were clanging and beeping, an unsympathetic doctor came in, new on the case and said monotonously, "Not all of you should be in the room at once. What is this, a death watch?" George's nurse, who we loved, chased him out. Fred leaned down to his ear and told George that we knew it was all just too much for him, that we were all there, that we loved him and it was OK for him to leave if he wanted to. He opened his eyes, he knew us all and then left as if he were going on a trip, my beautiful brother.

Ann:
We were all there when he died, except Walt. George was obviously trying to hang on and Fred told him that it was OK to take off. I have witnessed family deaths before but never like this one. His essence seems to have floated around for a beat and flew out the window. Harry Koutoukas, a good friend, was with us. Harry looked up at the ceiling and said, "Won't you reconsider?" I'll always love him for that.

Eloise:
We went home. Mary Lou and Mom stayed in George's apartment. After they had fallen asleep, Mary Lou said she woke up and saw something swaying back and forth next to one of his tall plants. She tried to wake my mother but she remained asleep. Soon, George's face and body appeared... a bit cloudy but definitely a distinct form. Mary Lou said George was reaching his hands out to her. In a regretful moment of panic, she told him to go and he faded away.

Mary Lou:
That night the family went back to Hibiscus' apartment and made a strained effort at an Irish wake with pizza and beer. My mother and I slept in his apartment. In the middle of the night I saw a small white object rocking back and forth in the air. Nervously, I tried to wake my mother, but she would not rouse. As I stared at the moving white object, George's ghost began to appear around what turned out to be his teeth. He was crying and reaching out to me with his arms. I desperately tried to shake my mother, who is normally a light sleeper, with no success. I would regret my next action for the rest of my life. I screamed out... "GO AWAY!" and he vanished.

Eloise:
Afterward, my parents lived in George's apartment. Whenever I felt upset, I could go there and feel safe and at peace. Since then I've seen changes in myself. I'm more driven to

accomplish things. Things I still have from his apartment remind me of how much he used to make me laugh or tell me to work harder. I can hear his voice coming out of the wall. George was a wonderful person and I loved him with all my heart.

Jayne Anne:
His life was cut short at age 32, but he filled it with what he wanted to do and on his own terms: performing and bringing entertainment to people and having a total blast along the way. I think of him a lot and feel that he is still with us.

Every year in some way, shape or form, he comes up whether it is the famous photo by Bernie Boston, of George putting carnations in soldiers' rifles or a fashion industry person utilizing things he had done back in the late 60's and early 70's in San Francisco. He was ahead of his time.

Robert Patrick, playwright and family friend:
What greater scope he might have had waiting for us, we will never know, for George became the first person I knew who was taken away from us by AIDS. One day I passed Ann in the lobby of Theater For the New City, and casually asked how George was. Her eyes wide with wonder and puzzlement, she said, "He's sick. He's really sick." And a week or a little more later, I heard the dreadful news.

Ann:
After that, so many of our artist friends joined him in paradise.

622 Greenwich Street
Hibiscus' last address

George Edgerly Harris III   Hibiscus de la Blossom
Brian Wolfe

September 6, 1949 - May 6, 1982

The benefit was beautiful. I feel he was there and somehow helped us put the show together. The 9th Street Stompers played and performed better than they ever had. We did "St. James Infirmary," "Over The Rainbow," and "When The Saints Go Marching In." The Screaming Violets sang like they were inspired by some incredible force. Likewise Fred and the rock band. John Herbert McDowell was beautiful and so was Fred - performing 'Disaster Bay.' The replacement for Hibiscus (Tommy Matthews) was terrific. The cast of 'Tinsel Town Tirade' and Ann, with a short speech, were all magnificent.

It was a beautiful show. Truly magic, Hibiscus magic.

- George, Sr.

Chapter 18
I Will Survive

George, Sr.:
I was brokenhearted and in shock over Hibiscus' death, as all of us were.

Ann:
We were heartbroken and no one wanted to do anything.

Mary Lou:
Our event at Danceteria, originally organized as a benefit for Hibiscus' medical costs, instead became a memorial.

Jayne Anne:
Jim Fouratt was kind enough to donate the space at Danceteria for the memorial. A host of performers sang and spoke about his life. It was very moving and ended with a spotlight on a microphone onstage with his boots and cape. His voice came over the sound system singing our disco version of "A Whiter Shade of Pale."

Mary Lou:
Our family had been such a large part of George's magical world... we were stunned... permanently. So as a family, we bravely forged ahead without our beloved, fun and inspiring brother.

Walter Michael:
When Hibiscus died, I was the only family member not at his bedside. In the three year gap between *Sky High* and the day of his death, George and I had drifted apart again for no particular reason. We were both preoccupied with our individual projects. No worries, it was a pattern we were accustomed to. His sudden passing hit me like a sledgehammer. I knew he wasn't well, but I believed he was in good hands with his doctors and the family and would recover. My absence at his deathbed left an irreconcilable hole in my heart.

Angel Jack:
When he was ready to do *Tinsel Town Tirade* I had told George he could use the costumes. George had no taste when it came to how things looked onstage. The way he was acting was driving me nuts. The twinkle was gone from his eye. Finally I left New York. I just had to get away. Soon I was back home in Florida, having a heavy discussion with Bette, my mom, and my brother Jimmy about being on my own, being myself - when the phone rang. George had tracked me down. He called me whenever and wherever I was. I don't know how he did it. He called me from the airport and said, "Jackie, don't leave me or I'll die!" I said to myself, "I won't call him. He'll be in Greece in three months if I'm there, so I won't tell him where I'm going." That's the last I spoke to him.

Walter Michael:
Living on Mykonos, Jack found peace and a renewed sense of creativity. He got clean, got healthy, exercised and started performing in local clubs. He received a telegram from his mother, Bette, "George is in the hospital, he's not expected to live."

Angel Jack:
I thought he was "crying wolf" like so many times before. I fell asleep for a really long time, then went to town and did my show. I overheard co-workers talking about George, that he'd died. I flipped out. Spent a lot of time standing by the edge of the sea. Went to a Greek baptism in a church that was pure sequins, pure George. I went up on a hill and cried like a donkey for hours.

George has come to me several times. He would do strange things. A picture on a wall would move. I said, "If you're really there, make a waterfall come on TV." Lo and behold, I turned it on and there was Olive Oyl singing "By a Waterfall" on TV! I swear it's true.

I should feel really stupid. By dying George let me know years ago how dangerous HIV is. I do know and I did know and I should have listened. Right now I'm secure. I have a message, something to say, and I lived for the right to say it. I chose my own road and am very proud of myself – proud of what I've done. I don't want to be anyone else but me. When I was younger I would have been anyone but me. I regret so <u>so</u> much of the drugs – I realize I'm not as godlike as I thought.

Walter Michael:
Angel Jack passed away not long after my interview with him.

Eloise:
Long after they broke up, Jack and George remained in touch although they had definitely gone different ways. Jack never got over George's death. It pained him right up until the end of his life. As our true brother outlaw it was pure chaos. Jack's family was ravaged by the AIDS epidemic. He and his brother Mij (Jim spelled backwards) both suffered with the virus.

Mary Lou:
George and Jack's deaths contrasted as much as their lives. Hibiscus had a fast, magical, spiritual and artistic passing, which resulted in him being deemed an important artist of his day, whereas Angel Jack, being placed on the pill cocktail for AIDS patients, elongated his decay. His end was long, painful and not glamorous the way he would have wanted it. Both Jack and his brother Jimmy were critically ill for many years before they passed. We did not find out Jack was gone until we were told by two antique dealers in Florida who also told us that his mother Bette Coe, who lived with him, was missing. My mother wrote in a song, "You never know what tomorrow may bring - you go to turn a corner and bing!" Bette finally turned up, of all places, where we started - Clearwater, Florida.

Eloise:
We were sitting on the porch at The Amherst, a vacation hotel where we often stayed in Ocean Grove, New Jersey – Jack, a young boyfriend he had picked up under the boardwalk

at Asbury Park, and me. The boyfriend reminded me of the character Flick from Lanford Wilson's play, *The Hot L Baltimore.* Jack was chain-smoking Marlboros. They were living and sleeping under the boardwalk. The progress of AIDS had started to ravage Jack's body, his mind, and his understanding of what he was doing or how he was living.

Unlike Hibiscus, who died soon after he was diagnosed, Jack's life was extended by a killer cocktail of pills. Because of them he was in his right mind enough to sustain living on his own terms, without unwanted interference. But those who knew him well knew something was not right. He called us onto the porch and insisted we sit and listen closely to the song he was about to play on an archaic, taped up old boom box he was cradling. It was Billy Vera's hit, "At This Moment," blasted at top decibels. Jack began to cry, inhaled his cigarette harshly and sang to me in his bratty, out of tune voice with tears in his eyes:

> *What do you think I would give at this moment?*
> *If you'd stay I'd subtract twenty years from my life*
> *I'd fall down on my knees*
> *Kiss the ground that you walk on, baby*
> *If I could just hold you... again.*

© *William David McCord*

There was no consoling Jack. I was completely shocked at how stupid I had been about his toxic-angry shell. He had been in love all this time with George and carried incredible pain all those years. He did not respond to the call when we told him George was dying. Jack was in Greece and thought it was just another of George's false alarms. Only this time it wasn't.

That was the last time I saw the authentic Jack Coe, the young kind-hearted boy who appeared on my doorstep at 319 East Ninth Street so many years ago. As bratty as he could be, he was still my brother-in-law. I felt helpless and awful that I could not help him. There was nothing to do but cry.

Ann:
Holly Woodlawn had a gig at SNAFU one night and sang "The Champagne Song" which I had written. She saw the girls in the audience and said to them, "Get back up here!" (onto the stage), and they did.

Mary Lou:
Holly Woodlawn booked herself and The Screaming Violets immediately into SNAFU, a club owned by Lewis Friedman, who also became another casualty of this mysterious disease that was claiming many of our friends and fellow artists.

Jayne Anne:
Louis Friedman extended the run at SNAFU. It was duly noted on the infamous Page Six of The New York Post.

Jack told me he hitchhiked to California at age eighteen with his friend Doe, whose father was chancellor of the University of California Medical Center. 'I went straight to where the queens were,' said Jack, 'in a Frank Lloyd Wright house on top of Parnassus.'

- Walter Michael

Clockwise from top left: Angel Jack's portrait in multimedia by Sterling Powell; backstage at 'Sky High'; and his beautiful mother Bette Coe when she was crowned Miss Long Branch, NJ. (1940's)

Ann:

The years after Hibiscus died were busy and sad. We missed him a lot. The girls took off with their trio singing 40's music. They played most all the clubs and discos in New York including Studio 54, Tatou, and The Rainbow Room. They were also featured on Geraldo Rivera's television show. I remember one night we were sitting in the dressing room at the Red Parrott waiting to go on. It was pouring rain and I looked out the window at the street below. There stood a camel, from the circus I guess. There was a party for Brooke Shields inside. I don't know if the camel had anything to do with it or not, but for me, it summed up the magic of what had gone before and what was yet to come.

George, Sr. had a part in the movie *Speak No Evil, Hear No Evil* with Gene Wilder. When that was finished, he worked with Gene on several short films depicting some of the challenges imposed by deafness. George had a hearing problem stemming from World War II. In the film he wore a hearing aid as part of the story. Funny though, the sound-man came over and told George that his hearing aid was making a buzz and to turn it off. So much for reality.

The girls sang at Grossinger's, icon of the Catskill "Borscht Belt," just before it closed. The manager, Michael Ettes, took us around the beautiful grounds and the fabulous hotel. The menu was scrumptious, especially the wonderful Borscht soup. It's sad that, one by one, those beautiful hotels closed. That way of life gave way to airplane trips to the Bahamas. Another sad note, a couple of months or so after he gave us that tour, Michael Ettes was killed in a helicopter crash in New York along with several other businessmen.

On Saturday mornings we "subwayed" to the Upper West Side for singing lessons. Tom Rosinsky opened the door to the "Rosinsky Method." He was a wonderful teacher and dear friend. Another good friend, classical oboist Bert Lucarelli, recommended Fred and his studio to Broadway songwriter Richard Adler *(The Pajama Game, Damn Yankees)*. Richard noticed a photo of the girls on the studio wall and asked about them. The upshot was that Richard invited them to record some of his songs with him. It was a magical experience. They learned a lot from both Richard and Don Smith, his accompanist. They performed live with Richard at such places as the Metropolitan Club, University of North Carolina at Chapel Hill, Lake Placid, and South Hampton.

On 'The Harris Sisters Sing Richard Adler' album we enjoyed interpreting many of Richard's 'hit parade' songs and included them in our road show. (1993)

In the early 1990s The Harris Sisters were booked to perform on the Holland America Line to Australia. The show, starring Donald O'Connor, was in part recreating the war years. The girls played The Andrews Sisters, reprising a tribute show they had done in New York. Upon their return via Fiji, Jayne and her husband Tom discovered they were expecting a child.

- Ann

Still image © Warren Steibel/Roxanne Co.

Ann as the lonely heart schoolteacher Doris Acker in the cult film classic 'The Honeymoon Killers.' (1970)

Harry Koutoukas ran into me on the street and told me to get back into action. I did three plays of his, one at La MaMa and two at Theater for the New City. I love his plays and he was a wonderful, caring director. He had us check the stage each night for nails as we were barefoot a lot. His attention to detail and marvelous sense of humor were awesome. His theatre was 'School for Gargoyles' and I was proud to be a Gargoyle. His telephone book listing in Manhattan was B. A. Gargoyle. (1992)

- Ann

Walter Michael:
A decade after George died I was inspired by Mom's poem, "From Another World," and by Eloise's essay about crying among his clothes in the closet. Seattle author Stan Henry and I collaborated on a musical about Hibiscus that traced our family's journey and the story of George's and my relationship.

> *Can you see me from another world?*
> *Is your other world*
> *Better than the one you had?*
> *Can you hear me from another world,*
> *Here in your yesterday.*
> *Still crying 'cause I feel so bad*
> *Can I find the place*
> *You went in outer space?*
> *Will our moments be erased*
> *As if they never were?*
> *But if they ever were,*
> *I'll see your face.*
>
> *And the echo of a thousand words,*
> *And the memory of a summer's day,*
> *Make the focus of the picture clear,*
> *Make the lonely hours melt away.*
> *And I'll hear you like I always did*
> *In the tune of half forgotten song*
> *Moving shadows where your laughter hid,*
> *Floating pictures where the dreams belong.*
>
> *Can you see me from another world*
> *Is your other world*
> *Better than the one we knew?*
> *Can you hear me from the other world*
> *Here in your yesterday?*
> *Still crying 'cause I'm not with you*
> *Can I find the place*
> *You went in outer space?*
> *Will our moments be erased*
> *As if they never were?*
>
> *But if they ever were*
> *I'll see your face*

The poem became a lyric, the lyric became a song, and the song became a show. The resulting musical, *Hibiscus,* began life as a workshop in Seattle and morphed in to a fully realized musical. Mom wrote new songs, working with composer Daniel Barry. My sisters came west to participate in the workshop at Pilgrim Center for the Arts, a Seattle "fringe" theater that I co-founded with Manuel R. Cawaling and Adam Othman, modeled on La

MaMa ETC, Caffe Cino and Judson Poets Theater. Ellen Stewart gave her blessing to bring the finished show to La MaMa, where it debuted in May, 1992 with a new book co-written with Rebecca Stone and Vida M. Benjamin and direction by the veteran La MaMa artist Jacque Lynn Colton. Although it was unnerving for the family to see themselves portrayed by others, the musical was well received by many who knew Hibiscus. It went a long way for me toward reconnecting with the zeitgeist of my brother, whom I loved.

Program cover by Skot Herrin

Jayne Anne:
We sisters played ourselves in the Pilgrim Center workshop production. I also played Hibiscus because George and I look very much alike and I could bring his character to life in a short time. When The Screaming Violets were onstage our director, Jonathan Harris (no relation), played me. It was like an out of body experience to be playing my brother Hibiscus while
"I," (Jonathan), was singing behind him. Two years later in New York, it was fantastic to see

Jayne Anne as Hibiscus

the show at La MaMa, our original artistic home. But it was weird seeing others playing us. Of course I wanted to be up there. My favorite scene was the juxtaposition of Hibiscus on one side of the stage scrubbing the floor of the commune as a Kitchen Slut while Walter Michael scrubbed the floor on the other side of the stage in his religious household. Two very different experiences yet very much the same. The following year, 1993, my sisters and I created a new musical of our own, *Cheek to Cheek,* inspired by our cabaret portrayal of The Andrews Sisters.

Walter Michael:
My sisters wrote the script and songs for *Cheek to Cheek,* and I co-produced the show with Ellen Stewart at La MaMa. In response to premiering our two newest musicals back-to-back at La MaMa, Ellen told me, "Baby, La MaMa is your home. You don't have to tell me *what* you want to do here, you only have to tell me *when.*"

Jayne Anne:
Ellen still called us her "babies." To anyone and everyone she recounted the story of Mary Lou at the age of three in *The Sheep and the Cheapskate* wearing a little bikini with the top riding up too high! She still saw us as children in her mind's eye but never dumbed down anything to us.

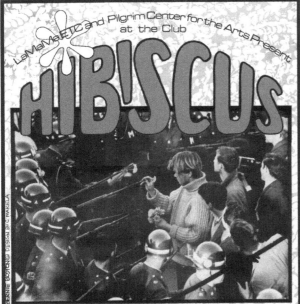

I was honored when my brother Walter asked us to come out to Seattle to take part in the workshop of his musical, 'Hibiscus.' It was cathartic to perform in a play written by him with Stan Henry as an homage to George. (1992)

- Jayne Anne

'Cheek to Cheek' was such a fun process for us. It was a breath of fresh air for The Harris Sisters, because for a long time we had been performing other peoples' material. We were returning to our roots, writing an original script, original music and lyrics with the talented Peter Kwaloff, making our own costumes, creating the choreography and co-producing the show at La MaMa with our brother and his Seattle fringe theater. (1993)

- Mary Lou

Mary Lou:
Cheek to Cheek is about a sister singing trio who had spent lives together being molded and primed for stardom on a popular radio show. We rehearsed at La MaMa's Annex for three weeks and had a successful two-week run in La MaMa's First Floor Theatre. It was so refreshing. It felt like coming home, only this time we could really appreciate the seasoned skills that we had learned over the years. In the production were musical sequences filled with harmony, counterpoint, tap dancing and impressive lighting and stage effects.

Ellen Stewart couldn't have been nicer to us. I secretly think she was happy to be working with the Harris family again.

- Mary Lou

Chapter 19
The Chrysalis

When friends desert you, you're all at sea
Do it yourself!
You can't depend on anybody
Do it yourself!

When peril's on the brink
There is no time to think
It's dark - you need a drink
To be a little stronger, live a little longer

Don't be afraid to act on your own
Do it yourself!
Don't lose your faith because you are grown
Do it yourself!
You think you've made a mess of this
You're hanging off the precipice
Hold on - And do it -yourself!

"Do It Yourself" from *Sky High*
Music and lyrics by Ann Harris

The Harris Sisters: Jayne Anne, Eloise and Mary Lou:
Growing up together in a bohemian soup set the stage for a lifetime of togetherness between us Harris girls. We shared roles and stages throughout the off-off-Broadway explosion. We toured Europe and struggled through school together, all the while developing from little kids to teens to young ladies. We spent decades exploring the planet and sorting out expectations.

We three sisters agree that we struggle with influences of duality provided by our father's bohemian DNA and our mother's upper crust Westchester roots. On our father's side, there are generations of artists and inventors prone to pick up stakes and wander. Among them are Myron Coloney, the newspaperman and inventor; and fine art painters Charles Xavier Harris and his son, George Edgerly Harris (Dad's grandfather and father, respectively). From our mother's side comes an appetite for wealthy, free-spirited living and Irish optimism, always looking on the sunny side like Auntie Mame. These two driving forces fueled reoccurring themes in the Harris sisters' lives.

After rigorous early years of off-off-Broadway, Angels of Light spectacles, rock 'n roll with The Harris Sisters, and Hibiscus and the Screaming Violets... in the blink of an eye ... a deafening silence. Our beautiful brother had suddenly died. We were devastated, demented, deranged, derailed and any other "de" you can possibly imagine... we were! Everything seemed to die with our precious brother – the music, fun, direction and our fearlessness. We had come to an unwilling grinding halt. As a family we were in shock and heartbroken. Our brother's death made us realize that we had been his live marionette dolls most of our lives. The combination of Hibiscus' tremendously over-shadowing personality and our parents' distraction left us exposed in the role of his foils. Don't get us wrong – it was fabulous beyond belief and filled with once-in-a-lifetime enviable experiences. However, once Hibiscus passed away, his dolls had no one to pull their strings. We waited lifelessly and completely freaked-out, trying to push the strings into other people's hands, but no one would put the dollies on their feet again the way that George (Hibiscus) had done. His death was our undoing, our unwinding. Now what do we do?

As children we dwelled for a long time in a perceived earthly paradise. Never once had we rebelled or made plans for our own futures. This dream-state led us to believe that, had our brother lived, we would have stayed in bliss forever. Moving on was a hard reality for us, and boy, were we sobbing about it! But as judgment and the ability to recognize our jeopardized futures entered into the picture, we chopped off the marionette strings and started fresh.

Thanks to Holly Woodlawn's insistence we got back on our feet and continued singing. It was fun but no longer effortless, euphoric or magical. However, we had our unique work ethic: find the greatest, most glittery spectacle and dive right in! We became a jazz trio managed by Carl Griffin, president of GRP records, as he was looking for a vocal trio to be the next Manhattan Transfer. We recorded an album with Broadway songwriter Richard Adler *(Damn Yankees* and *The Pajama Game),* toured Australia with our Andrews Sisters tribute show and performed and recorded as a trio and individually. We wrote songs for ourselves and for other artists including Phoenix (Atlantic Records); Carrie Nation (Think Big Records) and Michael Winslow (Epic Records).

Collaborating with the Harris Sisters looks more like fun than work.

Geraldo

JUNE 24, 1988
THE HARRIS SISTERS

DEAR HARRIS SISTERS:

I WANT TO THANK YOU SO MUCH FOR APPEARING ON OUR HOMELESS VETERANS
PROGRAM. WE ALL REALLY ENJOYED YOU. YOU WERE ALL BEAUTIFUL, TALENTED
AND TOTALLY PROFESSIONAL...BEST OF LUCK IN YOUR CAREER.

SINCERELY,

RICHARD ADLER
8 EAST 83RD STREET
NEW YORK, N.Y. 10028
—
(212) 744-8861

October 19, 1992

The Harris Sisters
622 Greenwich Street
Apt. 4E
New York, New York 10014

Dear Girls,

What a lovely card... I am, of course, referring to
your "late - early" card.

I have been very busy with many things but I must say
miss seeing you, and hope soon to be able to get together to finish the album and to see what we can
ultimately do with it.

Triple hugs and kisses to you.

Love,

Richard

PATRICIA BIRCH

Dear Harris Sisters —
Thank you — a belated
but none the less heart felt
thanks for singing at the
SOS Benefit. You all just
get better and better and
are a joy to listen to and
watch.
I wish the room had
been better for you — it
wasn't easy — & you still
were wonderful.
Do let me know when
the tape is ready & stay
in touch!
Thanks again,
Love,
— Pat

...REET, NEW YORK, NEW YORK 10021
261   FAX 212 794 ....

**The Harris Sisters worked
with many wonderful
people including TV host
Geraldo Rivera, Broadway
composer Richard Adler
and choreographer
Patricia Birch.**

THE HARRIS SISTERS

Photos © Nancy Brown

Attempting country & western, we recorded a four-song demo.
Top, L to R: Jayne Anne, Eloise, Mary Lou, Walter Michael.
Bottom: Mary Lou, Walter Michael Jayne Anne, Eloise. (1994)

The Harris Sisters: Jayne Anne, Eloise and Mary Lou:
The light and airy, free lovin' era of the 1960's had experienced its peak. The free-love concept continued into the 1970's, except the players were now drunk, money-driven and gross. Let's just say we have dated our share of lechers and lunatics! Through the next few years we Harris girls became masters at removing ourselves from dark and sticky situations.

Eloise:
While still in high school I had an offer to do a show with Hibiscus in San Francisco, *The Shocking Pink Life of Jayne Champagne.* I had to make a choice: stay home with my boyfriend, or leave him and my senior prom behind for the show. Of course I chose *Jayne Champagne.* When I was younger the shows and leaving seemed easier. As I became older, boyfriends, crushes and hormonal turbulence became more difficult. Drag queens are like cartoon characters. You can't go to a queen for a tampon or talk about love-sickness without getting weird advice like "Honey, all you need is some eye candy" or "Plug that up!"

One boyfriend, a European golf pro, treated me to a whirlwind romantic summer in Paris and Deauville, France. Back in New York another love, to surprise me on my birthday, landed a helicopter on my best friend's lawn in The Hamptons where I had fled following a tomato-faced quarrel. Some former boyfriends, like Tim Robbins, have remained friends throughout the years. Billy Breen is another. He was around several times in Margaretville and during the show we rehearsed in Tannersville before a European tour. Billy was a boy complete with long hair as desired in the 70's. George was trying to get his attention, but Billy was straight. The queens thought they could turn any man gay. Unfortunately for George, not this man. We had a wonderful time, but once again a goodbye was coming as the Europe tour loomed. It was time to go, drift apart and grow up.

Mary Lou:
Hibiscus gave me the best piece of advice, "Never do anything to your body that you can't wash off." He was right about that, as I needed my blank canvas to create new personas quite often. After *Sky High* I decided to go after television commercials. So, I washed off the glitter and sequins, got a haircut, bought several conservative outfits, enrolled in the Weist-Barron Television School and very quickly signed a one-year contract with the Marje Fields Agency. My assigned agent's name was Eileen Haves. She enrolled me in lessons on auditioning, make-up, clothing selection, and reading commercial-copy. In a very short time, I had landed three commercials: Charleston Chew, Heineken and Tampax. Eileen also sent me to audition for a role as a college student in *The Muppets Take Manhattan* movie, which I got. I was nervous but excited to work with Frank Oz, the director.

One day, I got a call from Eileen who said she was leaving the Marje Fields Agency and was inviting a few actors to join her new agency. Being young and foolish, I thought, I'd better stay with the "name" agency thinking that's what is helping me get all this work. I re-signed with Marje Fields and never got a call again. I wished I had stayed with the agent who was able to employ me as an actor on a regular basis. Commercial acting was such a short phase.

Even before George died, Jayne Anne solved our financial and social problems by getting all three of us hired to work Studio 54's coat rooms. "Studio" became our new Utopia. It was a playground for the rich, famous, fabulous, notorious and beautiful, and encouraged us into feeling our own jet-setting oats. It was the first time we were mature enough to enjoy freedom and money to burn.

The Harris Sisters: Jayne Anne, Eloise and Mary Lou:
Along with gainful employment, Studio 54 provided a new venue for The Harris Sisters to perform and all-access passes to concerts of emerging stars like Duran Duran, Culture Club and Madonna. Celebrities often used our coatroom to take a break from the crowds. We had carte blanche entreé to other chic clubs in New York City. We were there for a range of parties, from Michael Jackson's birthday party to Dr. Ruth's book launch.

Jayne Anne:
Working at Studio 54 saved us from the downward spiral of the era. So much went on, so many drugs, so much alcohol, so much money and so little sleep that you really had no choice but to fall from grace, either temporarily or sadly permanently, or become sober. It was pre-rehabs and before the wide spread of AIDS. People freely shared what drugs they

Eloise, Calliope, Lisa Wright-Overington and Jayne Anne at the Studio 54 coatroom.

had. The liquor flowed, the music was loud and happy, the people were beautiful and the night never seemed to end. After we got off our shift at five in the morning, we would find ourselves in after-hour clubs, go home when everyone else was heading to work, then wake up in the afternoon … and repeat! The hours were grueling and the work was extremely physical. We're not sure how we did it. We worked and eventually ran the coat rooms at Studio 54 until it closed in 1986.

Eloise:
Studio 54 offered weekly "Tea Dances" jam-packed with fun and gorgeous gay boys there to dance the night away. The coatroom was filled to the brim with identical leather motorcycle jackets. Front to back, they lined the coatroom like wallpaper. Euphoric boys would ultimately lose their coat check ticket and then saunter up to the counter with their dilemma. We would say very officially, "Can you identify anything in your pockets?" The answer was always the same, "Poppers and Pot!" As we contemplated this idea we scanned the coat racks, confused in the sea of "searching for the right coat" possibilities. Along with this problem, came the often and pungent popper spill which created a leather popper steam room. The vapor sent the now kaleidoscope-eyed coat check girls four feet off the ground for the rest of the night.

From the personal collection of L.J. Kirby

Photo © Nancy Brown

Studio 54 bartenders, our colleagues... God, did we ever wear shirts in those days? *Top photo, L to R:* Robert Ziehm, Dennis Lavalle, Greg Gunsch, Scott Baird and Bobby Farrell.

Mary Lou:

When A-List party promoter Robert Isabell, and Studio 54's head of security Chuck Garelick, asked us to run coat checks at their major events, Coat Check Inc. was born. We became executives overnight, working prestigious parties in Manhattan. Our new enterprise was given a nod by *Business Week* and *Crane's Magazine.* Our growing client list included Cartier, Victoria's Secret, Bloomberg LP, American Express, the American Museum of Natural History, The Bronx Zoo, Robert Isabell, George Trescher, Sotheby's, The Costume Ball, the Metropolitan Museum of Art, Phillips Auction House, *Today's Man*, Municipal Arts Society, *Sports Illustrated, The New Yorker* and MTV.

This new adventure enabled us to get out of working round-the-clock shifts at Studio 54 and allowed us to become daytime people with regular schedules. We were surprised at the mammoth scale of our new business.

Eloise:

Our largest event was for American Express at Madison Square Garden. Ten thousand people were slated to show up. We had generals, captains and patrol teams with walkie-talkies in order to keep every thing running smoothly. Coat Check Inc. had 225 people working at seven coat check locations. It was raining of course and the hordes of people came directly from work soaking wet with umbrellas, galoshes, raincoats, briefcases and... good-god... computers. We didn't lose a thing!

COAT CHECK, INC.

Jayne Anne:

We created elegant coat check concessions for an eight million dollar wedding. The rehearsal dinner and dance were in Battery Park in lower Manhattan. The party planners arranged for the city to kick out the homeless people and build a Chinese pagoda. They had movie trailers for bathrooms, cigar rooms for the men, touch-up rooms for the ladies, chandeliers and picture windows overlooking the Hudson River. The big finale was a spectacular firework display. Our main coatroom tent was situated at the entrance of the venue. At dusk, the guests arrived and strolled down the red carpet stopping to be photographed. The mother of the bride stepped out of her limo and strolled down the carpet in a fur coat. She stopped for a photo op and behind her was a giant rat, which I am sure had to be edited out! That's what happens at dusk in the city. They can kick out the homeless people but not the rats. Later on we had rats streaming through our coatroom tent. Fortunately one of our staff, Natalie Swan, was not afraid. Like the Pied Piper she shooed them away. The wedding itself was at the elegant Westbury Gardens on Long Island. The coatroom tent was placed behind the house. Generally, rental tents have side flaps to keep the rain out. The caterer forgot to order the flaps and of course it rained, sideways. The coats and furs got soaked and smelled like damp goats! Since it was early fall, most people just carried them to their limos.

Eloise:

Yearly paparazzi frenzy events included the Metropolitan Museum of Art Costume Ball and Mike Bloomberg's annual Christmas party at the American Museum of Natural History. Our coatrooms became an oasis for high profile politicians, celebrities, and socialites to hide from flashing cameras. Because the Angels of Light was our boot camp training, and Studio 54 our first work environment, we were unfazed by the extreme pressure.

Mary Lou:

After all that, it seemed we had finally settled down. We began to enjoy a new era of dating, marriages and loving life again. New York City was on an upswing of remodeling. Parks with flowers were created in place of corners where dark deeds once prospered. Wealthy families were moving into Manhattan. Telltale signs of neighborhoods being transformed were the lovely sights of mothers with strollers and beautiful gay couples walking vast breeds of petite dogs.

MARY LOU HARRIS   ELOISE HARRIS   JAYNE ANNE HARRIS

Coat Check Inc
1990-2003

Orchestrating swanky, high profile events for Coat Check provided a necessary chrysalis for us Harris girls to heal, transform and emerge with beauty, charisma and wings to fly.

- Mary Lou

It was a second wind for the Harris family. Walter Michael met the love of his life, married and began to build a beautiful world in Seattle. Fred, Jayne Anne, Eloise and Mary Lou were doing the very same thing on the East Coast. We girls experimented with college and, to our surprise, received our bachelors degrees with high honors. Mom and Dad loved living in Greenwich Village. They hosted parties, holiday celebrations and movie nights with family and friends.

The Harris children were starting families of their own. New grandchildren were beginning to make their debut. These new little babies were a ray of sunshine in all of our lives.

The beginning of many family trips to Ocean Grove at the Jersey Shore, mid-1990's. Left to right: baby Quinn, Eloise, Ann and George, Sr., who the grandkids affectionately called 'Shecky.'

Chapter 20
Head for the Hills

Jayne Anne:
It was a beautiful Manhattan day the morning of Tuesday, September 11, 2001. I had just dropped my six year old Quinn off at school and was on my way to the gym in Battery Park. I usually walked through the World Trade Center shopping malls to peruse the shoes and clothes. But today I came down the stairs of her school, P.S. 150, and saw an airliner so close overhead, I could read the writing on the side of the plane. I thought, "Wow, that plane is flying really low." Then it flew right into the World Trade Center with a disturbing sound.

We parents stood there in disbelief, thinking it was a horrible accident. Then suddenly the second plane hit. The fireball came up Greenwich Street, and I could feel the force of it go right through my body. That mobilized the parents to run up the stairs to get their kids, quickly realizing that we couldn't let them know. Sadly the children, including Quinn, witnessed unimaginable horrors. I called my husband Thomas on the fax machine from the school, and he came over and got us. We banded together with a few kids and their parents and made it a play date. Thankfully, we all made it to our apartment.

We had to live with the dust, smell, smoke, devastation and incredibly sad emotions for a very long time. Quinn's entire school was moved to one of many host schools. During the aftermath of 9/11 an army tank was stationed outside our door. Flattened cars and trucks were stacked four high on our street. To keep my six year old calm, I tried coping with humor and told Quinn that the guy in the tank was our new doorman. Two of our friends lost their lives: Keith Glascoe, who I worked with at Tatou; and Patrick Brown, who was Thomas's friend. They were both firemen.

In 2003, we decided to move to the Catskills. But not a day goes by that I don't think of the chaos and heartbreak of 9/11. In 2011 filmmaker Jacques Menasche, a parent from Quinn's school, made *The Class of 9/11*, a documentary shown on PBS. He interviewed the kids, now teens, and their parents, comparing then and now. It is a powerful piece.

Ann:
On 9/11 I was doing office work for Jayne's husband, Thomas, a CPA who worked from home. We heard the news on television and knew that Jayne Anne was at Quinn's first grade class, quite near the disaster. At first, they weren't letting any children out, but one of the parents, a detective, persuaded them otherwise. Jayne Anne came home with five other kids and we kept the television off.

Thomas and I went up to the roof. The office and their condo were on Broadway just below Canal Street. There were workers fixing the roof who told us when the first plane came in, they had to hit the ground (on the roof) because it flew so low. We stayed and witnessed the second plane hit the second building. I walked home around noon after two of the buildings collapsed. Besides the smoke there were knots of people listening to car radios and trying to figure out how to walk to Brooklyn. One of Thomas's employees walked all the way to the Bronx.

Photo © Robert J. Fisch/Creative Commons

For days after that, in order to get below Canal Street for work, we had to show a letter stating why we were there. For months you could smell the acrid smoke. The city provided special small buses to shuttle people around the area.

Susan Dale Rose:
After 9/11 I spoke with George, Sr. on the phone. He was heartbroken and angry and wanting to leave the city, but not wanting to leave the apartment because of the essence of G3 that lingered.

Ann:
In the summer of 2002 we decided to sell the Greenwich Village co-op and move upstate to Margaretville, George's childhood home in the Catskills. He was working as the advertising manager for The Allegro, the American Federation of Musicians, Local 802's newspaper. He wanted to retire because he wasn't feeling well. Fred and his family were already there in the neighboring town of Delhi. Jayne Anne and her family eventually also moved to Delhi. Eloise and family made a home in Andes, about ten miles from Margaretville. Mary Lou stayed in Manhattan with her family and Walter in Seattle with his.

Eloise:
Following 9/11 the events business in New York came to a halt, as it should have. Who felt like having a party? No one. My parents were moving to the country and we all felt ready to move as well. 9/11 pushed us over the edge. We offered to give our business to our best

employees, but I don't think they felt they could handle it. So we just walked away. We could not believe what had just happened and neither could anyone else.

Chapter 21
Butterflies

Down in the dark in the cavern below
There stands a white figure all covered with snow.
Old winter is leaving
And no one is grieving
Now spring can dance in on the tip of her toe
Now spring can dance in
And the world all aglow.

Poem by Ann Harris

Eloise:
When you're at the bottom of a large family it is hard to find an identity. Add in the Angels of Light and theater and it goes double. So many things my older brothers and sister did happened earlier than Mary Lou and I can remember. Their lives were rooted in a pre-theater family experience. When I performed in Invitation To A Beheading at Joe Papp's Public Theater, it should have been the seed of my identity. But somehow I lost the thread.

When I was about nine in the East Village in the 60's, I can remember donning a mirrored vest and walking along with political rallies of activism for peace. I remember someone calling me a "fake hippie." Maybe in some ways they were right. I really wasn't sure what I was doing, but I donned the clothing and modeled the actions of the time, like dancing with the Hare Krishnas, and then later on dancing at Studio 54 … being in the moment.

I loved doing the Angels of Light and wouldn't have given it up for anything. However, I wish I'd had more of my own identity to stand on when making choices. It was easy to get lost in the family amoeba. Being around such strong personalities who pushed, prodded and led, I learned to become a chameleon, taking on whatever color rock I happened to be sitting on. Other times, I would be able to find small bits and pieces of what seemed like my own personality.

Mary Lou:
Now that we are older and a little wiser, I can say with my whole heart that my parents were amazing. They created a Utopian society for their children under what could be considered dismal and downright scary conditions. We lived our lives totally based on fantasy, in the light and in Technicolor. Now we are in a different era where New York City is aimed at tourists and wealthy residents who demand outdoor cafes, glass and metal buildings, technology and expensive everything. We find ourselves living wonderful but very different lives. Our childhood Utopia has equipped us with optimism, adventurous spirits and unique energy to create our own caravans.

Whoo-ee! Weddings, children, diplomas, household moves and redirected careers began blooming as we clarified our priorities.

Our family must have had a guardian angel. The caravan was magical and glamorous, but also dangerous. As young children we were almost whisked away by Hare Krishna devotees because we were wearing identical costumes. During protest riots in France we were nearly trampled. We had eggs and tomatoes hurled at us by the audience because of sensitive dialogue in a politically charged show. Let's face it… we could have been killed!

Over the years we met talented rising stars and made lifelong friends, but we had also met some perilous lunatics. With all the dangerous choices any one of us could have made … we turned out to be a lucky and angel-protected Caravan.

- Mary Lou

Eloise:

Are we a postcard in time? Between the tricycle and today, life was wonderful, freaky, tiresome, exhausting, awesome and fabulous. George was a big fun, exhausting ball whose string I either held on to, or let go of when I needed a rest. Now I'm like a ball of yarn with a head, arms and legs sticking out rolling, unraveling and unraveling. I wonder when I will hit the end of the ball. But right now I am still rolling. Someday I will understand the mystery of it all.

Jayne Anne:

Looking back, being part of the caravan has given me a very different outlook on life. I have the ability to find humor in the darkest of times and situations. I can also take on any "role" depending on what company I find myself in. However, I always feel bohemian internally. That used to bother me, I have no idea why. But now, I see it as a good thing – I am who I am! We had a hell of a time back then and the world is so different now. It's fun to look back and realize how free we were. That's not to say it was all fun and games. Lots of my friends and acquaintances fell to drugs and lifestyle choices that ultimately ended their lives. I am proud to have been a part of a creative movement that was pushing barriers and cultural confinements.

Ann:

George, Sr. died of pancreatic cancer December 29, 2005. I was glad we made the move from Manhattan to Margaretville, in the Catskills. It gave him a chance to reconnect with old friends and neighbors and to build and fly his model airplanes. He joined a model airplane club in Oneonta and drove there to fly whenever the weather permitted.

Dad (left) with Bud Barnes, his flying buddy, in 2004

Walter Michael:

Shortly before Dad died he was in a coma and appeared unconscious. Still, we all read and sang to him believing he could hear through the haze. We told his favorite stupid jokes and made sure his grandkids got to spend time with him in his final hours. Knowing his love of flight, Mary Lou and her son Miles took Dad on an imaginary plane ride, recapping the main events of his life, soaring above the terrain over the village where he grew up and the city where his family succeeded in living their dreams.

Ann:

My Manhattan friends often ask me, "What do you do up there in the Catskills?" Whatever I do, I'm happy. So it's back to basics, I guess, but I wouldn't have missed it all for anything. I stay connected through friends like Robert Heide, John Gilman, Agosto Machado, Bob Patrick, Bob Dahdah, Magie Dominic, Crystal Field, George Bartenieff, Claris Nelson, Michael Warren Powell, Holly Woodlawn and the Cockettes on the West Coast.

So let's "Cut the hype and catch the fantasy." The next generation is coming up fast.

Ann in the Catskills

Here Comes Heaven
music and lyrics by Ann and Fred Harris

Up the stairs, one step at a time
Don't despair, it's gonna be fine
Don't you mope
You've got to to have hope in your heart
(the steps to Paradise - are really very nice)

Don't look down, you'll fall on your face
Drown that frown and smile in its place
Sing your own song
That's where the melody starts.

A sky of blue
Is there for you
There's gonna be
A rainbow too
I have a hunch
We'll muddle through
If we keep on hoping!

All your friends are gonna be there
Waiting at the top of the stair
Here comes heaven,
Let's make a dandy new start...

So whistle out the night
Everything's all right
Here comes heaven,
Let's make a dandy new start!

The Next Generation

Cousins! *Above, left to right:* Montana Damone, Miles Pietsch, Quinn Kelley. Their parents, in the same order, are Eloise and Joe, Mary Lou and Jim, Jayne Anne and Thomas. Below: These cousins are as close as siblings.

Walter Michael and Patricia's family, clockwise from top left of each photo:
Top of page: Jason, Irish, Joshua and James Green (aka "Jamie")
Bottom of page: Kristin Green, Chad Syme, Juniper and Avonlea Green.

Above: Ruby Harris, looking a bit pouty, on Lissa's shoulders; and happy *(inset),* with her parents, Lissa Harris and Julia Reischel. Lissa is Fred's daughter from his first marriage, and our family's first grandchild.
Right: Lissa's brother, Avery Jenkins, with his and Lissa's mom, Karen Dawn Harris.

Twice a year Mom organizes a family retreat on the Jersey Shore where our kids experience the sun, sand and ocean like we did in Florida.

Annual family vacations on the Jersey Shore keep our Caravan connected.

Photo by Patricia Harris

A Jersey Shore sunset at Ocean Grove.

Afterword

Jayne Anne, Eloise, Mary Lou and Walter Michael:
The motivation for this book was Mom's desire to document our family story. We found it daunting to recall the details and even more challenging to re-visit, reveal and re-live the emotions, joys, sorrows and unresolved issues that linger just beyond the horizon. Writing this memoir brought them thundering back in living color, and helped us understand and accept each other, then and now.

We've done our best to tell our story honestly for our children and theirs. We want everyone to know it's possible to work as artists while raising a family, and to simultaneously follow their dreams wherever they may lead.

One of Dad's most memorable Caffé Cino performances is the monologue "Take A Pew" by Alan Bennett from the British comedy revue *Beyond the Fringe.* Dad played a vicar giving a sermon. He loved this passage and quoted it often:

> "Life, you know, is rather like opening a tin of sardines. We are all of us looking for the key. And I wonder how many of you here tonight have wasted years of your lives looking behind the kitchen dressers of this life for that key. I know I have. Others think they've found the key, don't they? They roll back the lid of the sardine tin of life. They reveal the sardines, the riches of life, therein, and they get them out, and they enjoy them. But, you know, there's always a little bit in the corner you can't get out. I wonder, is there a little bit in the corner of your life? I know there is in mine!"

The Harris family's "tin of sardines" is a fully stocked pantry. In creating this memoir we've found the key, revealed the riches and dug out some of those little pieces in the corner. We're enjoying them now and hope you are too.

We thank our parents for the family's amazing Caravan to Oz and back. Our mother Ann sponsors our twice-a-year retreat to Ocean Grove, New Jersey, where our families come together to stay connected and so our kids can make sand castles in the sun like we did back in Florida. Mom's annual gift fuels our new utopia and enthusiasm to keep our family projects going.

We thank our lucky stars that led us to New York City, to Ellen Stewart, Joe Cino, and to the wildly creative, free-spirited community of risk-taking artists that founded off-off-Broadway. They embraced us with open arms, apartments, jobs, career opportunities, "Magic Time," artistic vision and human kindness.

We miss our father George, who the grandkids call Shecky. We miss our brother Hibiscus and all those golden boys who passed away from AIDS. We miss friends and family members with whom we have lost touch. We are thrilled with the books, plays, websites, film documentaries, blog references, tweets, museum exhibits, archives and anecdotes in which they are remembered and honored.

We strive to cultivate the seeds of creativity and adventure in our children that our parents imparted to us. True to our roots, we expect to continue sharing that fearless, euphoric (but not effortless) feeling in future books, lectures, films, and... who knows?

Maybe another show!

We thank you for sharing our journey and dedicate this memoir to all free spirits who are beginning their own Caravan to Oz.

Joshua and Miles dream ahead.

Photo by Patricia Harris

Our life in the arts endowed us with a broad range of transferrable skills. Here is a recent example of how Eloise deployed them with powerful results in service of education, youth empowerment, volunteer recruitment and community organizing.

Andes Gazette

$1 contribution

Now online at www.andesgazette.net

Vol. 16 No. 1

June 2014

STAR TREK GOES BROADWAY: THE BACKSTORY

By John Bernhardt

It's funny how one Saturday phone call can significantly change your life, even if only for a six-week period of time. That was the case when Dr. Robert Chakar called my house in mid March asking if I might play a role in putting together a last ditch effort to stage a musical production at Andes Central School this school year.

I have to admit, I had my doubts when Doc unveiled his dramatic vision that day. In most area schools, musical productions were in their final stages of development, the spring sport season was underway and music programs were busy preparing local youngsters to perform in All-County performances and at the NYSMAAs. It seemed unlikely that against those odds, we could harness the creativity and energy needed to stage a quality musical show.

It was only when Bob mentioned his hope that Eloise Harris would sign on to the project that I agreed. Previous experience with Eloise preparing Andes musical productions had left me wowed, amazed at her unlimited passion and energy for theater, and the lifetime of rich theater experiences she would bring to Bob's challenge.

There was no time to lose. The show that unfolded was the brainchild of Eloise. She understood the challenges and limitations we faced and crafted a show that could work within those confines. My doubts were enormous, but I had watched Eloise work wonders before and trusted she would work her magic again. She did not disappoint.

For much of my life I have worked in and around sports teams. Again and again, I have watched young people surpass expectations when they discover the power that comes with employing "we" over "me." As the architect of the Andes spring musical extravaganza, Eloise Harris tapped into the power of teamwork. Eloise stretched the ACS spring beyond the Drama Club making it a total school and community event.

Think about it. Where else but ACS would you find a home-grown musical production with a play script co-authored by a high school senior, Jonathan Andrews, and the co-musical directors, with a cast that included students from pre-school to the senior year in high school, and with teachers, staff and community members and even the Superintendent of Schools performing on stage. Over my long career in public education, I had never seen anything like it.

And, that's only speaking about what the viewing audience saw and enjoyed on the stage. Behind the scenes, Eloise wove together a network of support people, folks who labored to complete the sets, assist with the choreography, supervise the 'Little Players,' work on sound and lighting, complete programs with advertising, dig out or design and sew costumes, etc. On and on the list of contributions grew. However big or small a contribution one could make, everyone was welcomed and encouraged to support the effort in whatever way they could manage.

The end result was magical, a fast-paced night of rollicking fun with music and dance, Ed Sullivan, the Star Trek crew and lots of laughs. Andes has much to be proud of from their little school that could. With a forward thinking vision and the contributions of many heads and many hands, I think I can – I think I can – I think I can – turned into I knew I could – I knew I could – I knew I could – testimony once again of what can be achieved when people work together as a team. ~

Alexis Redden and Peter James DePierro singing "My Heart Will Go On" on the prow of the Titanic

Photo by Joe Damone

Jonathan Andrews as the ever-logical Mr. Spock

Photo by Joe Damone

Meet the Family

Bios, backstories and tales of today

George

George Edgerly Harris II

George Edgerly Harris II was born in Bronxville, New York, to Ruth Hoffman Colony and George Edgerly Harris (the first), both artists. His paternal grandfather was Charles Xavier Harris, a successful fine art painter, art professor and expert on the artists of New Amsterdam. George's mother, Ruth "Ruthie" Coloney SoRelle, was a talented photographer and a freelance journalist. His sister, Susan Joyce Harris Weimer, is a fine art painter and retired educator.

George II attended school in Margaretville and Scarsdale, NY, and served in the Air Force as a radio trainer during World War Two. He played drums through high school in a successful dance band formed with his cousin, Berrie Hall, who played piano. When they were kids their sailboat was disabled in a storm. They drifted across Long Island Sound from Sachems Head, Connecticut and landed miraculously on the tip of Long Island. The papers wrote that the boys were lost but they found a phone the next day and relayed this happy news.

Susan, Ruthie and George about 1925

After the war George attended Columbia University on the GI Bill. In 1948 he married Ann Marie McCanless of Bronxville, New York, where the first four of their six children were born. In 1958 the family relocated to Clearwater, Florida where the youngest two children were born. There the family became interested in theater, and in 1963 moved to New York City where they began successful professional careers. The family has spent their summers in Margaretville since the 1960s. George and Ann took up permanent residence there in 2002.

As an actor and director George was a regular in the early experimental off-off-Broadway movement. In 1968 he made his Broadway debut in *The Great White Hope* along with James Earl Jones and Jane Alexander. He worked steadily in movies, including *Superman,* on television and radio, in summer stock, often with Ann, and as a featured player in first-run national tours. During his long career he worked with pioneering producers and playwrights including Ellen Stewart, Joe Cino, Crystal Field and George Bartinieff, Al Carmines and Lanford Wilson; and with renowned actors Henry Fonda, Anne Meara, Billy D. Williams, Gene Wilder, Fred Astaire, Richard Pryor. and Frank Sinatra.

A lifelong musician and lover of big band music, George became a successful and respected bandleader in his own right during the 1970s, in New York City, where his Ninth Street Stompers were a popular act. The band featured many A-list musicians and launched or revived their careers. George worked on staff for the Musician's Union Local 802 in New York until his retirement. He was proud of his service during World War II and participated in the Memorial Day parade each year in Margaretville, NY, the town where he was born and where every day of his retirement was a new adventure.

Dad passed away in December, 2005. His proudest achievement was his family.

Dad said this about working with his son, Hibiscus:

"When I played God in *Sky High*, having worked in many shows where I learn my lines, I'm given the blocking and everything else – I said to Hibiscus, "what do you want me to do?" "Anything you want, Dad." I said, "Well, you got an idea how you want me to play this?" "Oh, no, anything you want to do!" "How 'bout the makeup?" "Anything you want." And so that's the way I did, you know, I got my idea, and I did it! He never came to me as a director will, and say, "I think you should consider incorporating this, changing that." He'd let you do anything you wanted to do. And it was amazing. He just had the fun of putting on a show. I've seen this sometimes in theater – a moment of pure magic. But with him, it's the whole show."

Ann

Ann Marie McCanless Harris

Ann Harris is an actress, dancer, playwright and songwriter. Her father was Fred McCanless, a successful Westchester dentist. Her mother, Anne, was musical, creative and the fiery daughter of Jim "Sol D" Driscoll, an Irish immigrant who distinguished himself in the St. Lawrence Seaway lumber business.

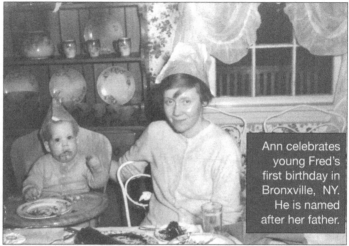

Ann celebrates young Fred's first birthday in Bronxville, NY. He is named after her father.

Ann wrote music and lyrics for the off-Broadway productions *Sky High, Speakeasy, Enchanted Miracle,* and *Hibiscus.* She has written songs for many other Harris family and Angels of Light shows including *Bluebeard, The Sheep and the Cheapskate, MacBee, There Is Method In Their Madness, Birdie Follies, Gossamer Wings, Razamatazz, Sky High* (the revival), *Tinsel Town Tirade* and *Dear Friends of Allegro Sanitation.* She performed in and/or choreographed dance numbers in most of them.

With her son Fred she co-wrote songs for *Hibiscus and the Screaming Violets'* performance art-rock show. Her children's musical *Bluebeard* has played from coast to coast. She toured Europe with the Angels of Light and has appeared at La MaMa ETC, Judson Poets Theater, Theater for the New City, the New York Shakespeare Festival Public Theater, Caffe Cino, at Lincoln Center and in summer stock.

L to R: Chandra, Ann and Java Jet

Ann originated the role of Martha Truitt in the world premiere of Lanford Wilson's *The Rimers of Eldritch* at La MaMa ETC, directed by the playwright. She has a growing fan base for her role as Doris Acker in the cult film classic, *The Honeymoon Killers,* often broadcast around Halloween on Turner Classic Movies.

She is a favorite actress of the late, great off-off-Broadway playwright H.M. Koutoukas and was directed by him in several of his plays. Ann, her children and her late husband George are considered pioneers in off-off-Broadway theater and performance art. She is often consulted by authors, filmmakers and scholars interested in the genres.

Hibiscus,
George Jr.,
George, G3

George Edgerly Harris III, 'Hibiscus'
by his brother, Walter Michael

Writer, director, producer and consummate performer, George Edgerly Harris III, aka 'Hibiscus,' was a loving son and brother who took his family on the journey of a lifetime. First-born to young Ann and George Harris was George III, whom the family called G3, and later, Hibiscus. He was a free spirit who packed more living into his 32 years on earth than most people do in a lifetime.

He was openly gay, and resisted limiting labels. He was a performance artist. Much has been documented about his creative life, especially during the intense twelve or so years he was known as Hibiscus, the name he chose for himself in the late 1960s, during the full bloom of the hippie movement. This book highlights the rest of his story.

From early childhood, George's creativity was in evidence. He expressed himself in pictures using found materials. He sang as soon as he could talk and was forever interested in how people behave. These elements were the foundation of his gift for social satire, always prominent in his shows. He absorbed his surroundings and incorporated them into his art, from the palm trees and flamingos of Florida and mythology learned in grade school to the social archetypes he loved to poke fun at.

Like his forebears, George was never content to stay in one place for long. However, for all his wanderlust, George was a dutiful son and faithful brother. No matter where his adventures took him around the world he sought to include his family, friends and even hapless bystanders whose paths crossed his. When distant from the family he kept in touch through letters and colorful postcards written with multicolored pens in his distinctive florid hand. When he was in town it was impossible for the family to resist his invitation to join whatever flight of fancy his inexhaustible imagination was dreaming up.

A born leader, G3 was a joyful soul whose passion inspired participation. It's fair to say he transformed lives and launched careers for better or for worse. He didn't care if you had little or no experience, he'd simply cast you in a role and push you onstage. If he felt you had even a glimmer of skills that he needed for sets, costumes, or publicity, he would put you in charge of that department. This approach succeeded more often than not. He could be maddening. He loved to push people's buttons and sit back and enjoy the result. But apart from the occasional lovers' quarrel, financial challenge or mischievous intrigue he was fun to be around. Hibiscus was a prolific reader and writer. Although formal schooling was never top of his list, he was a life-long learner with an appreciation for classic literature, instilled by his mother, and was a seeker of spiritual enlightenment.

George absorbed and synthesized religious influences from the Catholic Church to the Krishna Consciousness movement of the 1960s and the New Age "mystery school" his brother Walter Michael encountered in San Francisco. The worship of money and power so prevalent in Western society did not escape his notice and derision. All these influences turned up as characters and scenarios in his shows.

KARMA CHAMELEON

Hibiscus's appearance was outrageous even for the 1960's. Now, writes Horacio Silva, his Aquarian-age glamour is all over the catwalks.

Horacio Silva wrote a beautiful article on Hibiscus, his life and his influence on modern fashion for the New York Times Style Magazine, August 17, 2003.

Jon Teta, Hibiscus, Ann, and Fred

Hibiscus had a keen appreciation for the tremendous talents of his family members. His mother, Ann, was his chief writing partner. He found a place in a show for every lyric and note she wrote. He elicited creative participation from his parents and siblings whenever they were available and at whatever level they wished to participate. Hibiscus knew instinctively they were his strongest, most talented, loyal and reliable collaborators and co-performers.

Hibiscus and the Screaming Violets

In the final years of his short life, Hibiscus was drawn back to where he started, creating original performance art with his family. Continuing to absorb cultural influences and channeling them into a form of social satire that was highly energetic and entertaining, he went out at the top of his game. His influence continues to ripple out into the culture and into peoples' lives, especially all who knew, followed and loved him.

Walter Michael

Walter Michael Harris

Collaborating with my family on this memoir was a journey of discovery. My mother, sisters and I set out to tell the story of our family's theatrical history. In the process we helped each other fill in the human beings behind the makeup and glitter. As much as we thought we knew about each other, there was far more revealed in the course of writing this account. I so appreciate and admire my collaborators' willingness to dig deep, share their experiences and explore how they feel about them. It has brought us even closer.

A note on my name. Until age eighteen I was called Walter. After I left *HAIR* and followed Hibiscus to San Francisco, I started using my middle name, Michael. A new name seemed to go hand-in-hand with the journey of self-discovery I was on, and it stuck. Now I use both.

Soon after my brother George died something wonderful happened that changed everything forever. I met Patricia Mansfield. Patty and I met at a garden party her father and stepmother threw each year for their musician friends. Patty's then seven-year-old daughter, Kristin, joined me at the piano for a round of "Chopsticks" and "Heart And Soul." The latter title was appropriate, because Patty and I fell in love at that party and were married a year later. Kristin and her nine-year-old brother Jason made us an instant family. Patty is the woman of my dreams. She's beautiful, creative, kind and caring, intelligent, family centered and forward thinking. She has a great sense of humor, loves art and science and follows the Tour de France avidly. She has a bachelors degree in physical anthropology and is a life-long learner who reads several books a month. Her successful

career in project management contributed directly to the success of several Seattle area institutions, most notably Pacific Science Center. Patty is a master baker, a fan of good movies and music, and our family historian.

Sharing Kristin and Jason's childhood and coming of age has been the joyride of a lifetime. They are awesomely inventive, positive, well educated, resourceful, and self-directed. Now each happily married, they balance family life with successful careers. Jason and his wife Irish have two boys, Joshua, age nine; and Jamie, two. Kristin and her husband Chad have two daughters, Avonlea, five, and Juniper, three. Patty and I enjoy being grandparents to these four youngest members of our next generation. They amaze us every day with their creativity, intelligence, and joie de vivre as they discover the world and themselves.

When I left the cast of *HAIR* in 1969 I believed my theater career was over. Life as a new-age monk left little room for much else, although I did manage to sneak in some theater and music. My return to professional theater came about serendipitously in 1979 when I re-

Back row: Chad Syme, Irish and Jason Green. Front: Avonlea, Kristin and Joshua Green

joined the family caravan in *Sky High*. A few years later I left the religious community, met Patty and we married in 1984.

Theater called on me again in 1987 when I was invited to join the cast of *Voices of Christmas,* one of Seattle's most popular holiday shows. The creators of *Voices* were Ruben Sierra and Colleen Carpenter-Simmons of The Group, Seattle's multicultural theater. Its premise was simple: four singers and four actors celebrating holiday traditions around the world by sharing with the audience seasonal songs, poems, and personal memories from individual cast members. The personal stories gave Voices universal appeal and developed a large local audience. I performed in *Voices* and in other shows with The Group for nine seasons. In the 1990s I co-founded Pilgrim Center for the Arts, a venue for Seattle's "fringe" theater scene, analogous to off-off-Broadway. At Pilgrim Center, co-founder Manuel R. Cawaling and I gave emerging artists a place to experiment, show and grow just as Ellen Stewart, Joe Cino, Crystal Field and Al Carmines did for our family and so many others. Between 1989 and 1997 Manuel and I, along with a host of volunteers, produced or presented over 400 events showcasing new theater, dance, music and performance art. We co-produced two shows with Ellen Stewart at La MaMa in New York, brought artists from Russia and Iran to Seattle, gave hundreds of local artists an affordable venue and played a leadership role in the emerging fringe theater movement in our region.

with Patricia

241

In 2000 I was hired by ArtsWest Playhouse in Seattle as producing artistic director. Ellen Stewart put in a good word for me with the hiring committee. She wrote, "here at La MaMa, we think he is a genius!" Over five subscription seasons I put ArtsWest on solid financial footing, revived *Voices of Christmas,* and launched a summer theater conservatory for children. Through activist artists like Woody Guthrie and Pete Seeger I came to appreciate the power of song to spark a movement, bring communities together, and lift people's spirits. For the past forty years I have led sing-alongs for groups

Gil

of every kind. In Seattle I found many other musical opportunities including garage bands with two of my best friends, Tom Peters and John Savage – and membership in 'The Stubble Jumpers' band, led my friend and mentor Gil Kiesecker, a master fiddler, who teaches me about life, family and old-time music. Family life with Patty, our kids and our grandkids is my focus now, and nothing could be better.

with Avonlea and Juniper

with Joshua

Photo © Ellen Banner, Seattle Times

with Jamie

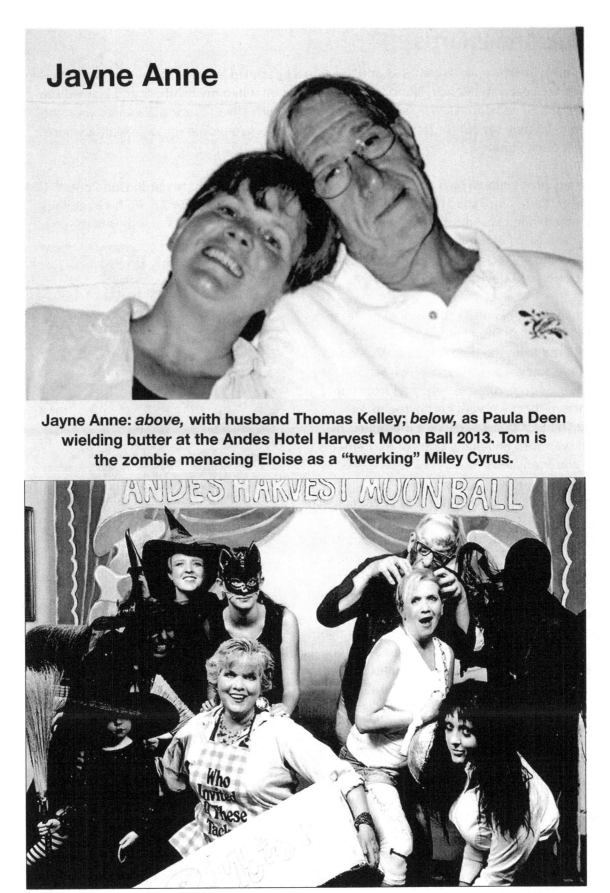

Jayne Anne

Jayne Anne: *above,* with husband Thomas Kelley; *below,* as Paula Deen wielding butter at the Andes Hotel Harvest Moon Ball 2013. Tom is the zombie menacing Eloise as a "twerking" Miley Cyrus.

Jayne Anne Harris

I was born in Bronxville, NY in 1955 and became a beach kid at age three when my family moved to Clearwater Beach, Florida. The acting bug bit when my brothers and I joined the Little Theater's Children's Workshop and continued with The El Dorado Players. I was nine when my family set out for New York City's East Village. We picked up at La MaMa where we left off in Florida.

So many productions! I worked frequently off-off-Broadway, primarily at Judson Poets Theater, Caffe Cino, and Theater for the New City. I also modeled for J.C. Penney catalogs and acted in television commercials, television shows and films. I'm a member of the American Guild of Variety Artists, Actor's Equity Association and Screen Actors Guild/American Federation of Television and Radio Artists.

Balancing school and a professional career was challenging. I attended public school and graduated from the High School of Music and Art (now known as LaGuardia High School). My brother George/Hibiscus returned from San Francisco that year with his boyfriend Angel Jack. The East Coast version of the Angels of Light was born and many years of excitement and glitter ensued!

With my sisters I worked as a trio in various singing groups ranging from rock and roll to jazz. We worked with songwriter Richard Adler (*Damn Yankees* and *Pajama Game*) on a new recording of his songs. As a trio we performed on the East and West Coasts, across Europe and many places in between. My favorite was Australia! In between gigs I worked survival jobs as a coat check girl in such places as The Park Avenue Armory Antique Show, Studio 54, Tatou and Gauguin. As co-founders of Coat Check Inc., my sisters and I worked fabulous parties and employed actor friends who were in between jobs.

I met Thomas Kelley at a "silly hats party" that Tim Robbins threw. It was a birthday party for his sister Gabrielle. Thomas is a CPA by trade, specializing in artists. Tim invited Eloise, Mary Lou and myself. They had to drag me out of my apartment as I had recently been through a nasty divorce and was busy consuming coffee flavored Hagen-Daz in my blue terrycloth robe while watching *Little House on the Prairie* reruns. I put on my black leather skirt and blue paisley jacket and the three of us headed on down to the party in an

apartment building on LaGuardia Place. The building was a Dutch style walkup where the stairs just keep going up forever. The apartment was on the first landing. Standing there was a 6' 4" gentleman with a cream colored Brooks Brothers sweater, tight brown leather pants and a paper bag rolled up and stuck on top of his head (remember, silly hats party)! I saw my life flash before me and knew this was it.

We talked for the rest of the evening and exchanged phone numbers. Three days later I called him and asked, "Were you going to wait two weeks to call me?" (An unwritten rule of dating back then). He said "yes." I said, "Well, let's just skip that and go out!" Our first date was the movie *Blue Velvet*. We and maybe two other people were the only ones laughing in the theater. That was 1986 and we are still together!

Quinn Taylor Kelley was born in 1995, is now nineteen and never ceases to amaze us. A natural artist, Quinn is a talented musician who plays piano, drums, guitar and sings.

Quinn with Cajun Betty

Quinn also raises and shows chickens and rabbits, has a rescue horse named Cajun Betty and is an animal lover who has birds, rats, guinea pigs, turtles, fish, snakes, hermit crabs and lizards. Quinn graduated high school with honors in 2013 and follows in the family tradition by studying theater in college, with the ultimate goal of pursuing the art of special effects makeup. Quinn is always running around the house made up with missing eyeballs, bruises and cuts!

I help with our entrepreneurial child's homemade soap business, provide animal care and perform with local community theaters. We reside in the pastoral Catskill Mountains of New York State with lots of animals.

Jayne Anne *(center)* catching up with classmates Susan Allen and Rita Irwin at their High School of Music & Art reunion, 2013

Eloise

Eloise (clockwise from upper left): with Dad; 1990s headshot; sipping coffee; teaching daughter Montana how to catch a New York cab; "Monty" with shades.

Eloise Alice Harris

In the 1960s I moved from the white sand beaches of Florida to the hippie-psychedelic-Ukrainian neighborhood of NYC's East Village at the age of five. The political and gender anarchy counterculture there was incredible.

Theater became our other home. At age nine I received my Actors Equity union card playing the role of Emmy in Nabokov's *Invitation To A Beheading* at Joseph Papp's Public Theater as my first order of professional business. WOW! The next two decades saw my family and I performing original musicals in New York and across Europe as the Angels of Light Free Theater troupe.

Inspired by the beat of disco, punk and MTV, the Harris Sisters trio began its singing journey, performing first gigs at popular clubs of the 70s including Gildersleeves, RT Firefly, Bonds, Danceteria and The Peppermint Lounge. We were lucky to find our first adult job at Studio 54 between gigs, the perfect combination of flexible hours and managers that understood the artist's way.

Hibiscus could not be parted from his beloved sisters for long so he jumped on stage with a ukulele at one of our gigs and professed he wanted to form Hibiscus and the Screaming Violets. "HSV" played every major club in NYC during 1981-82. As we were about to embark on a tour of Japan and make a video for then-startup MTV, Hibiscus died. Thanks to Holly Woodlawn's consistent encouragement The Harris Sisters went on to warm up for The Spinners, Buster Poindexter and toured Australia with our *Life of The Andrews Sisters* revue. In between we worked doing television gigs on *Muggable Mary, Street Cop, Bill On His Own* (with Mickey Rooney) and films including *Nighthawks*. We were signed by producer Carl Griffin for his GRP Records label and recorded with Michael Winslow. For Broadway

Jayne Anne   Eloise   Mary Lou

composer Richard Adler we recorded an album, *The Harris Sisters sing Richard Adler*. In 1993 my sisters and I wrote and co-produced our own musical *Cheek to Cheek* at La MaMa. At the same time we decided it was time for college.

I met Joe Damone, my husband, while singing in the musical production *Count Dracula* at Merkin Hall, NY. Asked to recommend a drummer, I gave the producers a list to choose from. Joe showed up and was hired. Later he asked me to watch him play with his band, The Rhythm Dogs, at a bar. I waited the appropriate three weeks and went. After the set Joe asked if I played racquetball. "Oh, of course!" I said. It looked like tennis. How hard could it be? So I found Joe at the West Village racquetball court. He smiled warmly and said, "Are you ready? I nodded "yes" with confidence, heard the serve and proceeded to try to find the little ball that went whizzing by me. It was hitting the floor, walls and ceiling like the Harry Potter game "Quidditch" without the brooms.

Between our respective gigs we didn't speak for a month. A job occurred where I needed a drummer so I called Joe. "Do you want to go out again?" he asked, and I said "Not with you. I don't want to play racquetball and I don't want lunch, I want flowers and dinner." He said, "How about tonight?" He showed up with flowers and took me to a lovely dinner. In our first year together I gave Joe his first camera, an underwater Nikon. I spent all year paying for the thing at B&H, a New York photography supply store. The staff cheered when I finally finished my payments and walked out with my gift-wrapped camera. Joe opened it and said, "What am I going to do with this?" Now "professional photographer" is added to his resume, and he is a great one.

Once back from Australia I was ready, really ready, to start a family. On my first attempt I lost a baby boy, Jackson, to a premature birth. I was determined more than ever to try again. I interviewed doctors at ten major New York City hospitals and finally settled on Dr. Parveen Sondi, a female doctor from Northern India, at St. Vincent's Hospital in New York. I was

As valedictorian of her class, Eloise delivers a stirring speech at Madison Square Garden.

Joe and Eloise

extremely nervous about going through the whole process again and make decisions about amniocentesis and other tests. At 40 years old, I was in for a scary ride and shell shocked from the last time.

Montana Eloise Parveen Damone was born at 29 weeks. She is now fifteen and a very tall beautiful girl. The doctors and nurses at St. Vincent's were angels. We are truly, truly grateful to them and to Dr. Sondi for our beautiful daughter. We are forever grateful to all who helped us along with Monty, the best production of my life. Although Hibiscus never got a chance to see Montana, I know he would've loved her. She attends school in Andes, NY. She enjoys piano, theater, sports, drama club and her friends. The apple doesn't fall far from the tree!

Monty then

I became a dedicated mom while simultaneously earning a masters degree and starting a career as a therapist for children with special needs. I help with Monty's theater productions at her school and provide choreography for other shows at neighboring schools. Children of all ages enjoy dancing and theater. It is wonderful for me to be able to pass on the legacy.

Monty now

I live between our homes in New York City and upstate with my loving husband Joe, my fantastic daughter Montana and our two pug dogs, Abigail and Frankie. Joe and I share a love of scuba diving in Bonaire and raising our amazing daughter. We have traveled to wonderful destinations together as a family, Rome being my favorite. Montana was able to see the Sistine Chapel and the unbelievable fresco, *The Last Judgment*, while attending second grade.

I have some wonderful lifelong friends (Angel, Julie, Wendy, Nancy, Bobby, Billy and Tim) who I love very much. I enjoy building my own world. It is getting easier to turn the external volume down and hear my own voice. I love the line from the movie, *Forrest Gump,* "Life is like a box of chocolates. You never know what you're going to get." Well, I guess I've had some exotic fillings!

Above: Eloise and friends in Agistri, Greece, circa 1984. Bottom: Scuba diving with Monty at Bonaire, 'the diver's paradise.' (2014) Photo by Joe Damone with his underwater Nikon.

Family photo by Michael Ian

Mary Lou

Top: **Mary Lou Harris during her Phoenix music project.**
Bottom: **Mary Lou with her husband, James, and son, Miles.**

Mary Lou Harris

Photo by Michael Ian

the actor

Born in Clearwater Beach, Florida, I am the youngest of the Harris Family Caravan. Being immersed in the arts from the beginning, indoctrinated my early years of repertory in New York City's La MaMa ETC, Theater for the New City and Judson Poets Theater. My brief television commercial career included, "Flight Captain Game," "Heineken Beer," and "Charleston Chew Candy." My even shorter movie career included a role in the film, *The Muppets Take Manhattan.*

In 1972, my brother Hibiscus included his family when he formed his Angels Of Light theater troupe. While touring Europe with the Angels I was lucky to live in Paris, France and Mykonos, Greece.

As teenagers in New York City, my two sisters and I formed our own rock band, The Harris Sisters and Trouble. We played the downtown club scene and opened for Buster Poindexter in the late 70's. Next we joined forces with my brother Hibiscus, to form a new bejeweled rock band, Hibiscus and the Screaming Violets. As the band began to get popular, our plans to shoot a video and tour Japan were suddenly halted by the untimely and devastating death of Hibiscus.

the singer - about to rock the CBGB stage

In an effort to pick up the pieces, I attended City University of New York. In 1987, I graduated magna cum laude with a bachelor's degree in English Literature and a minor in music. I began songwriting. Lady Luck smiled upon me, as several of my songs were published and subsequently recorded by a variety of artists including Carrie Nation (Appollon Records), Phoenix, (Polygram Records) and Carolyn Leigh (JVC Music).

Desperately missing the Harris caravan, I teamed up with my sisters again and recorded an album for a Broadway composer titled, *The Harris Sisters Sing Richard Adler.* We also wrote and produced a new musical, *Cheek to Cheek,* and premiered it at La MaMa ETC in 1993. In April of 2005, La MaMa featured the Harris family in its *Coffeehouse Chronicles* series where we shared publicly our family's theatrical contribution to the off-off-Broadway movement. Playwright Robert Patrick proclaimed our family, "the Lunts of off-off-Broadway." I wish Hibiscus could have been there.

Photo © Michael Ian

Jim Pietsch

Shot by Cupid's dart, I met my husband-to-be on the downtown #1 subway train in New York City. Jim Pietsch is a sweet, loving humorist who works as a video editor in the television industry. He romantically proposed on top of the Empire State Building and we were married in New Canaan, Connecticut in the year 2000. Jim wrote, illustrated and published *The New York City Cab Driver's Joke Book* series and is an accomplished drummer with Broadway shows to his credit.

On December 1st, 2002, an intoxicating event happened for both Jim and myself...the birth of our beautiful and amazing son, Miles Vincent Pietsch. Miles attends school in New York City, plays electric keyboard, loves swimming, is a technological wiz and has many friends.

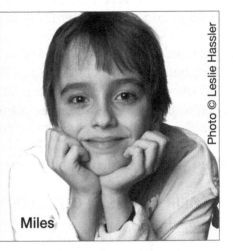

Photo © Leslie Hassler

Miles

Over the years, I went back to school for my master's degree. Currently I work for New York City schools as a therapeutic teacher and literacy specialist for young children. My lovely family and I live in the Chelsea section of Manhattan in New York City.

My deep appreciation to all of my personal friends along the way, as you have taught me the art of autonomy and have made my life rich.

The Pietsch Family

Photo © Michael Ian

Special Thanks

The family thanks the following folks who proofread, asked questions, offered feedback and encouraged us to dig deep: James D. Gossage, Patricia Harris, Skot Herrin, Eric Laschever, Jim Pietsch and Susan Dale Rose. Thanks to Kristin Green and Peter Thall for their expertise and to Judy Corcoran for sharing her publishing experience and marketing tips. Thanks to David Weissman for putting us in touch with hard-to-find photographers. Thanks to Chad Syme for restoring damaged photos and for taking new ones we needed. Thanks also to Chad and to Jodi Steele for interpreting our El Dorado Books USA logo so creatively. We like them so much we are using both! Thanks to Mary Lou Harris for our cover design, inspired by a Patricia Harris collage, and to Jodi for rendering it in final form.

Thanks to all the authors and photographers who graciously gave us permission to quote and include their work in the book and on the cover. We thank the late Ritsaert ten Cate for championing our work in Europe and opening doors for us there. Thanks to Horacio Silva, Elissa Auter and Adam Lerner for raising awareness of Hibiscus' work and influence.

Finally, thanks to Ellen Stewart, Al Carmines, Joe Cino, Crystal Field and George Bartinieff, Maurice Bejart, Michael Butler, Louis Friedman, Norman "Speedy" Hartman, Tom Eyen, Paul Foster, Larry Kornfeld, Harry Koutoukas, Marshall W. Mason, Tom O'Horgan, Robert Patrick, Ron Tavel, Lanford Wilson, James Waring and the countless other pioneering producers, playwrights and directors who believed in us, put us to work and helped us along the way.

Without you our journey would have remained only a dream.

FOR THEIR VOICES IN OUR STORY
(in order of appearance):

Tim Robbins
An Academy Award-winning actor, director, screenwriter, producer, musician, and activist. His many awards and works can be found online. He is also a father and a humanitarian. Tim founded and directs The Actor's Gang, an experimental theater company based in Los Angeles. http://www.theactorsgang.com

Robert Heide
Plays include *The Bed* and *Moon* at the Caffe Cino; *Why Tuesday Never Has a Blue Monday* at La MaMa; and *Crisis of Identity* at Theater for the New City. Robert Heide and John Gilman have co-written books on pop culture and on the state of New Jersey, plus articles for periodicals. Visit Bob and John at: http://robertheideandjohngilman.blogspot.com/

Scott Morris
An independent master filmmaker and editor, Scott's work encompasses diverse techniques including clay animation, documentaries, dramatic short subjects, and music videos. His animated film, *The Intruder,* was broadcast on PBS and won a Cine Golden Eagle. Visit Scott at www.scottmorrisproductions.com

Robert Patrick

Robert Patrick is an American playwright, poet, lyricist, short-story writer and novelist. He is the author of the hit play *Kennedy's Children* plus over sixty published plays, novels and articles. Via the internet, Bob keeps our far-flung off-off-Broadway community connected and informed. Visit: http://en.wikipedia.org/wiki/Robert_Patrick_%28playwright%29

Crystal Field

An early adopter of, and collaborator with, the Harris family, Crystal is an OBIE Award winning actress and is the co-founder and Artistic Director of Theater For the New City in New York. Visit Crystal at www.theaterforthenewcity.net

Mike Figgis

Mike is an acclaimed English film director, screenwriter and composer who befriended us when the family was new to the theater scene in Europe. Mike performed with us, invited our participation in his work and gave Ann and Fred a much needed place to stay during a hiatus in the Angels' European tour. Visit Mike's web site at http://www.mikefiggis.co.uk

John Bernhardt

John is an accomplished educator, administrator, coach and sports writer in upstate New York. We thank John for his fine article on *Star Trek Goes Broadway* in The Andes Gazette. Tune in to http://wioxradio.org Fridays at 8:00am EST for *Tip Off with John Bernhardt.*

FOR THEIR PICTURES, WORTH A THOUSAND WORDS

Andrew Sherwood

An "early adopter" of the Harris family when we arrived in New York City from Florida, Andrew became our piano and voice teacher, family photographer and loyal friend. Thanks to his artistry we always had the best promotional and show photos in town. Andrew lives in Paris, visits when he can and remains in close touch with our Mom, his dear friend.

James D. Gossage

Jim is off-off-Broadway's premier photojournalist and a close family friend who resides in Bellingham, Washington. He is a tireless champion of off-off-Broadway, the Caffe Cino, and the Harris family. His work is catalogued and archived at The Billy Rose Theatre Collection at Lincoln Center, New York City. http://jdgoobphotos.blogspot.com/

FOR JUMP-STARTING OUR WEB PRESENCE

Jodi Steele

As an artist raised in a creative family in Muskoka, Ontario, Jodi appreciates our family's journey. She read an early draft of Caravan and, on the spot, offered to design the awesome web site and blog we now enjoy supporting our book. Jodi lives in Seattle with her family and manages web marketing at Daniel Smith Inc. Visit Jodi at www.jodisteele.com.

TO ANYONE WE MISSED ... *Thank you!*

Appendix 1
The Harris Family's Career

HARRIS FAMILY SHOWS, original and collaborative:
        1962 – 64
THE EL DORADO PLAYERS in Clearwater, Florida:
Bluebeard, The Sheep and the Cheapskate, Camelot, Cleopatra,Queen of the Nile, The Unsinkable Titanic (film)
        1965-1966
THE EL DORADO PLAYERS in New York City:. At Judson Poets Theater: *The Sheep and the Cheapskate* and *Remember the Thirties.* At La MaMa ETC: Young Playwrights Series, in residence: *Bluebeard, The Sheep and the Cheapskate, MacBee, There Is Method In Their Madness.* Plus the El Dorado Player's unfinished second film: *It's New York City!*
        1969 –1971
THE COCKETTES in San Francisco, in collaboration with Hibiscus:
Gone With The Showboat To Oklahoma, Hell's Harlots, Fairytale Extravaganza, Paste on Paste, Hollywood Babylon, Les Cockettes Folies de Paris, Pearls Over Shanghai, Les Ghouls, Tinsel Tarts in a Hot Coma, Madame Butterfly
        1970s
HIBISCUS' ANGELS OF LIGHT in San Francisco:
Nativity Midnight Mass at Grace Catherdral (as 'Blue Angels'), Flamingo Stampede, The Moroccan Opera, Myth Thing, Hot Voodoo, Kabaret, Earthquake!, Plaster of Paris, Flaming Hot Exotica Erotica, Titillating Tittress of de Amazon, Femme Fatale, The Planet Show, The Shocking Pink Life of Jayne Champagne

HIBISCUS' ANGELS OF LIGHT in New York at Theater for the New City: *Birdie Follies, Sky High (original version), Gossamer Wings, Femme Fatale,The Best of the Angels of Light*

HIBISCUS' ANGELS OF LIGHT in Europe (Mickery Theater, Festival du Mondial):
Enchanted Miracle, Razzamatazz

OFF BROADWAY
Speakeasy, Sky High (Entermedia Theater and Player's Theater versions)
        1980s
The Harris Sisters / The Harris Sisters and Trouble
Hibiscus and the Screaming Violets (at New York area music clubs)
Tinsel Town Tirade (Theater for the New City)
The Screaming Violets (at New York area music clubs)
        1990s
PILGRIM CENTER FOR THE ARTS in Seattle, WA
Bluebeard, Hibiscus (the musical), Dear Friends of Allegro Sanitation

LA MAMA ETC
Hibiscus (the musical), Cheek to Cheek, The Coffeehouse Chronicles

SHOWS FEATURING ONE OR MORE HARRIS FAMILY MEMBERS:

BROADWAY
The Porcelain Year, 1965; *HAIR,* 1968; *The Great White Hope,* 1968; National Tour of *The Great White Hope,* 1969

OFF BROADWAY
Wide Open Cage, The Peace Creeps, Gorilla Queen, Invitation to a Beheading, Lemonade for an Angel, An Enemy of the People, Little Mary Sunshine, Dracula Sabat

OFF-OFF-BROADWAY
Caffe Cino:
>*This is the Rill Speaking* by Lanford Wilson, 1965
>*The Death of Tintagiles* by Maurice Maeterlinck, 1966
>*Palm Sunday Spectacular aka More, More, I Want More!* by OOB all-stars, 1966
>*Eyen on Eyen* by Tom Eyen, 1966
>*The Clown* by Claris Nelson, 1967
>A *Funny Walk Home* by Jeff Weiss, 1967
>*The Brown Crown* by Haal Borske, 1967

La MaMa Experimental Theater Club:
>*The Sand Castle* by Lanford Wilson, 1965 and 1967 w/extension at the Cino
>*The Madonna In The Orc*hard by Paul Foster, 1965 and 1967
>*Miss Nefertiti Regrets* by Tom Eyen (three editions, 1965 and 1966
>*The Rimers of Eldritch* by Lanford Wilson, 1966
>*Give My Regards to Off-Off-Broadway* by Tom Eyen, 1966
>*Myrtilus* by Edward de Grazia, 1967

Ellen Stewart's Young Playwrights Series at La MaMa, starring The El Dorado Players:
>*Bluebeard* by Ann Harris, 1965
>*The Sheep and the Cheapskate* by Ann Harris, 1965
>*MacBee!* by Ann, George and Walter Harris, 1966
>*There is Method in their Madness* by Ann, George and Walter, 1966

Judson Poets Theater:
>*Sing Ho! for a Bear* adapted from A. A. Milne, music by Al Carmines, 1964
>*The Sheep and the Cheapskate* by Ann Harris, feat. El Dorado Players,1965
>*Remember the Thirties* by the El Dorado Players, 1965
>*Pomegranada,* an operetta by H.M. Koutoukas and Al Carmines, 1966
>*Gorilla Queen* by Ron Tavel, 1967
>*The Poor Little Little Match Girl* by Arthur Miller, Al Carmines, 1968
>*James Waring and Company* annual dance concert, 1968

The New Dramatists Committee:
>*The Little Birds Fly* by Harding Lemay, 1965
>*The Peace Creeps* by John Wolfson, 1966

Equity Library Theater:
>*Once Upon A Mattress* by Rodgers, Barer, Thompson and Fuller, 1966
>*Damn Yankees* by Abbott, Bissell, Adler and Ross, 1967
>*An Enemy of the People* by Henrik Ibsen, 1968

Bowery Lane Theater:
> *It's A Mod, Mod World,* a musical revue, 1966

The Electric Circus:
> *Alice Through The Looking Glass (Lightly)* by Tom Eyen, 1968

Off-Off-Broadway on tour:
> *Pomegranada* by H.M. Koutoukas and Al Carmines at Sundance Summer Theater in Upper Black Eddy, PA; Michael Smith, producer, 1966
> *The Madonna in the Orchard* by Paul Foster at the Eugene O'Neill New Playwrights Conference in Waterford, CT, 1966

The Old Reliable Theater Tavern:
> *Dynel* by Robert Patrick, music by the playwright and Walter Harris, 1968
> *Joyce Dynel* by Robert Patrick, music by the playwright and Walter, 1969
> *Silver Skies* by Robert Patrick, 1969

Theater for the New City:
> *Dracula Sabbat, Prosperall Rising, Monding The Store* (Street Theater Tour), *The Celebration: Jooz/Guns/Movies/The Abyss,* Olmstead (in Central Park), *The Co-Op, The Litle Prince, Undercover Cop & Sky Salesman* (Street Theater Tour), *Halloween #1, Morning to Midnight, The Time They Turned The Water Off*

COMMUNITY THEATER, TOURING & SUMMER STOCK

The Nuremburg Stove, Mrs. McThing, Hop O' My Thumb and the Seven League Boots, Macbeth, Anna Christie, The Bells Are Ringing, The Best Man, Cradle Song, Detective Story, Everybody Loves Opal, Front Page, His and Hers, Lovers and Other Strangers, King Lear, No Place to Be Somebody, Norman, Is That You?, The Trial of A. Lincoln, Mame, The Story of Woodstock, Star Trek Goes Broadway - The Backstory

FEATURE FILMS & DOCUMENTARIES

The Amityville Horror, dir Stuart Rosenberg, 1979
Angels of Light, dir Mary Jordan (unreleased work in progress)
Any Wednesday, dir Roger Ellis Miller, 1966
The Cockettes, dir Bill Weber and David Weissman, 2002
Come See The Paradise, dir Alan Parker, 1990
Cops and Robbers, dir Aram Avakian, 1973
The First Deadly Sin, dir Brian G. Hutton, 1980
Fort Apache, The Bronx, dir Daniel Petrie, 1981
The French Connection, dir William Friedkin, 1971
Hear No Evil, See No Evil, dir Arthur Hiller, 1989
The Hospital, dir Arthur Hiller, 1971
The Honeymoon Killers, dir Leonard Castle, 1969
I, The Jury, dir Richard T. Heffron, 1982
Julian Po, dir Alan Wade, 1997
Last Address, a film by Ira Sachs, 2010
The Muppets Take Manhattan, dir Frank Oz, 1984
The Panic in Needle Park, dir Jerry Schatzberg, 1971
Pickup's Tricks, dir Gregory Pickup, 1973
The Prisoner of Second Avenue, dir Melvin Frank, 1975

Ragtime, dir Milos Forman, 1981
Some Kind of a Nut, dir Garson Kanin
Superman, dir Richard Donner
Times Square, dir Allan Moyle, 1980
What's Up, Doc? (aka *A Glimpse of Tiger*), dir Allan Harvey, 1972
For the Want of a Nail, dir Frank Lewailen, 2007

FEATURE VIDEO FOR TELEVISION AND NEWS MEDIA
The Class of 9/11, Jacques Menasche, PBS
The Ninth Street Stompers – PBS
Film for French TV of 1975 Festival Mondial du Theatre, Nancy
(the Angels of Light took top honors at this festival)

NETWORK AND CABLE TELEVISION SHOWS
Bill, starring Mickey Rooney, 1981
The Ed Sullivan Show (casts of *HAIR* and *The Great White Hope*), 1969
The Garry Moore Show, 1966
Geraldo Rivera Show – Harris Sisters performance, 1987
Love of Life, (soap opera) CBS
Another World (soap operas) NBC
Muggable Mary, Street Cop, 1982
Orphan Annie Goes To The Moon, WNYU TV,
Tattinger's, drama series, NBC,1988
The Tonight Show starring Johnny Carson (cast of *HAIR),* 1969
Texas Soap Opera, NBC, 1980
Way Off Broadway with Joy Behar, Lifetime Channel, 1987
Veterans Ensemble Theater Company - HBO

TELEVISION COMMERCIALS & VOICEOVERS
Blue Cross of New York, Charleston Chew Candy, Dream Whip, Dove for Dishes, Gaines Burgers (for dogs), GE Portable Color TV, Heineken Beer, Tampax, Maytag Washers, Mazda Car & Light Co. (Paris), Sunshine Crackers

IMPROV
The Madcaps, Clearwater, Florida, 1960-1963

RADIO
The Star Pit by Samuel R. Delany, Mind's Eye Theater, WBAI 1967
The Celebration by Arthur Sainer, Theater for the New City, WBAI, 1972
The Harris Sisters for Veterans Ensemble Theater Company, WBAI, 1986
The Harris Sisters Sing on WKRB, 1988
Voices of Christmas interview with Walter Michael, KUOW, 1988
Sandy Bradley's Pot Luck, KUOW, 1990 performance by Walter Michael

RECORD ALBUMS and OTHER RECORDINGS
HAIR – Walter Michael on the Original Broadway Cast Album, RCA, 1968 (13 weeks at #1)
Brenda Bell & the Ninth Street Stompers, Dad, Spivey Records #1032, 1980
The KEZX Album Project – Walt performs George Leroy Poole's "Seattle, Washington," 1982
The Harris Sisters Sing Richard Adler, recorded with and for Richard Adler

Butterfly – The Jazz Police perform Ann's "From Another World," BopCop, 1994
Phoenix (Mary Lou Harris):
 *Cool Planet to Land On, In This Experience, Think Big Records, 1996
 *Lost Voices, The Songs of Hendrix, Joplin and Morrison, Polygram 1998
 *Songwriter for recording artists: Carrie Nation and Michael Winslow, 1999
New York Country – The Harris Sisters & Walt Original Songs demo, 1990

ORCHESTRAS and CRUISE SHIPS
Lincoln Center with Burt Lucarelli
Holland America, Australia and Fiji, 1994
Emory Davis Orchestra
Kingsborough Orchestra
Vince Giordano and the Nighthawks

SOCIETY EVENTS
Mary Tyler Moore & Gordon White; Chuck Scarborough; Patricia Birch; Kitty Carlisle; The Duke & Duchess of Marlborough; Jamie Spencer-Churchill, Marquess of Blandford; Lady Henrietta Spencer-Churchill; Andy Warhol; Gurumayi, Chidvilasananda

LEGACY EXHIBITIONS
Caffe Cino and its Legacy, a ten-week exhibit at the Vincent Astor Gallery of the New
 York Public Library for the Performing Arts at Lincoln Center, 1985
The Coffeehouse Chronicles, spotlight on The Harris Family – La MaMa, 2005
The Cockettes Are Coming! Performance event at Theater for the New City
 celebrating donation of the Martin Worman/Cockettes/Gay Theater Archives to the
New York Public Library for the Performing Arts, Billy Rose Theater Division at Lincoln
Center, New York City, 2008
Last Address, based on a film by Ira Sachs, 2010 www.lastaddress.org
West of Center: Art and the Counterculture Experiment in America, 1965-1977 –   Museum
of Contemporary Art, Denver, CO, plus touring exhibit, 2012-2013

BROADCAST MEDIA INTERVIEWS
Lifestyles of the Rich & Famous - Robin Leach interviews
 Hibiscus and the Screaming Violets
The Harris Sisters on the Joe Franklin, Joey Adams and Geraldo Rivera shows

PRINT MEDIA PROFILES & INTERVIEWS
"Young Scene," Walter Harris profile, Scholastic News, 1967
"At Home With Hibiscus" - The San Francisco Oracle, 1968
The Berkeley Barb's coverage of The Cockettes, 1968-1970
"Les Cockettes," Rolling Stone #93 – 971
Richard Adler and The Harris Sisters – Sheet Music Magazine, 1988
The Harris Sisters – Profile, Catskill Mountain News, 1990
Phoenix - Billboard Magazine, Daily News and Pro Sound News, 1999
"Karma Chameleon" – The New York Times Magazine – Horacio Silva, 2003
 PLUS reviews, profiles and press coverage of The El Dorado Players, both in Florida
and New York; The Cockettes, The Angels of Light, The Harris Sisters, Hibiscus and the
Screaming Violets, Pilgrim Center for the Arts and ArtsWest Playhouse.

CLUBS and CABARET

The Harris Sisters / Solo Shows / The Harris Sisters and Trouble / Hibiscus and the Screaming Violets / The Screaming Violets

Most venues listed are in New York City.

1018
Studio 54
AGVA Tours
The Apollo Theater
Arizona Arts Festival
The Ballroom
The Bitter End
BONDS
CBGB
Copacabana
Danceteria
Delaware & Ulster Railroad
Don't Tell Mama
Downtime
The Duplex
Earth Day Festival (Catskills)
Eighty Eights
F Sharp
Great Gildersleeves
Grossinger's Catskill Resort
Holland America Line
Horn of Plenty
The Ice Palace, Fire Island
The Ice Palace, New York City
The Limelight
Ludlow Cafe
Malibu Club
Merkin Concert Hall
Metropolitan Club
Club Monaco
Mudd Club
Municipal Arts Society, NYC
New York Athletic Club
New York City Municipal Events
Pallsons
Paradise
Peppermint Lounge
The Red Parrot

Roses Turn
The Roxy
The Rainbow Room
The Reggae Lounge
R.T. Firefly
SNAFU
Songwriter's Hall of Fame, NYC
The Swan Club
Sweet Basil
Sweetwaters
Swing 46
Tatou
Tunnel
Underground
West Bank Cafe

PLUS:
Theater for the New City
    Halloween Cabaret, several years
Tarrytown Country Club
University of North Carolina
    /Chapel Hill
Phoenix performance at
    Denver Arts Festival, Colorado
Phoenix at The Songwriter's
    Hall of Fame, NYC
The Harris Sisters at
    The Waldorf Astoria, NYC
Opened for Buster Poindexter
    (Soho, NY)
Windows on the World, NYC
World Trade Center Promenade
    (New York City)

Appendix 2
Quote and Photo Credits

Thanks to all who kindly gave permission to include photos and quotes. Every effort has been made to acknowledge them correctly and to contact the copyright holder of every image and quoted text. Photos not otherwise credited are drawn from Harris family members' private collections and family archives. We apologize for any unintentional omissions or errors. They will be corrected in future editions of this book. Please send the information to info@caravantooz.com. *Thank you.*

QUOTATIONS

Alice Ashe, *Bernie Boston: View Finder,* 73. from *Curio Magazine,* © James Madison
    University, 2005, pp. 11-14
John Bernhardt, *Star Trek Goes Broadway - The Backstory,* 227. © Andes Gazette, Volume
    16, No. 1, June 2014, www.andesgazette.net
Gary Comenas, Mark Lancaster interview, 71. http://www.warholstars.org/andywarhol
interview/mark/lancaster.html, last accessed 1.13.14
John Gruen, The New Bohemia: 49, 50. *A Cappella Books (November 1990)*
James Rado and Gerome Ragni, lyric excerpt, "Aquarius," 80. Music by Galt MacDermot.
    From the Broadway musical *HAIR,* © 1967, 1968, 2008, 2013
William David McCord, lyric to "At This Moment," sung by Billy Vera, © 2002, 190.
Ellen Stewart, 7, 48. Courtesy Ellen Stewart / La MaMa ETC, New York City, NY
Ronald Tavel, *Gorilla Queen* excerpt, 69. © Ronald Tavel
Ritsaert ten Cate interview: 142. *Research Workshop - Artistic Explorations in Cultural
    Memory,* © Leiden University, Faculty of Creative and Performing Arts; Edited by
    Colleen Scott
Mark Thompson, *Gay Spirit: Myth and Meaning:* 88, 97 © Mark Thompson. White
    Crane Books; Reprint edition (June 1, 2005)
David Weissman and Bill Weber, 97. *The Cockettes, a brief history.* © GranDelusion.com
    http://www.cockettes.com/history1.html

PHOTO CREDITS

Front and back covers: James D. Gossage, Andrew Sherwood, Sheyla Baykal, Bernie Boston/ RIT Archive Collections, Rochester Institute of Technology, Jim Bowers/CapedWonder.com, Michael Butler, Charles Caron, Kenn Duncan, Ingeborg Gerdes, George Harris Sr., Jayne Anne Harris, Michael Ian, Dagmar Krajnc, David Loehr, Paris Theater, Campaign Premier, Roxanne Co., Ruth Sorelle and Warner Brothers Studios.

Inside the book: The page numbers on which each image appears are listed below, along with the locator legend: (t=top, b=bottom, l=left, c=center, r=right). Where all photos on a page are from the same source, only the page number is listed without directionals.

James D. Gossage: 7 (br), 27 (t), 40 (tr), 48 (tr), 49 (tr), 50, 56, 58 (tr, tl, bl), 59, 60, 61 (b), 62, 63, 64, 70, 75, 162 (tr, br), 229 (b), 244 (t)

Andrew Sherwood: 4, 37 - 38 (all photos), 51, 61 (t), 120 (b), 128 (t), 130 (br), 131 (t), 134, 135 (t, bl), 141, 146 (t), 152 (t), 159

Robert Altman: 89

Sheyla Baykal: 118, 127, 128 (b), 130 (t), 131 (b), 133 (t), 136, 137 (all photos), 154, 156

Bernie Boston/RIT Archive Collections, Rochester Institute of Technology, front cover and page 73

Nancy Brown: 202, 205 (b)

Dagmar Krajnc: (HAIR's official photographer): 76, 79, 82 (bl), 84, 85

Joe Damone: 213 (bl), 215 (cl), 226, 243, 245, 247 (b), 248 (b), 249 (c,b), 250 (b)

Kenn Duncan: 83, 91 (b), 177 (t), 190, 247 (b)

Ingeborg Gerdes: 90, 112 (t)

Michael Ian: 162 (tl) 207, 228 (tr), 251 (b), 252 (t), 253 (t,b) 256 (t), 257 (t) (b)

Gregory Pickup: 91 (t), 112 (all)

Chad Syme: 71 (photograph of David Hockney drawing), 220 (b), 223 (tr,cl), 242 (cl)

Irene Young: 177 (b), 179 (tr), 181 (Topman Magazine layout)

Plus:

Phil Banko: 239; Ellen Banner, Seattle Times: 243 (tr); H. Blum, 223 (b); Jane Bown, David Hockney 1966 portrait: 71 (tr inset); Jim Bowers/CapedWonder.com/Warner Bros. Pictures: 158, 160, 228 (b); Kenny Burgess: 40 (br); Michael Butler: 82 (cr); Charles Caron: 36, 122, 231; Don Hogan Charles/NY Times: 47 (tr); Valerie Coe: 121 (b); Steve Clagett, 214 (tr), 240; Michal Daniel: 86 (t); Wren de Antonio: 74; Festival Mondial 1975: 148; Robert J. Fisch/ Creative Commons: 210; Clay Geerdes: 95 (b); Herve Gloaguen/Rapho, Realities: 45, 48 (t); Randolph Graf: 43 (t); Jason & Irish Green: 220 (t); George Harris Sr.: 32; Jayne Anne Harris: 253 (tl, cr), 255 (t); Karen Harris: 221 (br); Lissa Harris & Julia Reischel: 221 (center and inset); Patricia Harris 223 (t), 225, 242 (bl); Leslie Hassler: 257 (c); Skot Herrin: 196 (t), 197 (b); Judson Memorial Church: 7 (bl); L.J. Kirby Collection: 205 (t); Timothy Krause, Crystal Field: 101, courtesy Theater for the New City; La MaMa ETC: 7 (t); Mark Lancaster/David Hockney: 71 (b); Bud Lee: 96 (t); David Loehr: 120 (t); 137; Glyn Lowe, 211; Mickery Theater, Amsterdam: 142 (t); Scott Morris: 67, 213 (tl), 232 (b), 245 (t); newblackman.blogspot.com/ 2011/01/in-tribute-to-ellen-stewart-roger.html: 47 (tl); New York Shakespeare Festival Public Theater: 58 (br), 86 (t), 87 (br); New York Times Magazine: 236; Paris Theater, Campaign Premier: 149, 153; Robert Patrick: *The Haunted Host* flyer, 40 (bl), 48 (tl); Richard Peterson: 125; Doug Plummer: 242 (tr); Sterling Powell: 191 (tl); Bobby Reed: 175; Billy Rafford: 135 (br); Lovro Rumiha, creativecommons.org/licenses/by/4.0/legalcode, 7 (t); Dave Simons/Hollywood Art Service NYC.: 173, 178 ; Ruth Sorelle: 12 (b), 14, 229 (t); Warren Steibel/Roxanne Co., 109, 194 (t); Theater for the New City: 7 (c), 102 (b), 107 (t); Reyn van Koolwijk/The Guardian: 142 (t); Allan Warren: 171; Conrad Ward: 43 (tl, br).

Appendix 3
Links and Resources

For additional content and news, please visit our Caravan to Oz web site and blog:
www.caravantooz.com

They Acted Everywhere: The Harris Family on Robert Patrick's Cino Pages
http://caffecino.wordpress.com/1938/01/01/harris-family/

Angels of Light: History of Shows
http://angelsoflight.wordpress.com

Caffe Cino: Robert Patrick's Cino Pages
http://caffecino.wordpress.com/

The Cockettes (documentary film by David Weissman and Bill Weber)
http://www.cockettes.com/

Gorilla Queen
http://www.outhistory.org/wiki/David_Kerry_Heefner:_Remembering_Ronald_Tavel's_
%22Gorilla_Queen,%22_March_1967

The Billy Rose Theatre Collection
http://www.nypl.org/find-archival-materials
    Caffe Cino / Joe Cino Collection
    Magie Dominic Collection
    James Gossage Collection
    Circle Theater Collection

HAIR the musical
http://www.michaelbutler.com/hair/holding/Hair.html
Dagmar Krajnc, HAIR's photographer: www.dagmarfoto.com

George E. Harris, Sr. – essay by Walter Michael Harris
http://www.capedwonder.com/george-harris-officer-mooney/

Hibiscus: Flower Power photo by Bernie Boston
http://www.washingtonpost.com/wp-dyn/content/article/2007/03/17/
AR2007031701300.html

Hibiscus: interviews with collaborators
http://www.peacheschrist.com/?p=9512

Hibiscus Rising: a glittery, Technicolor Fashion Homage to the Cockettes
http://www.papermag.com/2013/10/
hibiscus_rising_haight_ashbury_cockettes_fashion_editorial.php
photographed by Holly Falconer / styling & set design by John William

Holy Order of MANS
http://www.has.vcu.edu/wrs/profiles/HolyOrderOfMans.htm

La MaMa Experimental Theater Club, NYC
http://lamama.org/

Pickup's Tricks, a 1973 film by Gregory Pickup featuring Hibiscus, the Cockettes, Allen Ginsberg and the San Francisco Angels of Light. www.pickupstricks.com

Studio 54
http://en.wikipedia.org/wiki/Studio_54

Theater for the New City
http://www.theaterforthenewcity.net

BOOKS WE ARE IN OR ARE CONNECTED TO:

Adler, Richard, and Lee Davis. *You Gotta Have Heart.* New York: D.I. Fine, 1990.

Auther, Elissa and Lerner, Adam, ed. *West of Center: art and the counterculture experiment in america, 1965-1977.* Minneapolis: University Of Minnesota Press, 2011.

Berger, Dan. *The Hidden 1970s: histories of radicalism.* New Brunswick: Rutgers University Press, 2010.

Bottoms, Stephen. *Playing Underground: a critical history of the 1960s off-off-broadway movement.* Ann Arbor: The University of Michigan Press, 2006.

Brooks, Adrian and Daniel Nicoletta. *Flights of Angels.* Vancouver: Los Angeles: Arsenal Pulp Press, 2008.

Crespy, David Allison. *Off-Off-Broadway Explosion: how provocative playwrights of the 1960s ignited a new American theater.* New York: Back Stage Books, 2003.

Dominic, Magie, and Smith, Michael, ed. *H.M. Koutoukas 1937–2010, remembered by his friends.* Silverton: Fast Books, 2010.

Farr, Kendall, Montague, Sarah and Bennett, George. *Pugs in Public.* New York: Stewart Tabori & Chang, 1999.

Gamson, Joshua. *The Fabulous Sylvester: the legend, the music, the seventies in San Francisco. New York:* Henry Holt & Company, 2005.

Grode, Eric. *HAIR : the story of the show that defined a generation.* Philadelphia: Running Press, 2010.

Gruen, John. *The New Bohemia.* New York: Shorecrest, Inc., 1966.

Haden-Guest, Anthony, and Niels Kummer; Felice Quinto; Domitilla Sartogo; et al. *Studio 54 : The Legend.* New York: te Neues, 1997.

Heide, Robert, and John Gilman. *Greenwich Village: a primo guide to shopping, eating, and making merry in true Bohemia.* New York: St. Martins Griffin ed., 1995.

Horn, Barbara Lee. T*he Age of HAIR: evolution and impact of broadway's first rock musical.* Westport: Greenwood Press, 1991.

Kolsbun, Ken, and Michael *Sweeny. Peace: the biography of a symbol.* Washington: National Geographic, 2008.

Lake, Bambi, and Alvin Orloff. *The Unsinkable Bambi Lake: a fairy tale containing the dish on Cockettes, punks & angels*. San Francisco: Manic D Press, 1996.

Lucas, Phillip. *The Odyssey of a New Religion: the Holy Order of MANS from new age to orthodoxy*. Bloomington: Indiana University Press, 1995.

Rose, Susan Dale. *Upon Our Westward Way: Myron Coloney, Josephine Artemisia Coloney, and an american adventure*. Lexington: Blue Horse Books, 2012.

Smith, Michael, ed. *The Best of Off-Off-Broadway*. New York: E.P. Dutton Inc,.1969.

Stone, Wendell. *Caffe Cino : the birthplace of off-off-Broadway*. Carbondale: Southern Illinois University Press, 2005.

Susoyev, Steve and George Birimisa. *Return to the Caffe Cino*. San Francisco: Moving Finger Press, 2007.

Tent, Pam. *Midnight at the Palace: my life as a fabulous Cockette*. Los Angeles: Alyson Books, 2004.

Thompson, Mark. *Gay Spirit - myth and meaning*. New York: St. Martin's Press, 1987.

Trinidad, David. *Plasticville - poems*. London: Turnaround, 2000.

Wilson, Lanford. *The Rimers of Eldritch and Other Plays*. New York: Hill and Wang, 1967.

Woodlawn, Holly. *A Low Life in High Heels*. New York: St. Martins Press. 1991.

EL DORADO
BOOKS
USA

© Copyright 2014

caravantooz.com

85884492R00148

Made in the USA
Columbia, SC
05 January 2018